EDUCATION FOR SPIRITUAL, MORAL, SOCIAL AND CULTURAL DEVELOPMENT

Also available:

Ron Best (ed.): *Education, Spirituality and the Whole Child*

Ron Best, Peter Lang, Caroline Lodge and Chris Watkins (eds): *Pastoral Care and PSE: Entitlement and Provision*

Mike Calvert and Jenny Henderson (eds): *Managing Pastoral Care*

Steve Decker, Sandy Kirby, Angela Greenwood and Dudley Moore (eds): *Taking Children Seriously*

John McGuinness: *Counselling in Schools: New Perspectives*

Louise O'Connor, Denis O'Connor and Rachel Best (eds): *Drugs: Partnerships for Policy, Prevention and Education*

Sally Power: *The Pastoral and the Academic: Conflict and Contradiction in the Curriculum*

Jasper Ungoed-Thomas: *Vision of a School: The Good School in the Good Society*

CONTINUUM STUDIES IN PASTORAL CARE AND PERSONAL
AND SOCIAL EDUCATION

EDUCATION FOR SPIRITUAL, MORAL, SOCIAL AND CULTURAL DEVELOPMENT

Edited by
Ron Best

CONTINUUM
London and New York

Continuum

Wellington House
125 Strand
London WC2R 0BB

370 Lexington Avenue
New York
New York 10017-6503

First published 2000

British Library Cataloguing-in-Publication Data
A catalogue record for this book is available from the British Library.

ISBN: 0 8264 4802 X

Typeset by BookEns Ltd, Royston, Herts
Printed and bound in Great Britain by Cromwell Press Ltd, Trowbridge, Wiltshire

Contents

Contributors

Ron Best is Professor and Dean of Education, University of Surrey Roehampton

Stephen Bigger is head of applied education studies, University College Worcester.

Bridget Cooper is a research officer at the Computer Based Learning Unit in the University of Leeds. She is currently researching values education for her doctorate at Leeds Metropolitan University.

Jane Erricker is a principal lecturer in education and co-ordinator of science education and spiritual and moral education at King Alfred's College, Winchester. She co-directs the Children and Worldviews research project.

Raywen Ford is deputy principal of Froebel Institute College and senior lecturer in art education at University of Surrey Roehampton.

Jeannette Gill is senior lecturer in Humanities and Religious Education at the University of Plymouth.

Bill Law is Senior Fellow in the National Institute for Careers Education and Counselling (NICEC) and an independent education consultant working on organization- and staff-development in primary and secondary schools.

Kevin McCarthy teaches drama and religious education at a school in Worthing, Sussex, and is a director of the Re:membering Education Network.

Vanessa Ogden is Curriculum Manager for Humanities and Religious Education at Hurlingham and Chelsea School in Hammersmith and Fulham, and tutors in Religious Education on the MA (Education) course at London University Institute of Education.

Jack Priestley was principal of West Hill College in Birmingham from 1990 to 1997 and is now an honorary research fellow at the School of Education, University of Exeter.

Jonathan Roberts is a freelance trainer and educational consultant based in Durham.

Don Rowe is director of curriculum resources at The Citizenship Foundation in London.

David Smith is a researcher at the Stapleford Centre in Nottingham.

Marianne Talbot lectures in philosophy at Brasenose College Oxford and leads the work of the Qualifications and Curriculum Authority (QCA) on pupils' spiritual, moral, social and cultural development.

Marilyn Tew has been a teacher for over twenty years and is an educational consultant with Jenny Mosley Consultancies. She is currently undertaking doctoral research on social inclusion in secondary schools.

Margaret A. Warner is an Ofsted registered inspector with wide experience of inspecting schools' provision for religious education and SMSC. She is also involved in inservice training and consultancy as 'MAW Education'.

Paul Yates is a lecturer in the Graduate Research Centre for Education at the University of Sussex, and honorary curate at St Michael-in-Lewes.

Introduction: Where are we going with SMSC?

Ron Best

The much-quoted second paragraph of the 1988 Education Act asserts that the school curriculum should be one that is

a balanced and broadly-based curriculum which –
(a) promotes the spiritual, moral, cultural, mental and physical development of pupils and of society; and
(b) prepares such pupils for the opportunities, responsibilities and experiences of adult life.

This statement stresses the education of the whole person, rather than merely the cognitive domain which we associate with 'book learning', 'school work' and so on. It identifies four other domains – the physical, moral, spiritual and cultural – which schools must develop if they are fully to discharge their obligations under the Act, and it asserts that pupils should not merely be 'educated' in the conventional sense of acquiring 'book learning', passing examinations and acquiring certificates. They should be prepared for what will confront them as the 'opportunities, responsibilities and experiences of adult life'.

While the desirability of such an aim is difficult to dispute, what it might mean in practice is less easy to say. As adults, we know that adult life includes many *opportunities* including opportunities

to apply for jobs (but not necessarily get them);
to enter marriage (but also opportunities to leave marriage);
to fall in love (more than once, but also to fall out of love, even to fall into hate with another person);
to participate in the electoral and judicial systems of our society (to stand for election, to serve on a jury);
to seek ownership of property and the accumulation of wealth (but also opportunities to swindle, defraud and misappropriate property and wealth);
to serve the community (but also to undermine the community through antisocial behaviour);
to help those less fortunate than ourselves (but also opportunities to dominate and exploit them).

We know that adult life may be felt to carry many *responsibilities* including responsibility for our own actions; responsibility for our children's welfare; responsibility for aged parents; responsibilities associated with membership of organizations, clubs, societies; responsibilities as a citizen (to vote, to uphold the law, join the PTA. etc.).

We know that adult life will bring many *experiences*, some positive, some negative. For some of us adult life will bring experience of: sexual relations; childbirth; bereavement; poverty and wealth; war; illness; broken relationships; exploitation of others (and *by* others); disillusionment; wonderful holidays; getting drunk; smoking tobacco; taking illegal drugs; physical violence; driving a car; filling in an income tax return; operating a bank account; using credit cards; and disputing with a neighbour the right to grow a 20-foot high Leylandii hedge!

The connection between these opportunities, responsibilities and experiences and the school curriculum is by no means clear. We may well ask: what is the use of a great deal of the content of the conventional school curriculum? How does it prepare children for adult life?

These are not new questions, of course. Those of us involved in education in the 1960s and 1970s will be aware of the critiques of the 'de-schoolers', the 'free-schoolers' and the 'new romantics' – notably John Holt, Everet Reimer, Paul Goodman and Ivan Illich, and for me, typified by Postman and Wiengartner's (1971) incisive little book on *Teaching as a Subversive Activity* – all of which were trenchant in their criticisms of systems of schooling which, in their view, reproduced in schools the mind-numbing and soul-destroying experience of the factory production line. While their arguments are sometimes polemical rather than coolly dispassionate philosophies of education, the factory metaphor struck chords among a generation whose experiences of schooling, if less bleak, were not entirely dissimilar from those they described. But of course, the questioning of the relevance of the traditional teaching of a formal academic curriculum, remote from everyday life and taking little regard of the lived experiences of the learner, may be traced to all the 'great educators' of the eighteenth and nineteenth centuries (Rousseau, Froebel, Pestalozzi) and to a good many since. I suspect that many of the 'educational developments' of the late twentieth century would not meet with their approval. In particular, both the increasing influence of central government and the 'marketization' of education would, I think, be anathema to them all.

THE NATIONAL CURRICULUM AND ALL THAT

Whether state intervention in the determination of the curriculum is a good thing remains a matter for debate. It is clear that when left to their own devices, as many were in the 1960s and 1970s, schools showed that they could generate sensible curriculum reforms. These often broadened and balanced the curriculum so that, as well as initiation into the academic and technological curriculum, children and young people experienced courses in civics, PSE, health education and careers education. Bodies such as the Nuffield Foundation and the Schools Council promoted curriculum innovations which, were we to look at them today, would appear to be very appropriate to the requirements of paragraph 2 of the 1988 Act. In the age before educationists fell prey to what Stephen Ball (1990) has termed 'the discourse of derision', academics such as A. H. Halsey and Lawrence Stenhouse advocated programmes of action research which would encourage, especially for those categories of pupil and those neighbourhoods which were considered to be deprived or otherwise disadvantaged, activities which were relevant and interesting but still educational. In particular, the Schools Council's Humanities Curriculum Project (which Stenhouse directed) gave youngsters opportunities to study, in an integrated way, issues such as war, poverty, race and education. Interestingly, the rationale for this programme was not exclusively, or even primarily, in terms of promoting children's social and moral development; rather, it was to make the study of the humanities more interesting to children of average and below average ability, by treating topics with which (it was argued) youngsters were genuinely interested (Stenhouse, 1983).

Some curriculum initiatives of that era intentionally integrated traditional subject disciplines in order that what was seen as the 'seamless robe' of knowledge and experience would not be fragmented. Yet others stayed within the disciplinary boundaries but introduced new and intriguing pedagogy – such as the teaching of history through empathy, role-play and educational drama. Developments in health education, careers education and tutorial programmes like Active Tutorial Work were promoted and supported not only by the Schools Council, Nuffield and the like, but also by progressive LEAs such as Lancashire and the Inner London Education Authority. However, it is arguable that these developments were patchy and unco-ordinated – as, indeed, might be said of the curriculum as a whole – and for this, if for no other reason, one might have expected a warm welcome for a National Curriculum in the wake of the 1988 Act.

Whatever the merits of the ten programmes of study of the National Curriculum and of the Byzantine assessment procedures which accompanied them, the kinds of developments mentioned above were certainly not the beneficiaries. As might have been expected, the preoccupation with what was statutorily required led initially to the marginalization of those parts of the curriculum to do with personal and social development, including health education, careers education, tutorial work and, indeed, cross-curricular approaches in general. The Department of Education and Science was aware that 'more [than the statutory programmes] will be needed to secure the kind of curriculum required by section 1 of the ERA ....' (DES, 1989, para 3.9), and, within a year or two of the publication of the programmes of study, it was apparent that some pretty important aspects of human development were now missing from what was required of schools. Attempts were therefore made to identify, clarify and make good some obvious deficiencies.

In 1990–1, the NCC published a series of pamphlets under the heading 'Curriculum Guidance'. These dealt with cross-curricular elements: aspects of pupils' development which could not be left to any one subject department, let alone any one teacher. Schools were required to include in their curriculum planning a consideration of how, across the curriculum, they would deliver such dimensions as equal opportunities and preparation for life in a multicultural society, deal with such themes as Economic and Industrial

Understanding, Careers Education and Guidance and Health Education, and promote such skills as those of numeracy, information technology and problem-solving. However, as Watkins (1995, p. 123) has shown, the precise status of the cross-curricular elements was never entirely clear. They were not, it seems, a statutory requirement, or an entitlement. The lists of dimensions, themes and skills were indicative rather than compulsory. Quite how schools were expected to respond to this guidance is a matter for speculation, but it is likely that most schools who took it on board will have interpreted the lists as exhaustive. Their status became even less clear after Sir Ron Dearing undertook a much needed review of the National Curriculum in 1993, when the requirement on schools to plan for these elements seems to have disappeared. In this as in other aspects of the curriculum, however, the developing role of the Office for Standards in Education (Ofsted) in shaping curriculum planning through inspection is not to be underestimated. In so far as Ofsted assess schools' provision in an area, non-statutory guidance may be felt to be a requirement anyway!

Ofsted's particular interest in personal and social education can be seen to follow from the same key passage in the 1988 Act. Given that the mental and physical development of children might reasonably be expected to be covered within the National Curriculum programmes of study (including PE), and given that this passage makes specific reference to 'society' and to 'preparation for adult life', it was to *spiritual, moral, social* and *cultural* development that their attention turned. As Taylor has argued, the significance of Ofsted inspections is very considerable:

> Arguably, the single most propelling influence on schools' reconsideration of their values endeavours has been the statutory requirement that OFSTED inspections report on the spiritual, moral, social and cultural (SMSC) *development* of their pupils. (Taylor, 1998, p. 6)

But how this might be accomplished was problematic.

In 1994, we find Ofsted attempting to generate a debate from which, it was hoped, some clarity might emerge as to the precise meanings of, and relationships between, the four components. An intention seems also to have been to promote discussion in the schools themselves, and this is laudable. The discussion document produced by Ofsted in February of that year remains a rich source of questions for debate, including these:

> Is it reasonable to attempt to define spiritual development in a way which is acceptable to those of a non-religious perspective and to those with religious beliefs?

> What are the similarities and differences between social and moral development?

> What is the right balance between 'high' cultural and more immediate local cultural expressions?

> How can teachers present moral issues without moral abdication but also without indoctrination?

Whether such questions have any definitive answers is, of course, itself debatable, as is what might count as evidence that 'development' in SMSC is taking place. As Taylor (1998, p. 7) argues, judging schools on the extent to which pupils, for example, 'show respect for other people's feelings, values and beliefs' without a clear idea of the performance indicators of such behaviour is questionable. (For one account of how Ofsted inspectors go about their duties in this regard see Chapter 16 by Megan Warner in this volume.)

Questions of definition and demonstration were a problem for others, too. In 1996, the (then) Schools Curriculum and Assessment Authority (SCAA) set up a National Forum on Values in Education and the Community, charged with the task of identifying a set of core values on which there is a consensus and which could, therefore, be taught in our society without fear of charges of indoctrination. The outcome was to provide a basis for more than one initiative in developing the curriculum for SMSC, some of which are discussed below.

Then in 1997, careers education became a statutory requirement. Given that careers education was an area of considerable innovation in the 1970s and 1980s, eventually bringing together computer-assisted careers guidance with a careers education seen as preparation for life rather than, merely, for vocational choices, the reasons for its neglect and subsequent rediscovery invite speculation.

RECENT DEVELOPMENTS

So there was much to exercise the minds of those responsible for, and/or interested in, the whole area of personal and social development in the wake of the 1988 Act. But all this is as nothing compared with the flurry of activity in the last two years of the century. In anticipation of the revision of the National Curriculum for the year 2000, a number of groups, panels and associations have been busily examining, designing, advocating and trialling frameworks for curriculum design in the broad area of SMSC. Some are the product of action directly by the government or its agencies; others are pressure or interest groups, some professionally based, which have long-standing interests in this field.

In November 1997 QCA (the successor to SCAA) published draft guidance to schools on how to plan for the promotion of the spiritual, moral, social and cultural development of their charges (QCA, 1997). September of the following year saw the publication of the report of the Citizenship Advisory Group, chaired by Professor Bernard Crick (Crick, 1998). An advisory group for PSHE was also set up in 1998, and reported in May the following year. In December 1998, a panel looking at Education for Sustainable Development was established by the government as was an Advisory Group on Creative and Cultural Education, again giving emphasis to those aspects of development that are cross-curricular rather than the province of any one of the programmes of study.

Over the same period, a number of interest groups, aware of the impending review of the National Curriculum, had been generating debate and publication aimed at least at ensuring that the review produced a more balanced and holistic curriculum than then existed, and at best at winning a significant share of curriculum time for their own area of interest. These bodies include the National Association for Pastoral Care in Education (NAPCE), the Gulbenkian Foundation which has funded two initiatives in this area (see below) and the National Standing Committee of Advisers, Inspectors and Consultants of Personal and Social Education (NSCOPSE).

Finally, in May 1999, the Secretary of State for Education and Employment (David Blunkett) announced for consultation his plans for the National Curriculum to take effect from September 2000. Citizenship education is to be compulsory – i.e. a National Curriculum programme of study – for KS3 and 4 (secondary pupils) from 2002. There is non-statutory guidance for citizenship education for KS1 and 2 (primary pupils) where it is to be integrated into the curriculum for personal, social and health education and there is non-statutory guidance also for PSHE at KS3 and KS4. It is unclear precisely how, if at all, these decisions were influenced by the petitions and reports of the various groups mentioned above, some of which (like that of the National Advisory Group on Personal, Social and Health Education) were at the time yet to be published.

WHAT CAN BE SAID OF THESE DEVELOPMENTS?

I have reviewed a number of the documents which have emerged since 1994, several of which have already been mentioned. These include the SCAA discussion paper on *Education for Adult Life* (SCAA, 1996); the Crick Report (Crick, 1998); the Gulbenkian-funded *Passport* framework (Jenks and Plant, 1998); *Learning by Heart* (McCarthy, 1998); Community Service Volunteers' *Education for Citizenship* (Mitchell, 1999); QCA's draft guidance for pilot work on *The Promotion of Pupils' Spiritual, Moral, Social and Cultural Development* (QCA, 1997); the ATL-commissioned *Values Education and Values in Education* (Taylor, 1998); the report of the National Advisory Group on Personal, Social and Health Education entitled *Preparing Young People for Adult Life* (NAGPSHE, 1999); and Part 2 of The Secretary of State's proposals for the review of the national curriculum in England (QCA, 1999).

What have they in common and what issues do they raise?

To begin with, they pose interesting questions about the way in which school curricula are determined in a liberal democracy. I cannot help pondering the underlying motivations for these developments and the distribution of power by which they have been introduced. What significance are we to attach to the fact that, of all the initiatives listed earlier, it is the *citizenship* theme which the Secretary of State David Blunkett has chosen to adopt as the centrepiece of personal, social and moral education in the revised National Curriculum? Is it significant that Professor Bernard Crick was at one time David Blunkett's tutor at university? Is it taking too jaundiced a view to speak (as some have) of these developments as indicative of a period of 'moral panic' in which social conformity, cohesion and, therefore, order were felt to be under threat? This was the view of at least some of those involved in the January 1996 SCAA conference on 'Education for Adult Life: the spiritual and moral development of young people':

The conference was convened partly in response to public concern at a perceived degeneration in moral standards, especially among young people. Some delegates believed that we are living in a time of moral 'crisis', viewing society as rife with drug abuse, crime and violence. It was the view of some delegates that, although every generation expresses concern over the values of the young, a significant proportion of young people is now out of control. It was the behaviour of young people that gave the greatest cause for concern. (SCAA, 1996, p. 8)

The more or less subtle changes in the tone of political pronouncements since 1990, from the apparently religiously motivated statements of former Secretary of State John Patten through to the secular and civic concerns of the Crick Report, represent interesting shifts in emphasis, but there are grounds for arguing that a neoconservative preoccupation with both individualism and conformity provides the key thread of continuity. Some commentators have been quick to draw comparisons between the recent (September 1999) pronouncements by Prime Minister Tony Blair to the effect that we need a new moral purpose for our younger generation and the discredited call of his predecessor, John Major for the nation to 'get back to basics'. Is the continuity of concern an indication of a consensus among a power elite whose views will dominate regardless of how many panels, committees or focus groups may be established? Or do we have here a case of pluralistic democracy where the countervailing power of different veto groups leads to some kind of 'lowest common denominator' of what should be taught in schools?

The relative status and power of the bodies involved – especially where they are located on opposite sides of the line between government agency and independent pressure group (and, indeed, in the grey area of the 'quango' in between) – is clearly in some people's minds. Protocol matters. Thus Professor Crick thought it appropriate to include, as an appendix to his report, correspondence between himself and Professor John Tomlinson, chairman of the *Passport* project. While this may be read as an important clarification of the relationship between education for citizenship and the (apparently wider) field of SMSC, it can also be read as an exercise in the limitation of competition and the establishment of boundaries. That the spheres of influence of these two eminent chairpersons might also have been delineated in the process is a tantalizing thought! In turn, the authors of the *Passport* framework (e.g. Jenks and Plant, 1998, pp.1, 33) found it necessary to cross-refer to the QCA pilot materials. Interestingly, the co-ordinator of the latter – Marianne Talbot – was a member of the Crick Committee, the *Passport* Project Advisory Committee *and* the National Advisory Group on PSHE. She is a welcome contributor to this book (see Chapter 1), but the high visibility which she and one or two others have had in recent months suggests that a comparison of the full membership of these various groups might be an interesting exercise in determining just who the educational decision-makers are.

Meanwhile, the preoccupation with values, noted in early Ofsted deliberations (Ofsted, 1994), has continued. The twin spectres of indoctrination and relativism are much in evidence. As we have seen, the setting-up by SCAA of the National Forum on Values in Education and the Community was an explicit attempt to establish a core of values held by all members of society, such that teachers might reasonably suppose that there could be no objections to their teaching them. However, such an exercise inevitably leads to degrees of generality which require an enormous amount of work if they are to be translated into programmes.

There are doubts about the desirability of beginning with values anyway. These doubts have been tellingly articulated in regard to citizenship in a recent article by John Halliday (1999). Halliday argues that, even if the establishment of a substantial consensus on values in any detail and at any practical level were a realistic goal, this misunderstands what the substance of democratic life is about. We do not 'live' democracy through embracing, in some holistic way, a set of core values, but through

> a series of localised transitory agreements sharing no one thing in common but a series of family resemblances between different agreements made by neighbours and groups of neighbours in contingent association with one another .... In most cases it is neither useful nor possible to appeal explicitly to what might have been learnt as common ground between all members of society because there is no such common ground, merely shifting sands of agreement to which appeal can be made on a transitory basis. (Halliday, 1999, p. 49)

In other words, the attempt to work from values through outcomes to process may not be an appropriate way to approach curriculum planning in the realm of SMSC. It is a moot point whether *any* curriculum innovation lends itself to such an approach, as would argue those who (at least since the days of Lawrence Stenhouse) have advocated process or research-and-development models of curriculum development.

However, what seems to be common in the various approaches is what has traditionally been known as the *Objectives Model*. At the present time, this approach is most clearly exemplified in the QCA SMSC guidance materials currently being piloted in 100 schools across the country. They advise schools to proceed in the following order:

Consult the local community in establishing overall aims;
Identify Key Stage objectives;
Review current practice;
Plan and implement changes;
Monitor and evaluate progress; and
Recognize and reward success.

The SMSC guidance also most clearly illustrates how difficult it is to produce a straightforward system which will be based upon core values, prescribe outcomes, apply to everyone and cover all contingencies. The result is a complex three-dimensional matrix, to which is added a fourth dimension: that of the key stage for which the planning is being done. The pilot materials include a completed matrix and, expressly in order to protect the freedom of the school to determine how it structures its curriculum, there is also an 'empty matrix' to be filled in, after due consultation with the community and due debate among the staff.

Indeed, the specification of learning outcomes as a matrix appears to be the order of the day. Thus the Crick Report articulates three *strands*, four *essential elements* and five *aspects of society* which it proceeds to illustrate as a cube. The *Passport* framework, content with two dimensions, outlines, for each National Curriculum Key Stage, *skills, knowledge and understanding* and *attitudes and values* related to opportunities for pupils to 'develop self-awareness, develop a healthy lifestyle, learn to keep themselves and others safe, develop effective and satisfying relationships, learn to respect the differences between people, develop independence and responsibility, play an active role as members of society' and 'make the most of their abilities' (Jenks and Plant, 1998).

Now this approach to curriculum planning is not unattractive. For one thing, it appears extremely rational – indeed, this model is sometimes called the *'Rational* Objectivist Model'. It is also highly systematic and (by the sheer number of boxes to be filled in) gives the impression of being very comprehensive. But as Paul Yates argues in this book (see Chapter 2), this is an entirely modernist approach in which the faith of the Enlightenment in the powers of the intellect to resolve all issues and provide the foundation for all cultural construction may blind us to the transience, permeability and relativity of moral action.

It is also, says Yates, bureaucratic, and like all bureaucracies, impersonality and standardization are what it is all about. These outweigh individuality, idiosyncrasy and creativity. In short: bureaucracy replaces the human being with the *system*. And as Jack Priestley observes in Chapter 7 of this volume, '[i]t is systematization which destroys the spirit because it kills all movement' (p. 171).

However, there are significant differences between some of the schemes being advanced. In particular, although one may identify processual considerations in all the initiatives mentioned above, they vary in the relative emphasis they give to process and product. In stressing *opportunities to enable pupils ...*, the *Passport* project expresses, to a greater degree, I think, than either QCA or Crick, the importance of experiential learning in developing capabilities for action. But then, it is not entirely clear that the empowerment (through enabling) of pupils to engage in independent and negotiated thought and action is central in the political perspective which underpins much of the debate.

In the absence of a consensus (not withstanding the SCAA National Forum) one might infer that the best way to proceed is to focus upon *issues* rather than values. This has a good pedigree – including the Schools Council's Humanities Curriculum Project – and, as Don Rowe points out in Chapter 5, has become something of an orthodoxy in PSE and religious education. But according to Rowe, it has numerous weaknesses. In particularizing discussion, the kinds of moral reasoning which we want students to develop may become narrowed; they may even be excluded by an adversarial approach which rehearses dogmatic positions and substitutes rhetorical device for evidence and logic. Preferable, in Rowe's view, is a 'public discourse' model of moral philosophy with the teacher 'scaffolding pupils' arguments in a supportive, stimulating and increasingly sophisticated way around a framework of concepts ...' (p. 128). Like Halliday, Rowe believes the essence of moral behaviour in a civic context is talk; indeed, in this context talk *is* action.

But it is by no means the only action appropriate to education for citizenship or, indeed, to any aspect of SMSC. Earlier in this chapter, I used the categories of paragraph 2 of the 1988 Education Act – 'opportunities', 'responsibilities' and 'experiences' – to indicate the *open-endedness* of the idea of 'preparation for adult life'. Now, a set of circumstances in which one cannot act is no opportunity, and if one cannot act, then one cannot be held responsible for one's actions, or be expected to react to any experience. Essential to opportunities, responsibilities and experiences is *action* in its strongest sense of *engagement*. When we talk about experiential learning, we have in mind experience in which the pupil engages the world, whether the engagement is visual, auditory, tactile or linguistic. This is picked up by Crick (1998, p. 37) in advocating class, school or community projects which the pupils 'have helped to identify, plan, carry through and evaluate'. In this context, Community Service Volunteers' concept of 'active learning in the community' (Mitchell, 1999) is of some interest, not least because it emphasizes service to others in a way that is a refreshing contrast to what Yates has identified as an essentially conservative preoccupation with self (see Chapter 2).

AND WHAT OF SPIRITUALITY?

Although the annual Roehampton Institute conference on *Education, Spirituality and the Whole Child* (now in its seventh year) from which this book originates is conceived as covering the broad area of personal, social, moral and spiritual education, its title is indicative of an enduring preoccupation with the *spiritual*. This was very visible in the book which followed, and took its name from, the first conference (Best, 1996) and to which the present volume is something of a sequel. It remains the most thorny area of SMSC.

The contortions of SCAA/QCA, Ofsted and others in trying to define and distinguish between the moral, the spiritual, the cultural and the social testify to the challenge which faces any attempt to disaggregate human experience for purposes of analysis, however desirable this might appear. The dangers of attempting to specify, monitor and evaluate these as distinct aspects of schools' provision must by now be almost legendary. But of all experiences it is the spiritual which, it seems, is most resistant to operational definition. At its worst, attempts to pin it down lead only to a greater awareness of its intangibility and pervasiveness. Thus, the January 1996 SCAA conference report noted that delegates' views on what constitutes spirituality were many and varied, from 'development of inner life, insight and vision' to 'the quest for meaning in life, for truth and ultimate values', and went on to assert that

> [t]he spirituality of young people can be developed in many ways: for example, by religion, thinking, prayer, meditation or ritual. For some, spirituality is awakened through feelings of awe and wonder at nature and the universe. For others it comes through positive relationships with others. Apparently negative experiences can also contribute to spirituality, such as suffering mental or physical pain ... [but within this diversity] [t]he essential factor in cultivating spirituality is reflection and learning from one's experiences. (SCAA, 1996, pp. 6–7)

The quest for a better understanding of the spiritual and how it may be developed and researched through education is an explicit or implicit concern for several of the contributors to this volume, notably Priestley, Gill, Smith, Roberts and Erricker, all of whom presented papers or keynotes to the 1998 Roehampton conference. But to reach beyond the spiritual and to provide a more inclusive picture of SMSC, I have included chapters (such as those by Ford, Ogden, Cooper, Bigger and Tew) where the emphasis is more on values, culture and society, and by McCarthy where the emphasis is on emotional development. Three additional chapters (those by Talbot, Rowe and Law) were commissioned to ensure that the perspectives of QCA, citizenship and careers education were all represented.

CONCLUSION

In this introduction I have attempted to locate some of the more recent developments in education for SMSC in the narrative of post-1988 events. It is clear that the philosophical issues in the current debate are by no means new, but the more contentious of them have made on a new visibility in education precisely because of decisions made regarding the inclusion of SMSC (and particularly citizenship education) in the curriculum. The centralized determination of the curriculum is, itself, a challenge for those who hold that education in a liberal democracy must recognize if not celebrate diversity, but when this is applied to areas of social expectations, morality, cultural valuation and spiritual experience, the challenge is daunting, to say the least.

There can be few areas of education which are as rich in potential – and need – for philosophical analysis and empirical investigation. The chapters which follow each, in their own way, pick up the issues thrown up by a desire for an holistic, planned and meaningful education in the context of the shifting sands of late modernity. Together they provide important insights into the nature and the emergence of SMSC precisely at the moment when major decisions are being made about the school curriculum for the next century.

REFERENCES

Ball, S. J. (1990) *Politics and Policy Making in Education.* London: Routledge.

Best, R. (ed.) (1996) *Education, Spirituality and the Whole Child.* London: Cassell.

Crick, B (1998) *Education for Citizenship and Teaching of Democracy in Schools.* Report of the Advisory Group on Citizenship, London: Qualifications and Curriculum Authority (Crick Report).

DES (1989) *National Curriculum: From Policy to Practice.* Stanmore, Middx: Department of Education and Science.

Halliday, J. (1999) Political liberalism and citizenship education: towards curriculum reform. *British Journal of Educational Studies,* **47** (1), 43–55.

Jenks, J. and Plant, S. (1998) *Passport. Framework for Personal and Social Education.* 4th draft. Calouste Gulbenkian Foundation.

McCarthy, K. (1998) *Learning by Heart. The Role of Emotional Education in Raising School Achievement.* Brighton: Re:membering Education/ Gulbenkian.

McLaughlin, T. (1992) Citizenship, diversity and education: a philosophical perspective. *Journal of Moral Education,* **21** (3), 235–50.

Mitchell, P. (1999) *Education for Citizenship: The Contribution of Active Learning in the Community*. London: CSV Education for Citizenship.

NAGPSHE (1999) *Preparing Young People for Adult Life*. Report by the National Advisory Group on Personal, Social and Health Education. Nottingham: DfEE.

NCC (1990) *Curriculum Guidance 8: Education for Citizenship*. York: National Curriculum Council.

Ofsted (1994) *Spiritual, Moral, Social and Cultural Development*. Ofsted discussion paper, London: Office for Standards in Education.

QCA (1997) *The Promotion of Pupils' Spiritual, Moral, Social and Cultural Development: Draft Guidance for Pilot Work*. London: Qualifications and Curriculum Authority.

QCA (1999) *The Review of the National Curriculum in England: The Secretary of State's Proposals*. London: Qualifications and Curriculum Authority.

SCAA (1996) *Education for Adult Life: The Spiritual and Moral Development of Young People*. Discussion Paper No. 6, London: School Curriculum and Assessment Authority.

Stenhouse, L. (1983) *Authority, Education and Emancipation*. London: Heinemann.

Taylor, M. J. (1998) *Values Education and Values in Education*. London: Association of Teachers and Lecturers (ATL).

Watkins, C. (1995) Personal–social education and the whole curriculum. In Best, R., Lang, P., Lodge, C. and Watkins, C. (eds), *Pastoral Care and Personal–Social Education: Entitlement and Provision*. London: Cassell, pp. 118–40.

CHAPTER 1

Developing SMSC for the school curriculum

Marianne Talbot

INTRODUCTION

My aim in this chapter is to describe the work being done by the Qualifications and Curriculum Authority (QCA) to support schools in their promotion of pupils' spiritual, moral, social and cultural development. I shall start by briefly outlining the background to the work before going on to discuss its rationale and in particular the link – often left unexplained – between the values of a school and the work it does in this area. This will involve a philosophical discussion of the nature of values, and the existence and importance to schools of shared values. I shall then describe the guidance that QCA has produced and the nationwide pilot that QCA is carrying out on this guidance. I shall conclude by locating this work in its national context and in particular its relation to education for citizenship.

BACKGROUND

In January 1996 the School Curriculum and Assessment Authority (SCAA, one of QCA's predecessors) held a conference entitled *Preparation for Adult Life*. The purpose of the conference was to discuss section 1 of the Education Reform Act, now section 351 of the 1996 Education Act, which states that schools are required to provide a

balanced and broadly based curriculum which (a) promotes the spiritual, moral, cultural, mental and physical development of pupils at the school and of society; and (b) prepares such pupils for the opportunities, responsibilities and experiences of adult life.

The 200 delegates to the conference were asked whether there was reason to think that pupils' spiritual, moral, social and cultural development was not being addressed effectively and, if so, what might be done about it.

The conference agreed that schools were convinced about the importance of promoting pupils' spiritual, moral, social and cultural development, but that this was becoming increasingly difficult. The reasons, delegates thought, were not just the changes brought about by league tables and the National

Curriculum but also the perceived absence of support from society for schools' work in this area, and concerns that common values are not agreed in our pluralistic society. Schools were losing confidence in the appropriateness of promoting values of any kind, suggested delegates, fearing that by so doing they might be imposing values on children who ought to be encouraged to choose their values for themselves.

Delegates recommended that SCAA set up a National Forum for Values in Education and the Community, and give it a twofold remit:

- to decide whether there are any shared values in our pluralist society;
- to decide how schools might be supported in the promotion of pupils' spiritual, moral, social and cultural development.

The National Forum, consisting of 150 people drawn from different parts of society, met over the summer of 1996.

In response to the first part of their remit, Forum members agreed almost immediately that there are values common to everyone in society. Together they drafted a statement of these values. MORI then sent this statement to 3200 schools and 700 national organizations, and conducted an omnibus poll of 1500 adults. In each case they asked people whether they agreed with the values stated. Of those who responded 85–97 per cent agreed with them.

This consensus on common values formed the basis of the Forum's response to the second part of its remit. The Forum recommended that SCAA should use the statement of values to trigger debate about the existence and importance of shared values, to promote schools' confidence in the passing on of these values and to elicit society's support for schools' work in this area. SCAA should also produce guidance for schools' promotion of pupils' spiritual, moral, social and cultural development, based on the values and on existing good practice in schools. It is this work that I shall discuss in this chapter.

First, it is important to make explicit the relationship between values, schools' promotion of pupils' spiritual, moral, social and cultural development and the school ethos more generally. A secure understanding of this relationship is of great help in convincing people that the 'soft' areas listed are as intellectually accessible, in principle, as the 'harder' areas of National Curriculum subjects. This is a precondition of the confidence required to ground good practice.

VALUES: WHY THE PROMOTION OF PUPILS' SPIRITUAL, MORAL, SOCIAL AND CULTURAL DEVELOPMENT IS IMPORTANT

'Values' is a good candidate for the title 'buzzword of the 1990s'. The urge to do a year-end 'moral stocktake' seems very human, and the new millennium promised a veritable orgy of such stocktaking. Human beings are unique in the ability to value things for their own sake, and in their ability to reflect on their values and on whether they are living up to them. But something can be a common topic of conversation without being well understood. Teachers often say that, though they feel confident discussing their own subjects and school policies, they quail when it comes to topics like values. But values are accessible to anyone who is prepared to put in the intellectual effort. And this is amply rewarded by the creation of the ethos and relationships that bring a school alive.

The first question is: 'What are values?' My answer is:

Values are qualities that are in themselves worthy of esteem and that, in virtue of this, generate

a. principles (rules) that guide us in our actions and thoughts;
b. standards (ideals) against which we judge things.[1]

I adopt this account of values because I believe it captures all the elements of values that make them important to us.[2] Let me explain.

Our values *matter* to us because they are goods towards which we strive, qualities that we *want* to acquire or maintain. They encapsulate our most important goals. In so far as we value truth, for example, we seek to discern truth and we try to preserve truth in our beliefs, utterances, theories and accounts of the world. Truth is something towards which we strive, and its opposite, falsehood, something we try to avoid. So our values are goals that are important to us.

As goals our values set important constraints on our pursuit of other goals. In so far as we value truth, for example, we will believe that we should not lie, even to achieve something else that we want. This does not mean, of course, that we *will not* lie: sometimes our desires will get the better of us. Even then, our belief that we should not lie will manifest itself as guilt about the lie we have told.

Since our values are among our goals, and constrain our pursuit of other goals, they generate principles, fundamental rules that tell us how to act and what to think. In particular, they tell us what we *should* (and should not) do and how we *should* (and should not) think. 'Keep promises' might be one such rule, 'tell the truth' another, the former generated by our valuing trustworthiness, the latter by our valuing truth. Such rules give us little practical guidance until placed in context (until, for example, we have made a particular promise, or formed a belief about what the truth is in a particular case), but such is the nature of general principles or rules. Again, therefore, in so far as we value truth, we will embrace the principle 'do not lie', and we feel guilty if we find ourselves lying despite believing we should not lie.

Our values also generate standards against which we judge ourselves and others. They do this because of the principles that they generate. Our values are ideals towards which we strive, and like all ideals they make demands on us, which it is sometimes difficult to live up to. We measure ourselves and others by how far we generally live up to our values.

It might be objected that, even if our values do generate *personal* principles and standards, it would be wrong to impose our own values on others by expecting others to embrace the same principles or to live up to the same standards. But to say this is to misunderstand the nature of values. To believe that a quality is *in itself* worthy of esteem, is to believe that that quality is valuable quite independently of the needs, wants or goals of any individual, including oneself. To value some quality truly, rather than simply to pay lip-service to it, is to believe that others too should value that quality because it is in itself valuable.

This property of values is called *universalizability* by philosophers. It extends to the principles and the standards generated by our values. In so far as these principles or standards are generated by our *values,* rather than by our individual needs, wants or preferences, we will believe that they apply to other people just as much as to ourselves. If your belief in the principle 'do not lie' is generated simply by a personal preference for truth telling, then you will not extend it to anyone else. If the principle is generated by the value of truth you cannot *but* apply it to others. Similarly if you truly judge yourself in terms of your ability to resist lying because you value truth, rather than simply being afraid you will be caught, then you will judge others by the same standards.

Some might still say that we should resist the temptation to judge others by our own standards, because to do this is to insist that they share our beliefs and moral position. This would be unjustifiable because everyone has a right to choose their beliefs and their moral position.

But again this is to confuse personal preferences and values. There are no reasons to believe that others should adhere to principles and standards generated by personal preferences precisely because they are generated by personal preferences. And there is no reason to suppose that others do or should share one's personal preferences. But there is good reason to believe that others should adhere to principles and standards generated by values, because there is good reason to suppose that others do (or should) share one's values. This reason consists in the fact that values are worthy of esteem *in themselves*, not simply in virtue of our own individual wants. So we can offer persuasive arguments for values.

We all have reason to value truth, for example, because if people did not generally tell the truth, communication would be pointless. A primary purpose of communication is the exchange of information. Imagine if we could not generally rely on others to tell the truth. The lack of trust would make asking another for information pointless. We would still have to check everything for ourselves. Communicating would become a *waste* of time. Truth is valuable because without it communication, the glue that holds together our relationships, communities, societies and nations, would fail.

Even those who do not value truth as a quality in itself worthy of esteem have reason to value truth instrumentally (as a means to achieving their own ends). I cannot lie to you successfully unless you believe that I generally tell you the truth. If you think I *might* be lying you would be sensible to ignore what I say. If I want to take advantage of you, therefore, my best bet is to emphasize my trustworthiness. Dishonesty is parasitic on honesty. If a quality cannot be universalized in this way, if we cannot consistently wish that *everyone* valued that quality, then it is wrong to think of that quality as a value. Someone claiming to value it is expressing a personal preference, or a belief about how they prefer to achieve their own ends.[3]

Values, then, are qualities that are in themselves worthy of esteem. To value something is to have reason to believe that others value it, or that others should value it because it *is* valuable, independently of different individual preferences.

And values generate principles that guide our action and thought, and provide standards against which we measure ourselves and others. This explains the link between values and self-respect. If we live up to our values, we gain self-respect. This will help us to do better. If we fail to live up to our values, we tend to feel we have let ourselves down. If this happens often, it will lead either to loss of self-respect or to revising downwards one's values.

This link between values and self-respect is one reason why values are so important at school. Self-respect is the basis of many of the qualities which help people live what Aristotle called the 'good life'. Unless people respect themselves, furthermore, they cannot truly respect others. Bullies are people who lack self-respect and feel they have to do something drastic to force others to respect them, because no one will respect them just by virtue of who they are. Schools can encourage self-respect in pupils only if they pass on robust values, and help pupils to live up to those values.[4]

There is also an important link between our values and our reputations, the respect that others have for us. Some people merely pay lip-service to values: there will always be 'free riders' prepared to take advantage of others. There will also be moments of weakness when we fail to live up to our values. It is not only the unscrupulous who say one thing and do another, it is also the weak. And we are all weak on occasions.

But if someone consistently says one thing and does another it is not the words we should believe but the behaviour. These people will gain a reputation for untrustworthiness. Trust is an essential condition of a good relationship; untrustworthy people cannot maintain good relationships.

This is another reason why values are so important to schools. No school can function well if relationships are shaky. Pupils must feel able to trust teachers, teachers must feel able to trust the management team and each other, all must trust the head. A breakdown of these relationships can undermine the morale of the school. So relationships rest on trust, and trust depends on people doing what they say they will do, living up to the values they claim to have. Hence the values of a school (and of the individuals that make up the school) are a vital part of the school ethos.

Our values are an important determinant of who we are. It is difficult to love someone who rejects our values. Imagine that someone dear to you decides (perhaps through some traumatic life event such as the death of a child) completely to change their values. To all intents and purposes, he or she becomes a different person. Whether you are able to continue loving them (as opposed to feeling you *should* continue loving them) would become a very real question.

Organizations have values too, which play the same role as in the lives of individuals. They determine an organization's morale, reputation and identity. Every school, for example, has:

- values that are goals towards which it strives (e.g. excellence);
- values that constrain its pursuit of other goals;
- values that engender morale;
- values upon which their reputation in the community depends.

A school's values are often encapsulated in its mission statement. This is a statement of what the school would like to be and to believe about itself, and of what the school would like others to believe of it. If it lives up to these values, the school is likely to be successful because morale will be high and its reputation good, and in so far as it fails, its morale will be low and its reputation shaky. Mission statements should inform every aspect of the life of a school: they should be lived actively rather than being lists of 'feel-good' nouns in the front of the prospectus.

The values of a school have an added dimension of importance. They not only inform the daily life of school as a place of work, but are also the values that will be passed on to the next generation. These values should help their pupils live fulfilled, happy productive lives.

This can be difficult if the values of the school's community are at odds with those of the school. Living up to a robust set of values not shared by others is a continuous challenge. When one thinks that the only way to survive is to do as others in the community do, e.g. take advantage of everyone else, one loses sight of the fact that no community can survive for long on that basis. Members of the community may have revised their values downwards in response to such difficulties. But all of us have a responsibility to help the next generation embrace values that will enhance, rather than detract from, their chances of happiness.

Schools have a responsibility in law to promote pupils' spiritual, moral, social and cultural development. To do this effectively, the values in the school must be the right ones, they must really be worthy of esteem. Only if the school is a healthy community in which relationships are based on trust and concern for others, in which people value wisdom, truth, justice, courage and other such qualities, and in which people possess the virtues that enable them to live up to these values, is it likely that pupils will acquire these values (and the virtues associated with them) for themselves, will deem important the things that really are important and esteem those things that really are worthy of esteem. To learn such important truths is to have one's spiritual, moral, social and cultural development promoted in the best possible way.

The link between the values of a school and its successful promotion of pupils' spiritual, moral, social and cultural development is direct and indivisible. This is why the National Forum for Values in Education and the Community recommended that QCA produce guidance for schools' promotion of pupils' spiritual, moral, social and cultural development based on the values outlined in the Forum's statement. Let us now consider this draft guidance, how it was produced and the pilot project with schools.

GUIDANCE AND SUPPORT FOR SCHOOLS IN THEIR PROMOTION OF PUPILS' SPIRITUAL, MORAL, SOCIAL AND CULTURAL DEVELOPMENT

The National Forum for Values in Education and the Community recommended that the guidance should build on current best practice and make use of the expertise of those involved in the promotion of pupils' spiritual, moral, social and cultural development. QCA consulted headteachers, teachers, educationists and faith leaders, as well as numerous organizations (such as parents' organizations) whose work touched on these areas. This took six months, and the guidance was drafted in the light of views expressed.

Schools wanted practical guidance to help them not only to know what is involved in promoting SMSC but also what to do to enhance the school's provision in every area. The draft guidance recommends a six-step management process to create a vibrant whole-school approach. The six steps are:

1. Identify, together with your community, the values of your school and their relationship to the promotion of pupils' spiritual, moral, social and cultural development.
2. On the basis of step 1, identify concrete objectives for each key stage.
3. Review current practice to identify (a) current success and (b) opportunities for further work.
4. Plan and implement desirable changes.
5. Monitor and evaluate progress and achievement.
6. Recognize and reward effort and success on the part of both pupils and adults.

The first step enables the school to identify its values. Consulting with the community helps the school enlist its support. The Forum's statement of values is included to provide a trigger for the school's own debate about values. The values schools identify independently often prove to be similar to those outlined by the Forum. The second step ensures that the 'mission statement' which results from step 1 encapsulates a practical purpose, that it engages with school practice.[5] Step 3 often reveals that the school is already doing much good work and living its values. Those who contribute to this should be encouraged and used to champion the process. It is likely also to reveal gaps which need to be filled before the school can really claim to be living up to its values. (For example, the mission statement might claim that the school encourages pupils to make responsible decisions, yet actually there may be few opportunities for this.)

Step 5 indicates there is no point in having goals, and strategies to achieve them, without monitoring whether these strategies are in fact helping to achieve the desired goals, and without evaluating the success in achieving them. Step 6 makes explicit the importance of recognition and reward. This is vital if people – adults as well as pupils – are to feel that their efforts and successes are valued. Simple gestures such as public commendations and thanks are very powerful in the school community.

The National Forum recommended that the draft guidance be piloted in schools to ensure that the finished product was user-friendly. Over the last year, the guidance has been piloted in 150 schools nationwide. Some 100 schools were chosen at random, invited to take part in the pilot and sent the guidance, but offered no further help. They will be asked whether they have used the guidance, and for views about its usefulness, accessibility and user-friendliness. This will suggest ways in which the guidance can be improved and give evidence of what support and training schools may need if they are to make real progress in promoting pupils' SMSC development. The other 50 schools are acting as a 'development group'. They have received the guidance and been given extra training and a small budget so that they can help develop the guidance and implement it creatively.

Interim findings suggest that the guidance is useful, but that a shorter and simpler version is needed. The pilot schools have also mentioned the difficulty they have in trying to promote a robust set of values when other influences might reasonably cause pupils to question whether these are the actual values of society, rather than values to which lip-service is paid by adults.

THE NATIONAL CONTEXT

Alongside this work on the promotion of pupils' spiritual, moral, social and cultural development, the government set up Advisory Groups on Citizenship, Personal, Social and Health Education, Creativity and Culture, and Education for Sustainable Development, to make recommendations about how schools might best provide education in these areas. In the newly published National Curriculum documents, QCA has included a framework for the teaching of citizenship and PSHE. The values outlined by the Forum provide the rationale for both. If we value ourselves, our relationships, our society and our environment, children have both the right and the duty to be taught about their society, themselves and their relationships. Clearly neither citizenship nor personal and social development can be taught in an hour a week: any such classes must take place within the context of a healthy school ethos, one that vigorously promotes pupils' spiritual, moral, social and cultural development. In working through the six-step process schools will be able to see exactly where they are already teaching citizenship and PSHE and where there are opportunities for further work.

THE FUTURE

In this chapter I have briefly explored the nature of values and their importance to schools, both as institutions that rely on good relationships, morale and reputation, and as institutions that have a duty to help the young acquire the values that will enable them to fulfil their own potential and contribute to the society in which they live. I have also considered the guidance that QCA has been piloting relating it to the national context in which schools will do this work, in particular the new emphasis on citizenship and PSHE. But it is useful to go right back to basics and consider why education, and particularly education in values, is important.

Many of the changes in education over the last 20 years have focused on schools' responsibility to promote pupils' academic development. They tend to embody a rather instrumentalist view of education, as the means to qualifications and jobs. But every good teacher and parent knows there is more to education than this. Education must also be inspirational, it must help children to acquire a love of learning, a robust sense of themselves and a concern for the society in which they live. The current drive to recognize the importance of promoting pupils' spiritual, moral, social and cultural development, and of the areas, such as citizenship and PSHE, that contribute to it, is a necessary counterbalance to instrumentalist and economic pressures if we are to produce whole and rounded people capable of living good lives in the widest sense.

NOTES

1 The word 'thing' does not make the account of values imprecise because we *need* a word that does the yeoman service of 'thing'. We judge *all* sorts of things against the standards set by our values, e.g. we judge people (ourselves and others), institutions (schools, businesses ...), theories, thoughts and utterances, actions, properties of things and so on.

2 There are different kinds of values: intellectual (e.g. wisdom), moral (e.g. kindness), aesthetic (e.g. beauty), social (e.g. justice). It is important not to think of all values as moral values: there are qualities such as beauty, which are in themselves worthy of esteem but are not moral qualities.

3 It has been suggested at various seminars I have held that we should include on our list of values things like *violence* on the grounds that some people value violence. But to include something on the list of values simply because there are people that value that thing is to refuse to countenance the possibility of people *wrongly* valuing something. Yet human beings can make errors everywhere else, so why not in the area of values?

4 Values are often confused with virtues. Virtues are enduring character traits possession of which help us to live up to our values. Honesty, for example, is a virtue because to be honest is to be able to live up to the fact that we value truth.

5 Many mission statements sound very worthy, but when one tries to use them to formulate specific objectives they can be seen to be empty words.

CHAPTER 2

The spirit and the empty matrix: the social construction of spiritual, moral, social and cultural education

Paul Yates

Although Giddens (1986, 1991) uses the term 'late modernity' to distinguish his understanding of the current state of society from those who see modernity as having been replaced by postmodernity, the features of postmodernism are real enough, Tucker (1998, p. 125) describes the postmodern shift to an information-based culture as representing:

> a postindustrial, postmodern world, [is] characterized by the loss of old certainties in the context of the decline of industrial labor and its replacement by service work, the crisis of the nuclear family, the ubiquity of mass communications, and the ecological distrust of science. This ever-present change and sense of crisis translates into questions concerning the very nature of our selves and our communities, as demonstrated in the many debates on issues such as sexual orientation, multiculturalism, and nationalism. The lack of traditional moorings for our self-identity has accompanied the profusion of new identities, from gays and lesbians to religious fundamentalists, that influence societies throughout the world.

It is precisely this loss of certainty that schools as organizations and the educational agencies of government implicitly deny. Official educational discourse at every level is myopically modernist in its assumptions and in its explicit prescriptions (Hargreaves, 1994; Hartley, 1997; Woods et al., 1998).

While these novel social conditions are often represented as a quantum break with the modern period, Giddens sees them as developments within modernity rather than supplanting it. As Tucker (1998, p. 126) suggests 'Giddens rejects the postmodern claim of a surpassed modernity, stating that modernity's culture of incessant reflexivity creates a post-traditional social world.' Giddens's conception of the post-traditional society has implications for our understanding of education because he suggests that our social condition has changed significantly. Mullard and Spicker (1998, p. 132) identify the key element as a change in the nature of authority: 'it is a society which is post-traditional in the sense that we live in a social condition which is not anchored in tradition, authority and institutions ... a society which is seeking to come to terms with uncertainty.' It is this demise of the traditional and along with it notions of certainty and the absence of ambiguity which Giddens contrasts with prevailing social conditions. As I shall argue, it is precisely this vanished reality of a reliable monoculture which schools are attempting virtually to create and arguably thereby failing to address the real social conditions of their clients. While official school reality continues to be self-legitimated by the Enlightenment values of universal truth and the grand narratives of Man contained within the human sciences, the lives of pupils are being constructed within a different and contradictory framework. The danger is that school becomes a dissonant fragment in the landscape of the possible and the plausible.

Mullard and Spicker (1998) identify some key aspects of the post-traditional society which can be seen to qualify the role of school as a socializing agency of the state. In particular 'what Giddens calls a "generative" welfare state, [is] one which promotes the self-determination of individuals [and] sees people as citizens or individuals who are unique and with their own life projects' (Mullard and Spicker, 1998, p. 133). Critical for school is the issue of trust. The narratives of traditional society were held in place by 'the guardians of tradition' (Mullard and Spicker, 1998, p. 133). A range of institutions and persons enjoyed largely unquestioned authority in the sense that their narratives were not doubted. These included 'the church, philanthropic employers and professionals, including doctors and teachers. The trust in these guardians is broken' (p. 133). This has occurred through the proliferation of alternative knowledges which may in themselves conflict and thus, almost paradoxically, 'the new uncertainty of post-traditional society is founded on the growth of human knowledge' (Mullard and Spicker, 1998, p. 134). As Mullard and Spicker understand it:

> Rather than human knowledge leading to progress, as was argued by Enlightenment thinkers, the present levels of knowledge are creating new uncertainties. Rather than emancipation being dependent on history revealing itself through knowledge, emancipation in the context of postmodernity seems to depend on the ability of [sic] living with chaos. (p. 134).

There is also the issue of changes in the meaning of community which I shall turn to later.

Hargreaves (1994, p. 28) refers to the secondary school as a 'quintessentially modernist institution', while Hartley (1997, p. 125) outlines the signal features of modernity in education:

> The school is a monument to modernity. Virtually everything is arranged rationally, including space, time, curriculum, assessment and discipline ... The curriculum is rationally ordered, replete with aims, objectives and performance criteria ... A hierarchy of roles within the schools is deemed almost as natural. Schools are places where reason prevails over the emotions.

The point to be taken here is not that one would advocate the irrational organization of schooling but that the model of the person and what may be of value is severely circumscribed within rational modernity in ways that may fail to address pupils' actual social natures and political futures.

It is this reification of rationality that links schools into both Fordism as a mode of cognitive production and bureaucracy as a model of human relationships. The question is whether these fundamental, and increasingly pronounced, features of school are compatible with educating the late modern person. Fordism is the bureaucratic organization of the pursuit of identified objectives best exemplified by assembly line production. Following Weber, Brown and Lauder (1992, p. 11) list the attributes of bureaucracy as 'precision, speed, clarity, regularity, reliability and efficiency achieved through the fixed division of tasks, hierarchical supervision, and detailed rules and regulations.' Despite two decades of constant reform within education, Woods et al. (1998, p. 219) suggests 'schools still reflect the ideas, basic organisation and technology of the nineteenth century.' Centralization, however, is relatively new and its effect has been that 'democratic accountability at the local, micro-environmental level has been reduced drastically' (Woods et al., 1998, p. 203). In England the government's imposition of the National Literacy and Numeracy Schemes, with their heavy emphasis on targets and measured output, is a prescriptive intervention in the school curriculum which illustrates well the techniques of Fordism and centralized bureaucracy applied to education.

The impact of these aspects of commercial bureaucratic culture on school life are well documented (Ball, 1994; Brown and Lauder, 1992; Gewirtz et al., 1995; Whitty et al., 1998). Hargreaves (1994, p. 32) sees modernity as firmly entrenched in the public sector and argues that state bureaucracies including education in the late modern period have been characterized by 'narrowness of vision, inflexible decision-making, unwieldy structures, linear planning, unresponsiveness to clients' needs, the sacrifice of human emotion for clinical efficiency and the loss of meaningful senses of community'. This is wholly antithetical to any educational initiative aimed at increasing the social power and agency of pupils.

The increased emphasis on performativity, that is the equation of success with maximal cognitive output in tests and examinations, is a pragmatic response to central policy demands rather than to any assessment of clients' needs. Woods et al. (1998, p. 191) report that for parents the academic was not the single most important priority in school choice but was placed in a wider social and moral sphere; and indeed within schools 'the weight being given to the instrumental/academic over the intrinsic-personal/social does not reflect the broadly equal emphasis given to these by parents.'

Education policy has become to some extent a self-referential discourse. Much current writing emphasizes the narrow ideological base from which prescriptive policies are generated (Ball, 1992, 1994, 1995, Gewirtz et al., 1995). This would seem to be independent of the party of government. It may be that the cultural and intellectual sources of our educational policy and practice are drawn from an agenda that is rooted in a particular ideologically constructed past and may be failing to address emergent realities. McLean (1995, p. iv) suggests that 'the challenge to education comes from a global economy that makes work more complex and more mercurial.' For Hartley (1997, p. 106) 'global capitalism and post-Fordist work practices present education with an *economic* context far more turbulent than has been the case for much of the twentieth century' (original emphasis). Fink and Stoll (1997, p. 186) in a critique of teacher deskilling in current education suggest that 'the post-modern world requires a different model of schooling, one which is more in concert with the changing nature of economies and social structures.' While education in England and Wales becomes increasingly rigid through the expansion of standardization in curriculum and pedagogic practice, the domains of culture and economy are becoming more differentiated and diffuse in their nature.

It is the intensity of the focus on the end of schooling as one-off individual cognitive performances that has led to organizational goals being seen as sufficient in themselves and unrelated to social, economic or political futures. The motors of current social change are virtually absent from education policy and practice. Elliott (1998, p. 28) is critical of what he refers to as the 'objectives model' of curriculum planning on several grounds, not least that the basic epistemology of a system of learning which often presents knowledge as both external and immutable distorts its social nature. The real map of human knowledge is not a sequence of Platonic archetypes.

The objectives model constitutes a misrepresentation of knowledge, because within our *post-modern* culture we now tend to experience all knowledge as uncertain and unstable, as provisional and open to revision. This experience of knowledge as a *dynamic* rather than *static* quality may be positively embraced or it may evoke a desire to return to the old certainties and their promise of a rational foundation for living. (Elliott, 1998, p. 28.

Avis *et al.*'s (1996, p. 118) answer to the question of relativism is to advocate bringing to the surface of educational discourse an understanding of knowledge as social production.

The solution at school level ... is to reject notions of scientific certainty and move instead to those of situational certainty. Situational certainty derives not from the workings of scientific truth and knowledge, which are rendered problematic within post-modernism, but rather through open and honest discussion and dialogue that operate across a wide constituency and that respect the knowledge, skills and forms of expertise that various groups bring to the encounter. (p. 118)

The current focus in school on disembedded organizational goals may tend to alienate the organization from its social setting. The learning process needs to embed the sociality of pupils if it is to recognize a more complex model of the person. School also needs a focus outside of its narrow externally imposed goals, and one that is firmly rooted in the futures of pupils, so that the content of schooling will cease to be what it currently is, irrelevant to life.

SPIRITUAL, MORAL, SOCIAL AND CULTURAL EDUCATION

What I shall now focus upon is the question of whether the current conception of curriculum in English schools is antipathetic to anything we might call spiritual. The culture of bureaucracy produces schools 'balkanized into a maze of bureaucratic *cubbyholes* known as subject departments' (original emphasis) (Woods, *et al.*, 1998, p. 28). Whitty *et al.* (1998) express concern about the conditions of curriculum development and the creation of new school knowledges. Centralization, surveillance through accountability and the consequent lack of teacher involvement, combined with the 'increasingingly restricted opportunities for initial and continuing professional development', create the danger that 'curriculum change may stagnate' (Whitty *et al.*, 1998, p. 88).

In the school curriculum Ball (1995, p. 87) argues that cultural restorationism dominates, with a 'regressive traditionalism applied to all facets of educational practice'. This orientation represents, 'a hard line, old humanism based on a discourse that links education strongly with traditional social and political values and with social order' (p. 87). In the restorationist discourse, tradition is evoked and equated with the morally good but ' "traditional education" (and traditional values) is here a pastiche, a policy simulacrum – the identical copy for which no original has ever existed ... this simulacrum coincides perfectly with the broader agenda of restorationism and the neo-conservative project to re-establish *order and place*' (original emphasis) (Ball, 1994, p. 45). It is within this context that the discourse around the spiritual, moral, social and cultural curriculum (SMSC) can be located.

In the case of SMSC the notion that such complex and diffuse areas of social being could be the subject of surveillance via inspection requires the relocation of a very loosely framed and equivocal register into a tightly framed code which is capable of being objectified and understood as generally applicable.

However, even the concept of what a value might be is contested and elusive (Halstead and Taylor, 1996). Halstead (1996, p. 11) quotes the *Handbook for the Inspection of Schools* where 'a school is said to be exhibiting high standards in the area of pupils' personal development and behaviour "if its work is based upon clear principles and values expressed through its aims and evident in its practice".' Standards have two important elements, uniformity in application and conformity in expression, which may not be appropriate to the areas of the person indicated by SMSC.

Ball (1995, p. 100) is critical of the monoculturalism implicit in the National Curriculum which he describes as 'a fantasy curriculum', which fails to construct reliable knowledge of the world but attempts to 'conjure up and reproduce a fantasy of Englishness, classlessness, authority, legitimacy, moral order and consensus'. In this discourse the past is more real than the present which is constantly seen to fall short.

Ball quotes Pascall as chairman of the National Curriculum Council expressing a unitary and fixed view of culture where 'the culture of a society is defined by its political and social history, its religious and moral beliefs, and its intellectual and artistic traditions' (Ball, 1995, p. 100). Current realities seem not to impinge on the vision of a 'dominant culture' which is constructed by 'the Christian faith, the Greco-Roman influence, the Liberal enlightenment, romanticism, the development of modern humanism' (p. 100). As Ball (1995, p. 98) notes, 'we are to face the future by always looking backwards'. Pascall's notion of culture as 'a process of intellectual, spiritual and moral development' removes school knowledge from any connection with the cultural realities of pupils' lived experience. This means that there is no way of building a spirituality or a morality that is ontologically grounded, a precondition which might logically be seen as necessary for personal development.

The National Curriculum Council (1993) discussion paper attempts to unpack the spiritual and moral domains into a set of standard prescriptions. It is a classic document which, while apparently addressing concrete reality, touches no known social condition at any point. For example, spirituality 'has to do with the universal search for individual identity', a statement at odds with most theological, anthropological, historical and psychological understanding but consonant with neoconservative notions of the primacy of the individual.

The content of spirituality is a catalogue drawn from modernist religious education and includes beliefs, a sense of awe and wonder, feelings of transcendence, a search for meaning, self-knowledge, relationships, creativity and feelings and emotions. The rationale of this collection is not given nor is there any justification for their being constituted as valid knowledge within the school curriculum beyond the word 'spirituality' appearing in the preamble to the 1988 Education Reform Act. The authority of the text derives from its documentary form and its provenance in one of the agencies of the state. The School Curriculum and Assessment Authority's (SCAA, 1996a) statement on spiritual and moral development continues to address the same problem and is in the same genre. It has a clear concern with standardization, though this is presented as achieving consensus, a matter of no concern in the drawing up of the original National Curriculum. In the statement 'spirituality should be seen as a form of skill or aptitude', the limits of its conceptualization are rather firmly set (SCAA, 1996a, p. 6).

Under the heading of 'Defining spirituality', Pascall's neoconservative agenda is confirmed. Throughout the document there is no understanding of the autonomy of the social sphere; it exists only as a medium upon which the agency is to inscribe its will. And so in order 'to enable productive debate, key terms such as "values", "attitudes" and "morality" should have broadly agreed definitions' (SCAA, 1996a, p. 5) which is rationalist but unreal in the sense that it can only be asserted but never achieved. Similarly, 'traditional approaches to Personal and Social Education lack rigour', is unexplained but clearly pejorative (p. 5). The social is presented as a unified actor in thrall to the agency in the notion that 'society must express and affirm values and behaviours it expects schools to promote' (p. 5).

THE QCA *DRAFT GUIDANCE*

The implementation of the neoconservative model of the person in society as school curriculum is being pursued by the Qualification and Curriculum

Authority (QCA) which has issued a series of documents which are framed as *Draft Guidance for Pilot Work* (QCA, 1997). These documents repay careful analysis. (In this section, quotations are taken from the (non-paginated) QCA, 1997, unless otherwise indicated.)

That we are dealing with a bureaucratic construction of the spiritual, moral, social and cultural curriculum is made clear by the form and structure of the Guidance. It consists of nine (unpaginated) documents, two devoted to justification and description, two to the role of subject teaching in the main phases of schooling, one to 66 briefly sketched case studies of 'The promotion of pupils' spiritual, moral, social and cultural development', a list of resources and two matrices, one illustrative and one empty, subtitled 'a management tool' which 'will be a complete statement of school policy in this area' (QCA, 1997). Lastly there is a set of instructions on how the documents are to be used in order to create an enactment of their content and its own documentary legitimation in a whole school policy. In short, the Guidance documents are a do-it-yourself policy construction kit.

The Guidance is not constructed in continuous prose, which might encourage careful consideration, but in double columns of bullet points and boxes, a form which evokes the imperative mood and which belies the frequent exhortations to reflection. There is an immediate conflict between the often repeated message that these documents are merely aids 'designed to stimulate schools' own thinking in this area' and the level of comprehensive, and often prescriptive, detail contained in them. Instructions for use begin with an 'executive summary' which justifies the activity within a specific image of the school and lists seven advantages to the organization which 'the successful promotion of pupils' spiritual, moral, social and cultural development' can deliver. The first is that it will 'enable the school successfully to fulfil its statutory obligation(s)' and the second is that it will 'contribute to success in Ofsted inspections'. With this the exercise is immediately set within a forensic and coercive framework of legal duty and promised surveillance. It will also make people work harder by 'increasing pupil and teacher motivation'. The puritan virtue of hard work in the form of increased motivation is a constant reference throughout the documents. The affective areas of the person are referred to only once and in terms of an ideal and empirically meaningless end, that of ensuring 'that everyone in the school feels valued as an individual'. The notion that SMSC can make a 'contribution to school ethos' suggests that ethos is a planned and achievable condition rather than an undercurrent of school culture. This is explained by the last statement where achievement of this 'promotion' is to 'ensure that the values enshrined in the school's mission statement permeate every part of school life'. This last is a description of the perfectly rational bureaucratic organization where all idiosyncrasy is submerged under the weight of internalized and normalizing pressure.

The route to this perfect condition is carefully mapped in the form of rational management manuals by 'a six step process towards success'. This describes the process as one of establishing goals, turning them into key stage objectives, planning implementation and monitoring and evaluating outcomes. This will enable the filling in of the empty matrix and defines the activity as one of policy production, the creation of the perfect document which will in an undisclosed way order real-life social action in its image. In this process of conforming SMSC to the restorationist curriculum, the possibility of equivocation in these complex and diffuse areas is addressed through the provision of a 'Glossary of Key Terms', which may encourage clarity but also functions to regulate the meanings of words and thereby the boundaries of the discourse they produce and ultimately the meaning of the social action that they refer to.

The question of values is seen to be a key issue. The School Curriculum and Assessment Authority set up The National Forum for Values in Education and the Community in order first to establish a list of consensual values, and secondly to 'decide how schools might be supported in the important task of contributing to pupils' spiritual, moral, social and cultural development'. The deliberations of the National Forum, a group of one hundred and fifty people largely drawn from 'national organisations with concern for young people or education [*sic*]' resulted in the identification of four value areas, self, relationships, society and the environment, each with an associated set of 'principles for action' (SCAA, 1996b, p. 5). Within the guidance these principles are translated into a series of moral prescriptions under the four areas. First, the self, where for example 'we should: develop self-respect and self-discipline' (QCA, 1997). Secondly, relationships, where 'we should: respect the privacy and property of others'. Thirdly, society, where 'we should: support the institution of marriage'. Finally, the environment, where 'we should: understand the place of human beings within nature'. The neoconservative privileging of the individual over the social is established from the start in the statement 'the ordering [of the four value areas] reflects the belief of many that values in the context of the self must precede the development of the other values'. The idea that the construction of the self can in some mystical manner precede our sociality does not make sociological or psychological sense but is an ideological assertion. While our embodiment is individuated, any notion of the dimensions of the self can only be constructed within a socially generated lexicon.

As the guidance itself suggests, 'these values are so fundamental that they may appear unexceptional'. Which they very largely do, and so it is unsurprising that a poll of adults and a survey of 3200 schools and 7000 'organisations' overwhelmingly agreed with the values (although we are not given the response rate). A critical question here is why is there a need to establish a consensus on basic social values when we can be fairly assured of their content and existence? The National Forum was set up as a consequence of the SCAA conference, Education for Adult Life, which considered 'the spiritual and moral development of young people' (SCAA, 1996a). The 'key points' to come out of this conference were a neoconservative unpacking of the spiritual and moral around the implicit theme of social order where values became 'values and behaviour' which were the subject of an unsubstantiated 'current confusion'. Thus, the National Forum was to remove the confusion by establishing a national consensus. It is worth noting that such a consensus could only have moral authority within a populist political framework. Despite this, the demonstrated consensus is then used to remove the burden of the legitimation of a normalizing curriculum from the agency to an amorphous society. Thus,

Schools and teachers can have confidence that there is general agreement in society upon these values. They can therefore expect the support and encouragement of society if they base their teaching and the school ethos on these values'. (QCA, 1997)

The two propositions in the last sentence do not follow but are in line with the frequent references to 'community' and the need to establish 'business partners'. The preamble to the statement of values is in exhortatory mode with an underlying appeal to social order, 'their [the values] demanding nature is demonstrated both by our collective failure consistently to live up to them, and the moral challenge which acting on them in practice entails'. And so the development (which is the word used where one might expect to see 'education') of the pupil is towards perfect consonance with a moral condition determined by a government agency and expressed as a set of rational prescriptions. Given this, success might well be seen in terms of the degree of conformity that schools can manage to engineer.

The document on *The Promotion of Pupils' Spiritual, Moral, Social and Cultural Development*, gives advice on how to move through the six steps to a full matrix. This is headed 'the how', and is preceded by 'the why' and 'the who'. 'The why' reinforces the organizational boundaries of the project by emphasizing the point that the 'promotion' of spiritual, moral, social and cultural 'development' is 'an essential ingredient of school success'. The original orientation of the SCAA conference, that this curriculum area was to be primarily concerned with preparation for life outside of school, is lost. The advantages are confirmed in output terms as increased motivation for both pupils and teachers. 'The who' locates responsibility for the curriculum area with the senior management team and outlines the necessary personal and professional attributes of a co-ordinator.

The bulk of the document is given over to detailing the process of policy production. The empty matrix is even suggested as a conforming device for schools 'with well-established policies' who 'may find completing the empty matrix useful for auditing their existing practice' (QCA, 1997). For those who know schools and teachers well there is a credibility gap between much of the advice contained in the guidance and the assumptions it makes and the actual conditions of teachers' lives and work. The echo of consensus is here translated as success being dependent upon 'consistency of pupils' experiences and relationships'. The references to consistency in the guidance may have more to do with the aesthetics of regimentation than with the preparation of pupils for adult life. Part of the achievement of local consensus is consultation with the social segment called 'the community'. In 'extended' form this comprises an apparently random group of 'parents, employers and business partners, local shopkeepers, religious and faith groups, youth associations, the legal and emergency services and the local media'. It is assumed that all these groups can be enticed to 'evening meetings at which people can discuss these issues face to face'.

The advice on key stage objectives is to turn them into a prescriptive socialization programme by identifying 'the knowledge and understanding, skills, qualities and attitudes that pupils should be acquiring if they are to be developing those identified in the school's overall goals' which will 'facilitate a secure and practical understanding' for all concerned. The aesthetic of rational consistency in the bureaucratic model of the pupil is again evidenced by the advice to ensure 'breadth and balance' so that 'pupils' social development is not promoted *at the expense of* pupils' spiritual development' (original emphasis). How such an unbalanced state of affairs can be determined to exist is not ventured.

The review of current practice is to be thorough and is to include not only 'subject areas' and what is referred to as the 'broader curriculum' (a phrase which brings the informal aspects of school under official gaze) but also 'school structures, systems, processes and rules'. A range of advice on how to do this is given including teachers spending a whole day shadowing a pupil. No advice is offered on what to do with the fruits of this experience. However, perfect knowledge of the organization is the aim as the co-ordinator should be able 'to make sure that every part of school life is scrutinised and that everyone is clear about their contribution to this work'.

'Planning and implementing change' repeats the need for consistency; suggests that business partners and others in the community might 'lead and manage certain changes'; and gives advice on bidding for sponsorship from local and national businesses. The fifth step is evaluation which urges the need for 'reliable systems by which to gather, analyse and interpret evidence'. There is an assurance that 'reflection on lessons ... is good professional practice', and that 'systems and processes designed to test the collective mood of the school can boost morale'. These are to include informal mingling of 'staff and management', or us and them, where they might have a 'chance to unwind together'. On the difficult matter of detecting pupil development the illustrative matrix suggests that annual reports to parents might be based on 'regular questionnaires, quizzes or short exams of pupils' acquisition and development ... as outlined in the statement of concrete goals for the appropriate educational stage'. This is a clear statement that we are engaged in a process of cognitive acquisition not with the engagement with what might be valuable but open-ended discursive knowledge. Neither here nor in the illustrative matrix is there any reference to the wealth of advice on monitoring and evaluation to be found in the many practitioner researcher manuals designed for schools such as Altrichter, Posch and Somekh (1993) or Hitchcock and Hughes (1995).

The final step is 'recognising and rewarding pupil and adult achievement' with the illustrative matrix justifying rewards on the grounds of increased motivation. Within the Guidance as to what this might mean in practice, clarity of exposition masks the real difficulty in determining what achievement in these areas might look like.

The list of rewards reinforces the ideal of conformity to organizational goals through offering greater participation as recognition for achievement. These include 'the right to do coveted tasks ... to achieve status and reward by taking on responsibility ... to represent the school at public events ... to take responsibility, with teachers, for press coverage of school activities ... become members of committees that have real power' and, most blatantly demonstrating the notion of reward as trusteeship of the organization and its goals, 'to cooperate with teachers and senior management in the practical aspects of running the school'. These last used to be called prefects.

This is followed by a section headed 'A Discussion'. After disclaiming the prescriptive authority of what is to follow, there are four sections devoted to the development and promotion of the spiritual, moral, social and cultural curricular areas. In the discussion of the spiritual area, any notion of consistency is abandoned in an equivocal set of references to social order and the metaphysical. It is asserted that spirit 'is our essential *self*' (original emphasis) which moreover 'when it is strong, enables us to survive hardship, exercise fortitude and overcome difficulties and temptations'. Temptation is a clear theme. Evidence of moral development is seen in being 'able to deal effectively with moral conflict and temptation'. The point of moral development is that it will 'help them [pupils] exercise their will in resisting temptation'. Similarly, the internalization of 'rules' will 'enable them to resist the temptations they inevitably face'. The human essence or spirit of self becomes reduced to mood with a reference to 'spirits' which can be high or low. The work ethic is appealed to in that 'spiritual growth is the key to human motivation' and its presence can be detected by 'learning and striving throughout life'. This undeclared, and vaguely protestant, individualism runs through the whole discussion, which is full of exhortations to be motivated, to work harder and to be obedient. For example, evidence of moral development is 'a determination to obey rules'. There is reference to pupils discussing, reflecting and analysing but only as a route to conformity and within a barely mediated transmission pedagogy.

> Pupils will make these values [identified by the National Forum] their own only if they have been encouraged to discuss them, to subject them to criticism and see *why* these values are the ones that, in the light of reason and fellow feeling, they *should* hold and *why* obedience to these rules is a necessary condition of social harmony. (QCA, 1997)

It is difficult to see the educational value of organizing so closed a discussion where the object is to maintain social order through conformity. However, this may be avoided as 'teachers uncomfortable with a discussion-based approach to moral issues' can replace the possibility of discursive or co-operative knowledge construction through their own demonstration of obedience: 'the example they set in their own behaviour'. An example given is doing 'marking promptly' which demonstrates to pupils that they are valued. This possible reluctance of teachers to move into the affective realm is raised again in the section of the discussion which addresses potential objections. Among 'common concerns' expressed by 'heads and teachers' are 'difficulties with feelings, emotions and the need for personal disclosures'. At this point the advice is that 'discussions of feelings and emotions can seem intrusive' but pupils need to 'learn to use their emotional, as well as their academic [*sic*] intelligence'. The model offered here has a repressive dynamic because 'the ability to understand, express and control feelings appropriately is the basis of the ability to form good relationships'. The reluctant confessor is again reassured that 'personal disclosures are not essential' but as with obedience the message can be coded in that 'teachers can indicate that all adults have wrestled with the kind of choices and dilemmas that face young people.'

A section of the Discussion is headed 'Relations between the four areas', which it is asserted are interdependent. Interdependence is demonstrated with a range of assertions which are both reductionist and sociologically and psychologically naive. The spiritual is linked to the moral via individualism.

Moral development is achieved by the projection of self-love onto others. This moral development 'underpins social development' which in turn depends upon 'this sort of moral reasoning'. The links between the moral spiritual and cultural are established through our capacity for sentimentality: 'those moments when we are carried away by the sheer beauty of a piece of music ... enable us to understand the greatness of the universe.' The argument veers sharply from romanticism to social order in justifying the links between cultural and social development. The case put is that 'social cohesion depends on individuals being culturally developed'. The combining of the notions of culture and development is difficult to conceive of as a culture normally refers to a construction of what actually is, rather than something that we might incrementally instruct others in so as to cause recognizable or measurable development. While clearly aspects of socialization can be purposive and organized, for example, teaching table manners or the rules of public worship, this is part of a diffuse pattern of social reproduction rather than a mass induction controlled by the state. Society is a complex idea which is variously understood in the academic disciplines which seriously address its nature but in the discussion is reduced to being 'important ... in virtue of its having clear moral values and a strong sense of shared cultural inheritance'. Pauline morality is here briefly abandoned in favour of hedonism in the statement that '[society] creates the conditions in which human creativity, imagination and insight can be exercised in their highest form, in creation for the sheer pleasure it brings'.

In a separate document, 66 case studies, selected by Ofsted for QCA, are categorized according to the six steps of the matrix and the four areas identified by the National Forum. No indication of the criteria used for this assignment are given. The cases represent sometimes moving testimony to the creativity of the human spirit in the real capacities of children to organize and maintain their micro-communities and in the willing engagement of teachers in their pupils' sociality. But this humane discourse is absent because the guidance construes these activities as valuable only in so far as they produce rational cognitive performances that meet 'concrete objectives'.

This radical confusion of performativity and conformity with the exploration and expression of what it is to be human is also in the wider public domain. A recent newspaper education supplement article was headlined 'Spirituality and standards go hand in hand', with the sub-heading 'Schools can achieve better results by teaching moral values' (*Independent*, 21 Jan. 1999). The article explained how a 'struggling' primary school had introduced a behaviour modification programme based on 'golden rules' backed up by a token economy which had moved the school from the brink of special measures to an Ofsted judgement 'that it no longer even had "serious weaknesses" (*Independent*, 21 Jan. 1999). The easy fusion of the behavioural, which is to do with conformity, with the moral, which is to do with distinguishing the precepts that guide social action, turns what might be engagement with the responsibilities of autonomous selfhood into a simple exercise in obedience. This may produce social order but represents a developmental cul-de-sac. Both in the article and the Guidance what relationship there is between social order and spirituality can only be guessed at.

CODES, CONTROL AND CURRICULUM

I have employed this detailed textual analysis of the extensive documenta-
tion which constitutes the Qualifications and Curriculum Authority's
Guidance in order to elicit the subtextual themes of social order and
conformity within a restorationist model of society. In particular I have tried
to demonstrate the way in which the content of the concepts of spiritual,
moral, social and cultural in relation to school have been systematically
constructed within a narrow social order agenda and presented as broadly
suited to a transmission pedagogy where 'development' in these areas can
be measured and examined according to the level of conformity with the
authority's prescriptive elaboration of the National Forum's identified value
areas. The inclusion of an empty matrix is the perfect bureaucratic symbol
of apparent autonomy. That it is empty suggests the freedom to fill it;
however, the literally voluminous Guidance suggests that the exercise is
only really colouring in.

In order to pursue some of the consequences of this analysis it is instructive
to revisit Bernstein's (1973) model of curriculum codes. In Bernstein's (1973,
p. 238) terms the National Curriculum can be seen as a reassertion of school
knowledge as a collection code; that is to say as subjects between which 'the
contents are clearly bounded and insulated from each other.' Within such a
curriculum it is hard to see the mechanism by which the disparate domains of
spiritual, moral, social and cultural knowledge could be seen as legitimately
connected in the minds of either teachers or pupils because of the strong
classification of school subjects, where classification refers to 'the degree of
boundary maintenance between contents' (p. 231). The problems experienced
in implementing the NCC's earlier cross-curricular themes also illustrate the
strong classification of school subjects (Whitty et al., 1996).

The other key concept in Bernstein's analytical model is 'frame', which
refers to the 'strength of the boundary between what may be transmitted and
what may not be transmitted, in the pedagogical relationship' (Bernstein,
1973, p. 231). The National Curriculum is centrally determined and the
conditions under which it is realized would be strongly framed in Bernstein's
terms. This would favour instrumental involvement where the pupil has
simply to achieve predetermined objectives. Little scope would be afforded
for the learner to engage personally with forms of knowledge. Critically, this
is not a matter of choice for either pupils or teachers, for what is to count as
real knowledge is largely predetermined, as we have seen, and its legitimation
is through examination and certification. Whitty et al., (1996, p. 64), in a study
of conceptions of quality in Personal and Social Education (PSE), report that
for some pupils 'PSE was perceived to be superficial and lacking a focus, and
even its concern with practical issues was seen in negative terms.' Issues of
classification and frame were clearly evident: 'part of the difficulty lies in the
fact that in PSE there are no agreed conceptions about how to frame the
discourse. Potentially anything can be said and many teachers expressed
anxiety about how to limit the talk ... they were unsure about how much they
could allow pupils to say' (Whitty et al., 1996, p. 64). This echoes the concern
about 'discussion' reported in the Guidance.

Thus, an issue in thinking about the realization of spiritual, moral, social and cultural education is what it can contain and where to locate the boundaries of the subject given the strictures of the QCA's Guidance. A further issue is that of framing and legitimation within the prevailing epistemology of school. If pupils are to value the discourse it must be presented within the instrumental, unambiguous and examinable frame of the core subjects. However, to do this would be to destroy the potential of the discourse to serve the emerging maps of knowledge of self and the world existing outside bureaucratized knowledge.

CONCLUSION

I have attempted to outline above the determining conditions within which spiritual, moral, social and cultural education is currently to be realized. I have characterized the culture of school as a bureaucratized vehicle for the continuing restorationist agendas which have alienated the organization from its social and political contexts and from the urgent needs of pupils facing the continuing impact of globalization. The defeat of liberalism and the imposition of an arid and incomplete rationalism has made school knowledge superficial and unrelated to any meaningful post-school application. Ironically this is most apparent in the official Guidance for the construction of SMSC which came out of the *Education for Adult Life* report (SCAA, 1996a). This has been achieved through the centralized control of schooling, especially the curriculum and pedagogics. The de-professionalization of teaching has been a key strategic element in controlling the implementation of policy. SMSC, through its conceptualization within the normalizing focus of central curriculum planning is in the process of being ideologically constructed within the moral vision of restorationism. The remedy ultimately lies in seriously addressing the links between current school and likely futures. A beginning would be in the reinstatement of teachers as co-equals with the state in the construction of a curriculum grounded in the real conditions of pupils' lives. Spiritual, moral, social and cultural education could then contribute to the formation of knowledgeable and competent persons autonomously engaged in the construction of self and society.

REFERENCES

Altrichter, H., Posch, P. and Somekh, B. (1993) *Teachers Investigate Their Work, an Introduction to the Methods of Action Research*. London: Routledge.

Avis, J. (*et al.*) (1996) *Knowledge and Nationhood, Education, Politics and Work*. London: Cassell.

Ball, S. J. (1990) *Politics and Policy Making in Education: Explorations in Policy Sociology*. London: Routledge.

Ball, S. J. (1994) *Education Reform: A Critical and Post-Structural Approach*. Buckingham: Open University Press.

Ball, S. J. (1995) Culture, crisis and morality: the struggle over the National Curriculum. In Atkinson, P. (*et al.*) (eds), *Discourse and Reproduction, Essays in Honor of Basil Bernstein*, pp. 85–102. Cresskill, New Jersey: Hampton Press.

Bernstein, B. (1973) *Class, Codes and Control Volume 1: Theoretical Studies Towards a Sociology of Language*. St Albans: Paladin.

Brown, P. and Lauder, H. (eds) (1992) *Education for Economic Survival, From Fordism to Post-Fordism?* London: Routledge.

Elliott, J. (1998) *The Curriculum Experiment. Meeting the Challenge of Social Change.* Buckingham: Open University Press.

Fink, D. and Stoll, L. (1997) Weaving school and teacher development together. In Townsend, T. (ed.) *Restructuring and Quality: Issues for Tomorrow's Schools*, pp. 182–98. London: Routledge.

Gewirtz, S., Ball, S. J. and Bowe, R. S. (1995) *Markets Choice and Equity in Education.* Buckingham: Open University Press.

Giddens, A. (1986) *The Constitution of Society: Outline of a Theory of Structuration.* Cambridge: Polity Press.

Giddens, A. (1991) *Modernity and Self-identity: Self and Society in the Late Modern Age.* Cambridge: Polity Press.

Halstead. J. M. (1996) Values and values education in schools. In Halstead, J. M. and Taylor, M. J., *Values in Education and Education in Values*, pp. 3–14. London: Falmer Press.

Halstead, J. M. and Taylor, M. J. (1996) *Values in Education and Education in Values.* London: Falmer Press.

Hargreaves, A. (1994) *Changing Teachers, Changing Times. Teachers' Work and Culture in the Postmodern Age.* London: Cassell.

Hartley, D. (1997) *Re-Schooling Society.* London: Falmer Press.

Hitchcock, G. and Hughes, D. (1995) (2nd edn.) *Research and the Teacher.* London: Routledge.

McLean, M. (1995) *Educational Traditions Compared. Content, Teaching and Learning in Industrialised Countries.* London: David Fulton.

Mullard, M. and Spicker, P. (1998) *Social Policy in a Changing Society.* London: Routledge.

National Curriculum Council (NCC) (1993) *Spiritual and Moral Development – A Discussion Paper.* York: National Curriculum Council.

Qualifications and Curriculum Authority (QCA) (1997) *Draft Guidance for Pilot Work.* London: Qualifications and Curriculum Authority.

School Curriculum and Assessment Authority (SCAA) (1996a) *Education for Adult Life: The Spiritual and Moral Development of Young People.* London: SCAA.

School Curriculum and Assessment Authority (SCAA) (1996b) *Consultation on Values in Education and the Community.* Com/96/608. London: SCAA.

Tucker, K. H. (1998) *Anthony Giddens and Modern Social Theory.* London: Sage.

Whitty, G. (*et al.*) (1996) Competing conceptions of quality in social education: learning from the experience of the cross-curricular themes. In Hughes, M. (ed.), *Teaching and Learning in Changing Times.* Oxford: Blackwell.

Whitty, G., Power, S. and Halpin, D. (1998) *Devolution and Choice in Education. The School, the State and the Market.* Buckingham: Open University Press.

Woods, P. A., Bagley, C. and Glatter, R. (1998) *School Choice and Competition: Markets in the Public Interest?* London: Routledge.

CHAPTER 3

Practical ways for developing SMSC across the curriculum

Jonathan Roberts

Avid viewers of *Watchdog* know the story well enough. A teacher took a new job and moved house. The new house is in a picturesque development called 'Winterbourne'. All was normal until January when the garden turned into a permanent stream. Over coffee in the staffroom the English department followed advice on laundry with some lines from Keats:

It is a flaw
In happiness, to see beyond our bourn –
It forces our summer skies to mourn
It spoils the singing of the nightingale.[1]

The musicians said 'You mean "don't worry, be happy".' But the geographers asked where the house was, and explained that 'Winterbourne' is not just cute but describes the course of a stream that appears in winter as the water-table changes. The developers' act of naming the estate suggested that they knew the problem.

Spiritual, moral, social and cultural issues are intensely personal. We expect the teacher who bought the house to be irate, but think about how she or he might have responded. Spiritually, did that teacher feel like Noah, or a Ganges pilgrim or in touch with Gaia; or was the mud a pollution to be cleansed, a possession to be exorcised or purgatory? Morally, who was responsible? Socially, is it a sign of broken communication with the old residents who knew what happened at Winterbourne each year? Culturally, are we so attracted by an advertisement's metaphor, and so vague in our rich language, that we miss the reality behind the rhetoric? Did the teacher go to court or build a water garden?

The very personal nature of spiritual, moral, social and cultural issues creates a dilemma: on the one hand, pupils should have access to development in this key area of their lives: on the other, adult teachers come to the task with personal commitments to the questions that can make planning a programme for pupils' development hard. Training to do this needs to be open enough to allow for the wide range of teachers' lifestyle commitments and for the historic blocks to be dealt with.

My argument is that the very practical impact of spiritual, moral, social and cultural issues deep in the heart of our lives requires us to find practical ways forward across the whole curriculum. It arises from close work with primary and secondary schools in the city of Sunderland over the last five years and owes a good deal to the patience and kindness of teachers and LEA, particularly in Washington, who have made time to listen to me and try out some of the ideas. Time and priorities can make major initiatives hard but small practical steps can reflect the practical nature of the development involved in SMSC. I describe the journey we made and the interest lies as much there as in the individual results. I have tried to record insights that arose at various points on the journey as well as the sequence of events.

WE STARTED WITH COLLECTIVE WORSHIP

I know of no secondary school where this is not a nightmare. 'How can the whole school be together for it to be collective?' Let alone 'What do we do?' And 'Why?' The duty to be seen to be complying with Circular 1/94 and the need for inspectors to see something obvious often puts this up the list of priorities. Old habits of telling moralizing stories and gathering for rewards and reprimands do not seem adequate but it is not clear how to change. We have undertaken two ways forward: first to look at 'spiritual' and how it has corporate implications, and secondly to suggest some religious sources to create a 'broadly Christian' content.

While many at the end of the second millennium could attempt a discussion of moral, social and cultural, and would probably align themselves with all three words, 'spiritual' is more difficult. It seems more intensely personal and less a subject of public discussion. I found three contemporary approaches which seemed to make sense in schools:

> There's more to all this than all this. (David Jenkins, once Bishop of Durham)

> Spiritual Development relates to that aspect of inner life through which pupils acquire insights into their personal existence which are of enduring worth. It is characterised by reflection, the attribution of meaning to experience, valuing a non-material dimension to life and intimations of an enduring reality.

> Spiritual development, then, is concerned with how an individual acquires personal beliefs and values, especially on questions about religion, whether life has purpose, and the basis for personal and social behaviour – questions which are 'at the heart and root of existence'; it is therefore also about what a school provides – through its curriculum, through collective worship, through its ethos and climate – to help individuals make sense of these questions, and about what it does to help form pupils' response to life and to various forms of experience, or even to questions about the universe.

> Spiritual development is emphatically not another name for religious education, although there are close connections, and spiritual development may be both an aim for religious education and an outcome of it. Religious education certainly seeks to increase pupils' awareness and scrutiny of

ultimate questions surrounding existence. It is therefore right to expect religious education to play a major part in promoting pupil's spiritual development. (Stewart Sutherland, 1994)[2]

'Spirituality' describes those attitudes, beliefs and practices which animate people's lives and help them reach out to super sensible realities. But it needs further definition because, for example, Adolf Hitler was a man 'possessed' yet his spirit was surely evil. There are dangers of sentimentality and pietism. Heart may well speak to heart but the mind too needs to be cultivated. (Gordon Wakefield, 1983)[3]

These quotations stimulated a rich discussion of 'Why do we continue to teach?' 'Why do I teach here?' and 'Why I left another job to train as a teacher.' These are at the heart of spirituality in school and also mark the point of departure from understanding spirituality as private to understanding it as a dimension of a profession.

It is worth recording here some of the ways teachers saw their profession. The revealing aspect is that it was not a question of them 'professing maths' (for example) but their shared role as educators in the lives of their pupils. Some see their work as a calling, the best way that they can spend their lives within the wider purposes of God or the world, as they know it. Other reasons connected with the other three areas of SMSC. Teachers' moral role is to offer clear consistency in behaviour, to be fair and reliable in a world of confusion and deceit. Socially, the school offers a manageable place within which relationships can be built, roles taken up and diversity lived with. Culturally, the school may offer pupils the only access to a wider world than satellite football on TV and brutish parochialism. These outcomes were accidental; what they reveal is that a dialogue about spirituality, carried out in broad enough terms, is understood as important to teachers in their professional lives, as well as in their personal experience.

The task of creating a plan for collective worship involved a dialogue, with the school identifying the key issues at various points in the year and me suggesting the Bible passage which would work well with those themes. One of the factors governing my choice was the question 'what are the key texts with which a child is entitled to be familiar by the time they leave school?' In a secondary school it is reasonable to prepare a five-year cycle of readings if daily collective worship is offering variations on one text over a whole week. Certainly, a single year cycle seems inadequate and the drawbacks of repetition will soon show for staff and pupils with the content becoming predictable rather than stimulating, and the rich resources of spirituality being reduced to a basic greatest hits collection. A cycle like this also makes it easier for the school to suggest to visitors (from religious, charitable or public bodies) what they might like to offer.

BEGINNING TO WORK ON SMSC ACROSS THE CURRICULUM

When we began to work on SMSC across the curriculum, a positive view of SMSC was based on hope on my part and a duty to deliver a policy vision from government. There seemed little idea outside RE, music and English that it might be possible to build the links between SMSC and curriculum content. I worked with teachers who had usually no duty or responsibility in the area of collective worship. This meant that we were starting from a different perspective.

I began by working with teachers on their gut reactions to what they have heard or thought about SMSC. They identified these blocks when they were asked 'What is wrong with SMSC?'

- I find the whole thing hypocritical. How can you plan for a personal response?
- I hate dogmatism. How can I tell pupils what to believe and feel?
- Education is about helping people think for themselves. Moral education seems to replace real freedom with *the teacher tells me what to do.*
- I find it hard to talk about moral matters.
- I am bothered by cultural development. What if taking part depends on class or money, like opera?
- I can't see how it works for my subject.
- I think some moral stances are really stupid.

These seem to be real marks of something best avoided. But they are not the only points teachers have made. As well as straightforward praise or rejection, the conversations about SMSC have involved responses which suggest that the subject is 'interesting' in the sense that there are possibilities which it would be fulfilling to explore and see how they turn out. For example:

- SMSC needs time, which it has never had.
- SMSC is about values and a value-free school isn't possible, or desirable."
- We shouldn't be put off because SMSC is difficult to agree on; just because some knowledge at school is about facts and measurement, not all learning and development needs to be.
- SMSC could give pupils the chance to learn to discover balance, paradox and ambiguity.

This did not seem much progress but it was enough to get started. Above all it made a connection with the teachers who are self-consciously trying to develop values in their pupils. Like Friere,[4] the issue proved to be about a critical awareness of what makes us fully human and therefore Christians and Marxists proved natural allies. The conversation could continue.

THE PROBLEM OF MAKING JUDGEMENTS

The next substantial area of difficulty seemed to lie with the whole business of making judgements. Judgements seemed to some teachers to be a bad thing and especially in the area of SMSC. Here are some examples of the arguments.

- We are used to religion working in a private sphere with no real impact on public life, let alone the sort of controlled public action which schools represent. So, making a judgement in the spiritual area would require the sort of hard evidence we cannot have and it may invade a private interest.
- We are anxious about moral judgement, particularly at school age, because the pupils come from such a wide range of backgrounds and we do not wish to exclude by oversimple statements.
- We are therefore anxious about making a judgement that sets a social boundary. In a social context we put a value on understanding and affirmation.

- We are not always sure when a cultural judgement follows on as a development of previous cultural themes, or whether it arises because the work of art is really good art.

But if we allow ourselves to be totally constrained by such considerations, we may end up with no critical faculty. In fact I do make a judgement about what I consider beautiful and others will know when they enter a room I have decorated. I do choose how I will be in groups and which groups I will persist with. I do choose what to do with my time and money and I come to conclusions about some incidents in others' lives. I recognize incidents of spiritual significance and ways of growing. Finally, as one person put it, 'We all seek truth and to do the right thing. We know that we will be judged whether we like it or not when we die – whether or not people say it out loud.'

We thought about the value of making judgements and developing skills of judgement.[5] Teachers thought, from their work in schools, that we need judgement to:

- Accept the life experiences of others.
- Be aware of bias.
- Identify and correct mistakes when we make them.
- Put values into words and deeds.
- Know that justice is more than an opinion.

Understanding that making judgements underpins teaching can prevent the devaluing of a discussion with the killer phrase 'Everyone's entitled to their own opinion.' And 'Well, that's just how I see it.' These phrases deny any shared values which do exist and the courage it takes to make choices in public – which in fact teachers do all the time. Understanding judgements can begin to bridge the gap between moral truths and our own grasp of them. Understanding judgement can help us find the morality in politics and patriotism where choices are made very publicly.

This same issue is central to Fullan and Hargreaves's argument in *What's Worth Fighting for in Your School*. There teaching is seen as 'not just a technical business. It is a moral one too',[6] because schools provide influential moral environments (more so than church or family) and because teachers act as professionals. Professionals are people who are marked out by the kind of action and judgements they typically make. Fullan and Hargreaves quote Schön as they argue that 'professional action involves making *discretionary judgements in situations of unavoidable uncertainty*.'[7] Their argument is about the whole principle of teaching: there are strengths in teachers' professionalism which make the addressing of SMSC part and parcel of the way in which normal teaching is practised. This point correlates closely with what I found when working on collective worship.

THERE ARE SKILLS IN CRITICAL THINKING IN SMSC WHICH NEED PRACTISING IN PUBLIC.

The process of thinking critically needs to be applied to areas of school life which are linked to SMSC and cause serious thought anyway. In my work with teachers we dealt with two:

Table 3.1 What is the point in thinking about the spiritual?

	Positive	Negative	Interesting
For you	I may be honest, enthusiastic, challenged.	I may be vulnerable, or uncertain.	Putting things into words can lead to personal growth. I might try out something new.
In school	We may take pupils to the threshold of worship. We may give them access to something their families may deny them.	We may be involved in indoctrination, which could be inappropriate.	It is up to pupils to decide whether or not to cross thresholds. What will they show/reveal?
For our society	Lots of people pray, believe in God, have spiritual lives; so, it is a real agenda for people.	A society of many faiths can make this a diplomatic impossibility and we may risk racism, and can affect our lives together.	It is an abiding debate in public education – since 1800, or the Renaissance or Socrates.

Table 3.2 What do we think about fighting?

	Positive	Negative	Interesting
In school	We fight for budget. We fight to achieve targets. Sport seems to channel fighting into improving performance and teamwork.	We reject bullying. Fighting can place control in the hands of the strong or violent. We do not like the pain involved.	It can be a sign of life, energy and commitment. Fighting can produce the energy to learn.
In this city	The police may need knowledge of fighting to achieve public order.	It is awful for battered women. It is frightening for OAPs and young men. It undermines reason, democracy and justice.	It may change or publicize what cannot or will not be changed or publicized otherwise.
In our society	We need fighters in wartime. We need to manage others' violence.	It disrupts justice/work/life.	Survival: life–death. It can result in growth in groups. It can result in leadership.

- What is the point in thinking about the spiritual?
- What do we think about fighting?

One affects the responses to collective worship and the other deals with behaviour policy, i.e. one is about spiritual development and the other is about social development. To broaden the thinking we worked at the widening levels of society, asking in each case to find something positive, something negative and something interesting. The category 'Interesting' was used to invite care and subtlety in making judgements and to allow for the possibility of continued exploration and learning. The outcomes are shown in two tables (Tables 3.1 and 3.2).

We also carried out the same approach with 'dying' and 'Mozart' to continue the process of thinking around a subject rather than advocating neat answers. Teachers might like to try it and see what results they find. The outcomes of greater self-awareness in thinking and the willingness to seek a broader process of reaching a consensus enabled us to move to planning SMSC development within the curriculum.

THE ROLE OF SMSC IN A TIGHTLY PLANNED AND BUSY CLASS

Once we had begun to see how the issues of SMSC might be credible and justifiable we then had to see how they might be located in the curriculum. School time is always short and the suggestion that a particular subject area (e.g. RE) should be expected to deal with part of the SMSC (e.g. spiritual development) is explicitly argued against in DFE Circular 1/94.[8] If it is not a question of bolting on another lesson to the timetable and National Curriculum documents decide much of what is to be taught, how are teachers meant to plan for SMSC within the curriculum? Anxiety about SMSC development in schools did not appear from nowhere and it ought to be possible to connect this issue with other cross-curricular concerns. There might even be better ways of engaging with pupils in their learning. I wanted to challenge the schools to open this work up to all departments, to see what might be manageable for teachers and beneficial for pupils and it seemed to me that ways of understanding group process might offer a route forward. I therefore tried to put my argument before school staff. My paper presenting the argument was fairly telegraphic and I was fortunate that head teachers gave me time to talk through my ideas. Here is the advertising flier I sent to schools for the next stage of training and development:

Development within the curriculum
Schools are about a planned intervention into young people's lives.
Planning can be seen in what is set up, and what happens.
Development involves a movement from simplicity to complexity. For each person this is a complex process and open to influences and rates of progress often outside the school's control. And yet the school intervenes.
The investigation, inspection and planning in the areas of 'Spiritual, moral, social and cultural development' recognizes that there is always more to the curriculum than the curriculum, and that we can't expect the same view of life from everyone. We have the task of being aware of what else we are teaching and making overt choices.
The aim of this process is to have a dialogue between a curriculum area (e.g. geography) – the content; and a way of looking at the pupil's engagement with it (issues of SMSC Development) – the process.
The process issue is important because it can link: pupil's motivation and the curriculum; and the school and wider issues.
When we look at spiritual, moral, social and cultural issues can we identify some defining stimuli in a fluid world where there is greater anxiety about what is spirituality? Morality? Society? Culture? We can use the failure of the provincial world-view (I know what I like and I like

what I know) to let the fresh air of SMSC development give a fair wind to learning for life.

SMSC is best when it happens all the time throughout the curriculum.

But before we reach that we can set a target which could be to achieve one element in each of the four areas in each school year. By regular review we can develop other ideas about enriching the learning.

SMSC DEVELOPMENT AS AN ISSUE FOR SCHOOL MANAGEMENT

When an offer like this, to work on curriculum delivery, arrives in a school, there are not only the questions about whether individual teachers might want to take up this piece of learning: the school needs to see the point. Development in the area of SMSC is not just something which teachers worry about making judgements but it is also an area which appears so much part of the child that it may seem like trying to plan for physical growth.

Religious foundation schools have been set up precisely to nurture such development. Outside the overt religious sector of schooling, schools have been tackling racism and bullying as an essential activity. Approaches to behaviour such as Assertive Discipline[9] make conscious choices about personal decisions that pupils make while at school. Many good schools are conscious that their ethos and values do not happen without having an impact on the people who are part of the school. A school which chooses a non-religious approach to its life also chooses a particular form of spiritual development for its pupils. As institutions, schools cannot choose to be neutral. Ivan Illich[10] challenged the idea that planned institutions are neutral in their effects on people. Anti-racist educators would say that 'colour-blind' schools ensure that injustice goes unchallenged and black pupils do not receive their entitlement. I argue that schools that do not plan for SMSC disadvantage their pupils and may reinforce barriers of class that pupils bring with them to school. For example, it continues to be clear that universities that select, rather than recruit, are deeply influenced by the competence of candidates in demonstrating that they have developed in the areas of SMSC. This is deeply frustrating to teachers who have worked to a high academic standard with highly able pupils.

It might reasonably be asked, 'Where do we fit in SMSC development into a packed school week?' The way I chose to answer this was to use an insight from group work. In the study of how groups work, process issues (like belonging) underpin group content[11] (the fact that a group of people is building a bridge together). This provides an analogy for the way SMSC develops pupils as they engage with the content of the curriculum. Just as good workers with groups are sensitive to process as well as content, so teachers planning their lessons should be aware of the SMSC issues.

The analogy of group work also invites a certain modesty about what can be achieved on all occasions. Group workers expect groups to do particular things at different times in their life (e.g. one model of the life of groups expects 'forming, storming, norming and performing'). There are ways in which appropriate activities can help the process (e.g. finding out names at the beginning, and having time at the end to finish well). But each group has its own life and, while models help to think about what is going on, each precise working out of a group's life has its own characteristics. The role of the group worker has to be chosen carefully: with adult groups they will take up particular roles but not overwhelm the group; in a classroom a teacher takes on a more powerful role, but good teachers know well what their role is with the pupils they teach. The modesty is analogous to people surfing the sea: they try to read the waves and use the water's movement to ride their surfboard. Sometimes they have a good run when what they plan and what the water is doing move well together.

The best way forward is to develop teachers' ability to plan including SMSC development in their thoughts and practice. The outcomes can be a learning more sensitive to pupil's developmental needs and access to new opportunities.

A MODEL OF FAITH DEVELOPMENT AS A KEY TO SMSC PLANNING

Taking hold of SMSC so that these aspects of development can be planned requires a model of development. Many Ofsted inspections have looked for signs of SMSC within the curriculum in terms of 'awe and wonder'. So there may be SMSC in RE, English and a geography field trip to the Lakes. This is fine but many people of faith ask, 'Is that it?' Surely there is more to faith than Wordsworth. Every Ofsted report contains a paragraph assessing each school's planning and effectiveness in encouraging growth and development. When teachers who have been anxious about this aspect of inspection find out that inspectors appear to be interested only in this sort of material, they also ask, 'Is that it?' What if your subject does not stimulate plenty of 'awe and wonder'?

James Fowler's studies of faith development in the USA challenge the idea that we always respond spiritually in the same way. Christian educators use these studies to grasp the apparent discontinuities and differences in people's lives of faith so that appropriate ways of developing can be found. The work of Piaget[12] forms a useful underlying framework for these models.

Faith development models can create the impression that closeness to God can be planned and that there are rank on rank of increasingly superior believers. Most uses of 'Faith and Development' are not this crude. The main point of Fowler's work has been to look at human, generic faith rather than just religious faith. By 'generic faith' I mean the commitments and values which guide life and which may include conventional religious faith but are probably broader than a religious tradition. Certainly some of the developments happen by virtue of people getting older and some of the behaviour and meaning is not possible without adult freedom to choose and act. However, the model can be used to give an understanding of faith in adults when the faith does not seem to have developed much. As someone else once noticed, it does not matter how small faith might be: what is amazing is the potential for growth.[13] What follows is a way I present Fowler's model to open up all stages for adults. I hope that it plays to the strengths of his work. There are other popular versions in shorter or longer[14] form and also Fowler's own work.[15]

A FAITH DEVELOPMENT MODEL OF DIFFERENT RESPONSES TO SPIRITUAL EXPERIENCES: SEVEN STAGES OF THE SPIRITUAL LIFE OR STYLES OF RESPONSE TO THE SPIRITUAL

1. Fowler begins with the infant who, through touch and learning to use its limbs, finds out about relationships and also a basic sense of horror, delight and permanence. There is groundwork done for trust, autonomy and courage. If this learning does not happen, insecurities and difficulties arise. As an adult, I continue to develop in this very straightforward way. For example: I learn how to touch the sick and injured, or loved ones. I have a deep-seated gut reaction to the amazement, awe, wonder that comes into my life: when I saw my child born, the mountain top was climbed, Monet seen ...

2. Fowler describes how children think magically, experience dreams and fantasies as being indistinguishable from reality. They like single-factor explanations and may not be able to think logically or accept logical explanations. As an adult (though it is hard to declare this in prose which is meant to enable the reader to understand the sense of my argument) there are times when I am the same. How else do I explain the widespread fascination with horoscopes in newspapers, crystals, marrying obviously unsuitable partners and simplistic politics?

3. Fowler describes people as seeing themselves as the centre of everything. They like literal interpretations, can distinguish between reality and make-believe, can use logic and expect things to be fair. Storytelling is important at this stage. Other people are identified by the roles they have and the relationships that link them to others. As an adult, I too like things to be fair, I am delighted to tell people what has been happening to me, there are times when I long for a straightforward explanation and I deal with people in their roles at work.

4. Fowler finds this stage common in adolescence: how do they fit in and conform? Authority lies outside with 'them' (parents, teachers, police, leaders, etc.) and there is a network of expectations and duties to fit in with. They long for a significant other. Social relations are seen as extensions of personal relations rather than being patterns of networks, laws, rules and roles. As an adult I am part of a group with shared stories and rituals; football or hymn singing may be the focus or sheer fondness for my gang of friends. I am glad to belong.

5. Fowler sees young adults beginning to take responsibility for their own commitments, lifestyle, attitudes. There is increased awareness of how society works and the values expressed. Self-awareness, objectivity, new ideas are all important. As an adult it is not hard to see this stage, particularly in teachers entering their profession. It may also be expressed in marriage, successfully negotiating the birth of children. In religious faith, I know God to be my Father, Jesus is my personal Lord. This is my faith and it marks me out as an individual, sometimes from the rest of the world.

6. Here people see things as connected. Change in one place may affect other areas. They will accept reality so that truth is bigger than a model or theory or an idea. Encounters with people from other traditions prove interesting.

7. There are times when I know that 'all shall be well and all manner of things shall be well'.[16] Some people move from a personal focus to a commitment to love and justice for all. There is a strong focus on the present reality and looking to the future.

I apply this model to my professional practice by recognizing that there is probably one stage that tends to describe my preferred behaviour, but during a year I will probably know all seven. This is an approach which sees faith development not simply as stages which people pass through and leave behind. As each stage is real and valuable we may take on the characteristics of a particular stage rather than my preferred stage because we may not always find the features of our stage as the most straightforward way of responding in a particular situation. New experiences may especially make this occur. In part this is to say that we adopt styles of faith and in part to say that we are still developing. It is no great novelty to accept that adults do not always fully develop and it is clear that some adults remain at a particular stage.[17] Making progress from one stage to another may be something that happens more quickly in one area of life than another and it may be that it takes a number of significant transitions across a developmental boundary before the new preferred stage of faith is clear.

When it comes to having a dialogue with other people about developing faith, or planning how to develop another person's faith, there will be stages of faith in which the person doing the planning will constrain or open other's responses by virtue of the stage they themselves are at. The point is similar to that made in Transactional Analysis about whether the two people each take up harmonious or conflicting roles as Parent, Child and Adult. Look at how the faith development of the educator might affect their work as one trying to develop another spiritually. Thus it will be hard if the educator is inarticulate (Stage 1) to talk to anyone coherently about his or her response to spiritual matters but enthusiasm may be profoundly obvious. An educator at Stage 3 will have a good starting point for sharing a fund of stories and sayings. An educator at Stage 4 may expect membership to result, or may set up barriers to outsiders. An educator at Stage 5 may expect from young people the very risky step of standing out from their peers. An educator at Stage 6 may respond to the ambiguities of life and faith, but may be accused of selling the faith cheap or being vague. An educator at Stage 7 may offer stillness and affirmation, or be accused of being out of it altogether.

Clearly some responses to their faith experience will allow other people's responses to exist and others will not. This creates a threshold in the development of the teachers themselves which they will need to have crossed. However, a minimum of Stage 5 in the development of a teacher would connect with the normal professional expectations of a teacher working on his/her own with a class of pupils. The self-awareness that accompanies this stage could compensate for the educational destructive tendencies in earlier stages.

These insights can be used for planning spiritual, moral, social and cultural development.

The first point is to look for more than just awe and wonder. Awe and wonder are important and reflect Stage 1, but part of spiritual development is to recognize that it is not always a tangible high.

Stages 2, 3 and 4 offer the chance to connect with stories or well-known interpretations, and to affirm the value of transmitting the body of understood knowledge and interpretation in a particular subject. Teachers do this all the time. In planning for SMSC it is worth indentifying where and how the stories are told in the course of teaching the curriculum.

Stage 2 may also seek a passionate engagement with the subject where the creative arts offer the obvious opportunity, often cited in school SMSC documents. But people do stay up late utterly absorbed in the magic and in the beauty of maths or drawing what they can see at the end of a microscope. It is not insignificant in the making of scientists that they are confronted with something completely beyond their normal experience.

Making the transition from being absorbed and fascinated to seeing the experience as real is part of moving on to Stage 3. Stage 3 may be of more use when conducting scientific experiments as the data may be unaffected by agreed results which may be desired by pupils at Stage 4. The logic and fairness together with a wish to see what is really there is a good and appropriate basis for experimentation.

Stage 4 offers the enjoyment of systematic understanding. A big picture can be offered without each detail of exploring why being developed from first principles. So a periodic table gives quick access to the regular patterns of chemistry, verb patterns appear regular though they may be new and scales in music have regularity to them. For pupils growing through Stage 4 this is a great time to be on work experience learning the details of a trade.

It would be possible to stop with stage 4 and say that pupils do not need to know about what they cannot experience at school. This is not an argument we would use in other areas of school life. More important, Stages 5, 6 and 7 offer more resources which have been part of normal educational practice. Stage 5 is not just for teachers. There are issues to do with adolescent sexuality which demand that young people take responsibility for their own commitments, and it is clear that some do. The pupil at Stage 6 asks: Is war just? Is it ethical to do gene cloning? And it seeks to deal with the delight in both glaciation and Genesis.

Stage 7 is the justification for the amazing stories in assembly to be imitated. It can also give space for stillness and perspective in the curriculum. Ofsted are right to praise schools where there is no shouting – or where there are times of organized stillness, reflection and meditation.

SEEKING A PLACE TO START

Much of what I have described so far has had an interesting effect when I have used it in my work with teachers. Most were not trained in trying to identify SMSC in their work. Weaknesses arise from the separation of theology from the other disciplines and much religious practice is very uneven in the support it gives to different disciplines. But the invitation, which comes from using faith development models, is to look more widely for places where growth and development may happen. Teachers began to be able to see ways ahead. We agreed to set some precise targets and to be clear in thinking about them by now talking about SMSC as if it were a unity but by separating four areas of development. The aim of this splitting process was not to contradict the generic approach of Fowler's model that talks simply about 'Faith development' as we might talk about 'SMSC development', but to continue the approach of Fowler's model in emphasizing the value of difference as a way of achieving and recognizing development.

Separating the four areas of SMSC seems an obvious thing to do: it is what the inspection handbook does in giving guidance to inspectors[18] and it makes clearer the definition of what exactly the planning is aimed at. Despite this, many schools know that they will be inspected for SMSC but have not thought through the detailed implications of this for planning. Drawing on the four Ofsted paragraphs indicating what is intended in the four areas of 'distinct but interrelated aspects of pupils' development', we began to brainstorm possibilities for subject areas, aiming for one example in each of the areas in each year group's curriculum.

Table 3.3 Worksheets for SMSC development

Area of development	How?	What outcomes?
SPIRITUAL DEVELOPMENT: purpose and meaning of life; impact of religion on human history and culture; links between personal beliefs and social and cultural groups.		
MORAL DEVELOPMENT: ethics; personal values - what do I think is right? What does the law say? What do other people say is right?		
SOCIAL DEVELOPMENT: discover about living in society - who is in my community? What are the structures I deal with? How do I work in a team? Is it worth volunteering? How do I deal with conflict?		
CULTURAL DEVELOPMENT: what are pupil's cultural expressions/how can we broaden pupils' cultural experience?		

We used the worksheets in Table 3.3. The results have covered most areas of the curriculum. They provide foci for programmes currently being taught and we will review their effectiveness over the next academic year. To give a flavour of the outcomes of the brainstorming by the group, here are some examples from using maps in geography:

Spiritual: moving from local maps to global views gives a sense of our place in the universe. Mapping different religious groupings and the boundaries between them ... and places of conflict. Mediaeval maps put Jerusalem at the centre and Britain on the edge.

Moral: study of planning decisions and the impact on people's lives and feelings. Washington as a new town built over older settlements could offer the basis for research. Use maps to give an overview of distinct elements linking moral issues, e.g. the slave trading triangle. Mercator projection reflecting European perspective, Peter's projection reflecting a concern for world justice.

Social: what makes up our city? Where are my friends and relatives? Where is power exercised at different levels?

Cultural: Empire Day used to focus on the 'pink and proud' or was it 'red and bloodstained'? The beauty of map-making. Why do OS maps give so much detail?

This geography department understands why the range of maps on the classroom display is important and that the curriculum is not the only thing taught in its lessons. It expects to find issues bigger than its own subject and see pupils as more than containers for interesting facts. These geographers work with pupils who can grow in knowledge and as spiritual, moral, social, cultural human beings. Certainly it will not all happen in geography but each teacher makes a contribution.

CONCLUSION

The muddy teacher we began with knew the curiosity and intelligence of fellow teachers. The challenge of SMSC development for pupils requires precisely those qualities in teachers. Unlike the curriculum documents, which require a particular view to be put across, SMSC's very difficulties can offer opportunities for diversity, paradox and plurality. If we are willing to address the questions of spirituality, morality, society and culture, which have no grand narratives with straightforward answers, then we will find rich resources for the school. If we are willing to recognize the growth in stages of faith then our own viewpoint will be an enrichment rather than a hindrance. Finally, the modesty of finding small examples to use which really relate to what is being taught allows a growth in understanding, which could not be achieved with a bolt-on module.

Working with teachers on SMSC I cannot help being struck by the way in which the 'hidden' or 'implicit' curriculum can be made clear and explicit. Some of it has been done before under the heading of multicultural education or in the 'ghetto' of religious institutions. Some of it must be a challenge to teacher training institutions, not least those governed by religious groups. The hope that SMSC will simply offer an opportunity for transmitting orthodoxy does not do justice to the range of human experience and the limits of orthodoxy. There needs to be imaginative rigorous reflection built into teacher learning and development. Often the subtle listening of teachers to the local culture and context of the school will be most effectively done by experienced teachers and this will be a prerequisite for SMSC development to be appropriately planned. There is a final challenge to see who would be willing to work locally with schools in developing these skills more widely. I look forward to seeing the extent to which teachers and their pupils are empowered to work with a well-rounded curriculum.

NOTES

1 John Keats, *Epistle to J. H. Reynolds*, 1.82 (1818).
2 Stewart Sutherland, *OFSTED Handbook* (London: Ofsted, 1994).

3 G. S. Wakefield (1983) 'Spirituality', in *A Dictionary of Christian Spirituality* (London: SCM Press), pp. 361–3.
4 Paulo Friere, *Pedagogy of the Oppressed.* (London: Penguin, 1972), p. 17.
5 Some of the thinking underlying this was stimulated by Brenda Watson (July 1997) Reflections on moral relativism: a response to Values Education 3.3 (*Values Education,* 4.(1)) (St Martin's Lancaster).
6 Michael Fullan and Andy Hargreaves, *What's Worth Fighting For in Your School?* (Buckingham: Open University Press, 1992), p. 28.
7 Ibid., p. 28 (their italics).
8 Paragraphs 1 and 2 and footnote 2 referring to the National Curriculum Council's discussion paper on SMSC. Department For Education Circular 1/94, *Religious Education and Collective Worship* (London: HM Government, 1994).
9 L. Canter and M. Canter, *Assertive Discipline* (Santa Monica, USA: Lee Canter & Associates, 1992).
10 Ivan Illich, *Deschooling Society* (London: Penguin, 1973).
11 W. R. Bion, *Experiences in Groups* (London: Tavistock, 1961).
12 J. Piaget, *The Moral Judgement of the Child* (London: Penguin, 1977).
13 Matthew 13.31–32.
14 Jeff Astley, *How Faith Grows* (London: National Society/CHP, 1991).
15 e.g. James W. Fowler, *Stages of Faith* (New York: Harper & Row, 1981).
16 Julian of Norwich's conclusion in *The Revelations of Divine Love*, Chapter 27 (Harmondsworth: Penguin).
17 For example: were the Nuremberg trial accused who declared that they were following orders at Stage 2 (magical instructions that were incapable of amendment) or 3 (statements that cohered utterly with the way the plot was to unfold) or 4 (where authority is to be found in others) when the judges expected behaviour corresponding to Stages 5 (personal responsibility) or 6 (willingness to stand up for the truth and recognize the humanity of those who were being dehumanized) or 7 (where they may have joined the martyrs in their resistance)?
18 Ofsted, *Handbook* (May 1994) Part 4, p. 86.

REFERENCES

Astley, J. (1991) *How Faith Grows.* London: CHP/NS.
Bion, W. R. (1961) *Experiences in Groups.* London: Tavistock.
Canter, L. and Canter, M. (1992) *Assertive Discipline.* Santa Monica: Lee Canter & Associates
Fowler, J. W. *Stages of Faith.* San Francisco: Harper and Row.
Friere, P. (1972) *Pedagogy of the Oppressed.* London: Penguin.
Fullan, M. and Hargreaves, A. (1992) *What's Worth Fighting For in Your School.* Buckingham: Open University Press.
Illich, I. (1973) *Deschooling Society.* London: Penguin.
Piaget, J. (1977) *The Moral Judgement of the Child.* London: Penguin.
Wakefield, G. S. (1983) *A Dictionary of Christian Spirituality.* London: SCM.

CHAPTER 4

Spirituality and teaching methods: uneasy bedfellows?

David Smith

Recent times have seen a revival of interest in two educational issues which stand in a somewhat uneasy relationship to one another. On the one hand, *method* appears to be back in fashion; the much discussed new literacy and numeracy initiatives in particular have been presented to the world in terms of training teachers in new or correct methods which will raise standards in those areas. This is just the latest instance of a long-standing practice of promoting new ways of teaching as new *methods*, with all the aura of rigour, control and assured results which clings to the concept of method. On the other hand, *spirituality* has become the focus of a great deal of attention since the idea of spiritual development through the whole curriculum lumbered (whether as threat or promise) over the horizon. The aura here tends to be very different – more personal, holistic and affirming of the whole child or merely more vague, sentimental and fuzzy, depending on the observer's point of view. The two cultures represented by talk of method and talk of spirituality seem to be extremely unlikely bedfellows, and yet it appears that cohabit they must: the curriculum which is supposed to be shot through with concern for spiritual development is the same curriculum which is supposed to achieve the required standards through the application of the right methods.

Of course, in education we are fairly used to encountering demands which seem to pull us in different directions, and we are also fairly used to muddling through. One response to this particular tension might be for each side simply to throw up its hands at the other, lamenting respectively the lack of rigour, realism and concern for progress or the lack of a sense of mystery, wholeness and depth. Is this adequate? Must we simply choose sides and adopt the rhetoric which goes with the choice? Must we resign ourselves to seeing spirituality as wadding stuffed into the cracks of the curricular edifice, having little intimate connection with the real business of the school day? Or are there more productive ways of framing the issues?

Schön (1979, 1983) long ago pointed out that in tackling problems it can be more fruitful to focus first on how the problem has been posed than to set our sights immediately on solving it. It seems to me that if we are concerned to make something of the idea of spiritual development across the whole curriculum, then it quickly becomes necessary to ask whether ideas of spirituality and ideas of method which are simply at loggerheads will serve, or whether they just leave us locked in an insoluble dilemma. This is the question which I will begin to explore in this chapter, suggesting in the process that certain ideas of method and certain ideas of spirituality might have to give if teaching methods and spiritual development are to be more than irregular objects rammed into the same container. Let us first try to get a clearer sense of the dilemma.

METHOD AND SPIRITUALITY

The concept of method has played a prominent role in modern culture. Descartes, while not by any means carrying sole responsibility, had as much to do with this development as anyone, and his thoughts on the subject provide a particularly lucid example of some important features of a modern trust in method.

Descartes became convinced that 'our beliefs are based much more on custom and example than on any certain knowledge', and resolved to remedy this by seeking the 'true method of arriving at knowledge' (Descartes, 1968, pp. 39–40). In order to meet Descartes' ideals, this true method had to possess certain characteristics.

- It must admit nothing which was clouded in any way by custom, tradition, prejudice or any beliefs falling short of evident *certainty*, so that the results of its operation might have objective validity. It was allowing these kinds of contingent factors, mere traditions and beliefs, to hold sway in our thinking and knowing which had, according to Descartes, led to confusion and disagreement, and the existence of disagreement was for him a sure sign that we had not arrived at certain knowledge (Descartes, 1968, p. 32).
- The true method must, moreover, be rigorously, thoroughly and self-consciously *regulated* on the basis of disengaged reason, so that no contaminations might creep into the process and compromise its objective validity.
- It must be *repeatable* without variation, so that it can produce assured results at different times and in different places – this is necessary so that it can be regulated through rigorous checking.
- It must also be *comprehensive* in its grasp, so that the general validity of its conclusions might not be threatened by omissions – it needs to have all relevant factors under its control (Descartes, 1968).

Method thus conceived, and carried through by the expert without interference from general prejudices, would, Descartes hoped, carry us from disagreement and confusion to certain and reliable knowledge.

Descartes was not the sole author of the modern preoccupation with method, nor has his version been the only one. I am not suggesting that every modern enthusiast for some teaching method is a straightforward disciple of Descartes. Discussions of the role of controlled technique in various human endeavours are both wider and more ancient (Dunne, 1993). The point here is not a detailed treatment of the history of ideas, but simply to see in Descartes a particularly clear example of an influential set of ideals.

Descartes' description of his method expresses an ideal of a self-consciously controlled, self-enclosed, ahistorical, repeatable, encompassing and certain method which will deliver certain desired goods. Such ideals have been common enough themes in the modern period, particularly in its understanding of scientific knowledge. They were especially evident in the influential rise of positivism, for positivist thinkers adhered to scientific method in the hope of avoiding metaphysical commitments which might muddy the waters. Attempts to ground teaching methods scientifically have often reflected the same mindset, and a more general focus on the methodological or procedural has continued to be closely associated with the ideal of uncommitted neutrality on controversial matters of value, not least in educational discussions. We hardly need reminding that ideals of repeatability, assured results and rigorous checking have had some prominence in recent educational discourse.

The cultural significance of these themes is thrown into relief by the considerable efforts which have been invested in dismantling them in recent decades. To mention but some of the most well-known examples, Polanyi has argued that committed, personal knowledge rather than 'the vain pursuit of a formalized scientific method' provides 'the only relation in which we can believe something to be true' (Polanyi, 1958, p. 311). Gadamer denies that method can deliver the whole of the truth, and argues that the Enlightenment 'prejudice against prejudice' has obscured the positive enabling role which can be played by prior assumptions and judgements (Gadamer, 1989, p. 270). Feyerabend argues that the idea of a single, regulated method is likely to render potentially fruitful alternative routes of inquiry invisible (Feyerabend, 1975). Whatever one makes of the alternative programmes of these and other opponents of method, the prominence of their work signals both the importance of the idea of method in our culture and a certain loss of plausibility on the part of Cartesian or positivist ideals. The much discussed advent of postmodernity directly challenges every one of those ideals with a view of knowledge as plural, historical, uncertain, shifting, partial and influenced or controlled by a variety of extra-personal forces. The idea of method as standing above controversy and offering a clinically clean road to success is looking somewhat time-worn.

What of spirituality? Spiritual experiences and commitments are part of what the conception of method sketched above is supposed to exclude. This exclusion is reflected in the Romantic reaction to the rise of modern science. Romanticism denied that modernist method had truth within its grasp, and looked instead to the personal, the expressive, the numinous for access to reality. This reaction against the austerities of modern reason and science involved turning to 'a certain way of experiencing our lives, our ordinary desires and fulfilments, and the larger natural order in which we are set' as moral sources, emphasizing not the need for methodical rigour, but rather the need to 'experience these desires as rich, as full, as significant – to respond to the current of life in nature' (Taylor, 1989, p. 372). The educational tradition inaugurated by Rousseau follows this path, seeking to liberate the expressive learner from the constraints of an externally imposed schema. In this tradition, which in turn found itself opposed by the development this century of more rigorous empirical approaches to the study of human beings, feeling and intuition are valued above rational certainty and objective description

(Wright, 1997, p. 11). We continue to live with the cultural effects of the tension between these two sets of emphases (Gergen, 1991, p. 18–47).

The roots of much of the present debate concerning spiritual development lie not in the tradition which sought security in the method ideal, but in the counter-tradition which resisted it. The tradition of Romanticism in theology and education, with its distinctive understanding of the person, continues to shape many contributions to the debate (Wright, 1997, 1998). If spirituality has to do with the inner world, the undefinable, the ineffable, the intangible, the mystical, with individual personal experience and self-expression, then it would seem to be irreconcilable with the idea of reliable method outlined above. The two ideals grew up in mutual opposition. They seem designed to be at war, and any attempt to build a curriculum around both therefore raises interesting questions.

Although this remains a very sketchy outline, it does suggest that there are deep-seated issues which might need to be tackled if discussions of spiritual development and of teaching methods are to be brought into fruitful interaction. In approaching these issues I will draw upon some recent discussions of the nature of teaching methods in one area of the curriculum, namely modern language teaching. This choice not only reveals some of my background and interests, but also brings some benefits. First, recent discussions of spiritual development have tended to draw their examples from a restricted range of curriculum areas, and modern language education has been almost totally neglected. Second, and perhaps not unrelated, modern language education has been influenced in a particularly strong manner by the method ideal. Discussions in the field have tended to centre above all on questions of appropriate method. If we can find some clues as to how spiritual development might be relevant to teaching processes in this area, we may be on the way to answering some of the broader questions. Third, arising from this preoccupation with method, recent literature on foreign and second language teaching has included a vigorous reappraisal of the role and usefulness of 'method', a reappraisal which has raised issues which I think are relevant to spiritual development. For all of these reasons, modern language teaching may serve as a useful example for the purposes of looking in more detail at general questions of spirituality and teaching methods.

PROBLEMS WITH METHOD

First, let me sketch in some brief background. Modern applied linguistics got under way in the mid-twentieth century with a strong faith that the application of scientific method to the study of language teaching and learning could deliver a complete and correct teaching method. This went together with highly regimented and prescriptive recommendations for teaching. The role of the teacher was to implement the method correctly, following the prescribed sequence of actions, so that the scientifically assured results would follow.

In the 1970s the attempt to prescribe a single correct method gave way to a proliferation of diverse new language teaching methods (see e.g. Blair, 1982). A number of these, such as Community Language Learning or the Silent Way, resisted the idea that their authority should lie in their being validated by scientific reason (cf. Stevick, 1990). The ideals associated with method were not, however, all abandoned. The various methods proposed tended to be presented as complete, all-encompassing alternative packages, promising to deliver the right way to go about teaching languages. The attempt to find ways of empirically justifying methods continued (see Larsen-Freeman, 1991). Nevertheless, the plurality of methods being advocated forced attention towards the question of *why* there might be such diversity and how the various methods might be compared and described.

This led to a more basic discussion of the validity or desirability of the concept of method itself in relation to language teaching. The difficulties in making global empirical comparisons between whole 'methods' have led to scepticism concerning whether the idea of a comprehensive 'method' is the best way to think about teaching practices (Brumfit, 1991; Larsen-Freeman, 1991). The ideological diversity underlying the growing range of 'methods' available has also been increasingly recognized, making the idea of a purely empirical determination of the best 'method' still more remote (Davies, 1993; Pennycook, 1989). These problems, together with critique of the hierarchical way in which 'methods' have been imposed upon teachers by researchers, have led beyond discussions about which 'method' is best and into a debate concerning how we should navigate in what Kumaravadivelu has termed the 'post-method condition' (Kumaravadivelu, 1994). The question has become: are language teaching processes best thought of as an instance of 'method'? It is this discussion which, I suggest, might offer some resources for beginning to rethink the relationship between spirituality and the ways in which we go about trying to secure learning outcomes.

THE STRUCTURE OF TEACHING PROCESSES

Thus far I have suggested that some modern ideals which have kept close company with the idea of method have made it difficult in many contexts to speak of a spiritually oriented approach to 'teaching methods' and sound as if one were making much sense. I have also outlined some of the major reasons for a growing suspicion of those ideals in discussions of language teaching. It is now time to turn to a positive account of how spirituality might intersect with teaching processes.

I make no pretence in what follows to be offering an exhaustive account of how spirituality relates to teaching methods. I will be focusing on one particular line of investigation to see how far it helps us with the apparent dilemma which I have sketched. I will be looking at how particular spiritual beliefs and orientations might (to Descartes' discomfort) inhabit the structure of an allegedly neutral teaching method. As a way into this investigation I will first revisit and then progressively modify a classic attempt from the language teaching literature to define the structure of a 'teaching method'.

ANTHONY ON TEACHING METHODS

In 1963 Edward Anthony made what has become a classic distinction between *approach*, *method* and *technique* (Anthony, 1963). In his account, *techniques* are specific actions and technologies which are applied in the classroom to achieve specific objectives. They might include administering a vocabulary quiz, showing an image or asking a question. A visitor to a class sees mostly techniques (Anthony, 1963, p. 66). These techniques do not, however, occur

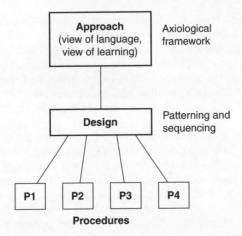

Figure 4.1 Anthony's model

randomly. They are organized and patterned in certain ways, making up a way of teaching which has an overall consistency. This general way of teaching, or constellation of techniques, is what Anthony terms a *method*. Method is, however, in turn dependent on a wider axiomatic framework of assumptions and beliefs; it is a way of realizing a certain vision of things. The overall coherence of a method, in spite of the variety of techniques which it may include, derives from its consistency with a set of beliefs about the nature of language and of language learning. This wider framework is termed by Anthony an *approach*. An approach 'states a point of view, a philosophy, an article of faith – something which one believes but cannot necessarily prove' (Anthony, 1963, p. 64). In sum, then, '*techniques* carry out a *method* which is consistent with an *approach*' (Anthony, 1963, p. 63).

Before considering the dynamics of this framework in more detail, some attention to terminology is in order. In view of the range of suspicions and connotations attached to the term 'method', Anthony's use of it as the middle term in his description invites potentially misleading preconceptions. Richards and Rogers replace Anthony's terms with 'approach', 'design' and 'procedure', and in what follows I shall adopt their usage (Richards and Rodgers, 1982; Richards and Rodgers, 1986, p. 19). *Procedures* are individual actions in the classroom, *designs* are repeatable patterns in the way teaching takes place, and *approaches* are the background beliefs, orientations and commitments which give rise to one pattern rather than another (Figure 4.1).

Starting from this basic model, we need to expand or qualify it in a number of ways if we are to do justice to the complexity and flexibility of the relationships between the various levels. I will suggest four issues for clarification or expansion.

What goes into an approach?
In the discussion which has followed in the wake of Anthony's paper, approach has received less attention than design and procedure. It is often assumed that its content can be described in terms of particular academic

disciplines which feed into language teaching. In fact its content has been restricted by some to theories from linguistics and psycholinguistics – theories about language and about how we learn it (Anthony, 1963, pp. 63–4; Richards, 1984, p. 7; Richards and Rodgers, 1986, pp. 16–19). This is far too narrow. If the idea of an approach is to be useful as a way of talking about all of the assumptions, orientations and influences which guide the shaping of procedures into patterned designs, then it must be expanded in at least two directions.

First, the range of theoretical assumptions which are seen as relevant must be broadened. The shaping of language teaching into distinctive patterns involves assumptions not only about the nature of language and of learning processes, but also social, political and economic assumptions (Pennycook, 1989; Pennycook, 1990; Williams, 1992), assumptions about the nature of the human persons involved in teaching and learning (Smith, 1997b; Yoshikawa, 1982), ethical assumptions (Smith, 1997a) and probably more besides. This will apply similarly to approaches to any other area of the curriculum. A way of teaching draws explicitly or implicitly on far more than a couple of academic disciplines specifically concerned with its subject matter. It draws upon our beliefs about a wide range of potentially relevant issues.

Second, we need to take account of non-theoretical influences on design. An approach to teaching may be significantly shaped by less consciously formulated elements. It is likely to consist partly of conscious principles and partly of unconscious assumptions and personal orientations drawn from such sources as experience, personality, social or cultural background, awareness of general educational practices, knowledge of particular students, a lived spirituality or a broad *Zeitgeist*. The influences on a particular constellation of practices may lie as much in the realm of what is taken for granted or unreflectively lived as in that of the consciously (let alone theoretically) formulated. Approaches will be to varying degrees consciously systematized and internally coherent, but given their basic 'where I'm looking from' status, they will not be completely articulated; one of the hardest things to discern is the full contour of our own implicit perspective on the world (Polanyi, 1958). An approach is not something which we grasp in its fullness in advance of any actions.

I shall refer to these two lines of expansion in terms of *beliefs* and *orientations*. By *beliefs* I mean to indicate our basic assumptions about any issue related to teaching. By *orientations* I mean to refer to the ways in which we are oriented in the world, ways which are intertwined with but not reducible to our conscious beliefs. I have in mind here unarticulated dimensions of our character, our spirituality and our belonging to communities, cultures and traditions.

How strongly does approach determine design?

A second point to note is that similar approaches may lead to or be consistent with a variety of designs (Anthony, 1963). A broad orientation or set of beliefs does not lead with rigid determinism to a single design. What we tend to find in practice are clusters of designs displaying family resemblances. They differ from one another, but also show a common consistency with various convictions characteristic of a general approach. In the 1970s, for instance, an influential set of ideas about the person and the learning process provided by humanistic psychology gave rise to a variety of ways of translating those ideas into specific ways of going about teaching languages (Stevick, 1990). Similarly, the belief that learners benefit from a clearly defined structure, or that children should be respected as responsible beings made in God's image, can give rise to a variety of teaching designs which are in part inspired by the belief.

A given design will fit well or badly with a given approach (Wolterstorff, 1984), but the approach is by its very nature *not* a set of detailed specifications for constructing a design, a blueprint which details the outcome in advance. A design is a creative construct developed in a particular context under the guidance of an approach, an attempt to translate an approach into a repeatable constellation of more detailed procedures at a particular place and time. The substitution of the term 'design' for 'method' accentuates this point: 'what links theory with practice ... is design' (Richards and Rodgers, 1986, p. 19; Weideman, 1987).

Does each design have its own procedures?

Third, a given procedure may appear in a variety of designs which are in turn related to divergent approaches. In other words, a design is not made up out of its own exclusive and unique set of procedures. It is a particular *combination* of procedures selected from the full range which is available or conceivable. This range may be restricted in particular contexts, for instance by available equipment or teaching space or the particular features of the language being taught, but some selection and prioritization within broad bounds of possibility is always present. A given approach or design may require, commend or exclude certain specific procedures (as, for instance, Community Language Learning excludes error correction during beginner level oral practice), and may permit a range of others in varying proportions (Allen, 1993). Taken individually, most of these procedures will be open to use by teachers holding a variety of approaches, and are perhaps the area most susceptible to empirical assessment in terms of whether they achieve what they set out to achieve.

What makes one design different from another, however, is basically the way in which a range of procedures is configured or *patterned* in a manner consistent with the approach adopted, yielding an educational experience with particular characteristic emphases and priorities (Brumfit, 1991, p. 138; Swaffar, Arens and Morgan, 1982). Seating learners in a circle or asking them to think of a topic for discussion are procedures which could be woven into a variety of designs. If the class are regularly seated in a circle and the teacher consistently remains outside it and refuses to take the initiative in terms of shaping the conversation then we have something which much more clearly expresses the philosophy of Community Language Learning. Much as the same notes, rhythms and instruments can be variously combined into very different pieces of music, so procedures are to be regarded with an awareness that 'their value depends on [*design*] and *approach*' (Anthony, 1963, p. 66). An approach is a belief-laden *orientation* which is embodied in various particular *implementations*.

Which comes first?

Finally, it must be emphasized that in the day-to-day life of approaches, designs and procedures the traffic is not one-way, beginning with approach and moving down to procedure, or moving from theory to practice. The development of a new procedure or new discoveries concerning the effects of a procedure may modify a design or the beliefs which make up an approach (consider, for instance, the significance of the development of new printing technologies for the picture-based pedagogy of Comenius' illustrated textbooks in the seventeenth century). As Richards and Rodgers note, language teachers may 'stumble on' a successful procedure and form beliefs which justify it later (Richards and Rodgers, 1986, p. 29). Equally, teachers typically begin their teaching career with some beliefs about teaching and learning which they are forced to abandon or modify as they interact with particular groups of learners.

Moreover, the creative construction process which goes into the design of an episode of language teaching draws upon particular skills, personality strengths, traditions, experiences, educational situations and awareness of a variety of constraints (age and background of students, parental expectations, budgetary limitations, etc.). This does not, however, mean that beliefs and orientations are irrelevant, any more than a recognition that the teacher does not produce or control every event in the classroom renders the teacher's input superfluous. A design is not a set of ideas dressed up for practical service. It is rather the fruit of an *interaction* between a set of beliefs (coherent or drawn from conflicting sources), personal qualities, goals, etc. and a set of available procedures, contexts, experiences and educational demands.

It follows from these points that it is mistaken to expect the beliefs and orientations which make up an approach to yield cleanly separate sets of distinctive procedures which can be deduced from them (although this possibility is not excluded; an example may be the use of the teacher's silence in the Silent Way (Stevick, 1990, p. 101–30)). This does not, however, mean that such beliefs or orientations only have any effect at the level of approach, remaining insignificant for the procedures adopted, for the beliefs and orientations making up the approach play a role in guiding the coherence of the design, a design which in turn structures the utilization of procedures. In a given episode of language teaching, approach, design and procedure are simultaneously operative. The creativity and loose fit between approach, design and procedure mean that beliefs and orientations do not correspond one-to-one with procedures; they do, however, have their impact on the choice, arrangement and development of procedures (Figure 4.2).

A teaching 'method', then, emerges from creative interactions between basic beliefs, assumptions and orientations and a range of available procedures, yielding a design for the teaching and learning process which exhibits a particular pattern. Where does spirituality come into all this?

PATTERNED SPIRITUALITY AND LANGUAGE TEACHING

I would like to suggest that it follows from the discussion thus far that both a general concern for spiritual development and particular spiritualities may

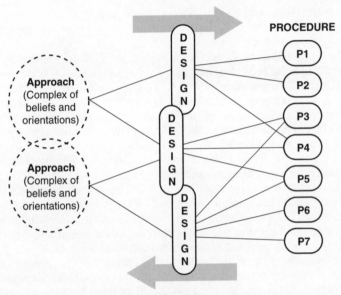

PROCEDURE

Figure 4.2 Approach, design and procedure in interaction

be relevant as part of an approach, both in terms of beliefs and of orientations. I shall consider each of these briefly in turn.

Spiritual beliefs and language teaching

If matters such as basic beliefs and assumptions about the ethics of teaching, the purpose of communication or the nature of the learner are a significant part of how teaching methods are shaped, then beliefs which are related to particular spiritual commitments might prove to be relevant in some way, for such commitments and assumptions may have confessional roots. Once 'approach' is broadened out beyond the confines of a couple of relevant academic disciplines, it begins to seem likely that the basic belief-laden orientations to the world, to others, to God, gods or God's absence, to life and learning which are the stuff of spirituality might form part of the ocean on which the ship of method plies its course.

Spirituality, like teaching, is typically patterned in significant ways, in ways which are interconnected with basic personal orientations and broader frameworks of belief (cf. Smith, 1999). It is this which makes it possible to speak of a mean or a humble spirit, of Christian, Jewish, Muslim or humanist spirituality or even of Protestant, Sufi or Beguine spirituality. A particular conception of spiritual *development* is likewise dependent upon a framework of beliefs and assumptions – it is therefore possible to speak of a Romantic, a humanist, a communitarian or a Christian approach. Focusing on spirituality in a way which emphasizes universality to the exclusion of particular commitments echoes the inadequacies of the similar attempt to exclude the particular in the Cartesian concept of method. A particular understanding of spirituality will be bound up with implicit or explicit assumptions about the nature of teacher and learner, about the relationship between spirituality, belief and knowledge, and so on. These frameworks of belief may guide methodological choices if they become an active part of an approach to teaching.

The beliefs ('articles of faith', as Anthony puts it) which make up an approach are a specialized (although not isolated) subset of a wider network of beliefs. If a world-view can be described as 'the integrative and interpretive framework by which order and disorder are judged, the standard by which reality is managed and pursued' (Olthuis, 1985), then a teaching approach is that more focused integrative and interpretive framework by which pedagogical order and disorder are judged and sound teaching practice is regulated and pursued. The beliefs which it incorporates are likely to include both the conclusions of research and experientially inspired hunches, both fresh insights and the received wisdom of the profession. They will include very mundane beliefs, such as the belief that children like books with pictures better than those without. They may also include more confessional beliefs, beliefs which are tied up with particular spiritual commitments and particular understandings of the spiritual nature of teacher and learner.

Consider, for instance, beliefs about the nature of the human person. Human beings appear in the classroom as teachers, as learners and as the characters who inhabit teaching materials of various kinds – story books, images in wall displays, videos, histories and so on. An implicit or explicit set of beliefs concerning the human beings who appear in these three roles must therefore be a significant part of any approach to teaching, and will play some role in the process of choosing and arranging materials and of organizing procedures into a design. If (for instance) there are characteristic Christian, Jewish or humanist beliefs concerning the nature of the human person, then the likelihood clearly exists that such beliefs may play a regulative role in this process (Smith, 1997c). They may play such a role in terms of the teacher's (or curriculum writer's) spirituality and of the teacher's understanding of the spirituality of both the learners who are present and the more distant humans who inhabit the content of the curriculum.

This is confirmed by the current literature which criticizes the concept of method. The confirmation is of two kinds. First, as discussed above, one of the features of method which has been conspicuously under attack is its claim to ahistorical neutrality. Second, the various alternative analyses which have been proposed confirm the dynamic outlined above. Kinginger has analysed the metaphors employed in teachers' descriptions of their own teaching in order to elucidate the 'coherence systems' through which they make sense of their practice (Kinginger, 1997). Prabhu talks of the need for particular teaching practices to resonate with teachers' 'sense of plausibility', which involves interconnected pedagogic perceptions rooted in a view of the world (Prabhu, 1987, 1990). Pennycook argues that changes in language teaching practices 'have represented different configurations of the same basic options rather than some linear, additive progress toward the present day, and that these changes are due principally to shifts in the social, cultural, political and philosophical climate' (Pennycook, 1989). Brumfit speaks of 'methods' as 'cultures socially emerging from human practices', leading to particular 'constellations of techniques' (Brumfit, 1991, pp. 136, 138).

All of these formulations are subversive of the modern ideal of method described at the start of this chapter. They certainly undermine the idea that an approach consists of theories discussed at the university and obediently implemented in the classroom. What should be clear, however, is that they all support the implication of Anthony's account that it is necessary to do justice to the ways in which particular practices are combined and emphasized in the light of certain beliefs and orientations. The various alternatives currently proposed to talk of methods seem to me, therefore, to strengthen rather than detract from the case made above for a consideration of the relevance of spiritual commitments to teaching practices being a sensible undertaking.

Spiritual orientation and language teaching

As I have emphasized above, there is more to an approach or a world-view than conscious beliefs and theories – we are more than what we consciously know. While I have argued that accounts of the significance of spirituality for education must have reference to beliefs and commitments, I do not wish to suggest that spirituality is no more than belief. It is therefore appropriate to consider the relevance of a more general orientation, a lived spirituality, to language teaching methods.

Discussion of spirituality in education in recent years has focused almost exclusively on the spirituality of children. Teachers too are spiritual beings and this is also relevant to educational processes. Paul Tench, in an article discussing Christian involvement in foreign and second language teaching, cites Strevens's finding that one of the strong recurrent reasons for success in the learning and teaching of foreign and second languages is that 'teachers cherish learners' (Tench, 1985, p. 42). Tench suggests that this is an area in which lived Christian spirituality should provide significant resources which impact the teaching situation. Stevick, in a review of Curran's work, which also focused on affective dimensions of language teaching and learning, suggested in a similar way that the warmth of the teacher's personal attitude towards students may be a significant factor causing variations in the results achieved by different exponents of the same method (Stevick, 1973).

Stevick cites the example of a teacher of his acquaintance who, despite using a textbook made up 'primarily of dialogs, grammar notes and ordinary drills' and methods which 'all language teachers that I know would find fault with at several points', consistently produces 'superior – often strikingly superior – results' (Stevick, 1973, pp. 267–8). He suggests that the affective attitudes of the teacher may be significant contributors to this state of affairs. If we assume that a teacher's spirituality may be interlinked with such affective attitudes, then such observations suggest that very unmethodological factors such as a teacher's lived spirituality may be significant factors in shaping teaching and learning. That something more than the merely affective is involved is evident as soon as we consider that a teacher may evidence a loving orientation towards students whom he or she dislikes on a personal level; what is at stake is a basic orientation towards the other which is expressed, among other ways, in terms of affective welcome.

This theme has recently been picked up in more general terms by Parker Palmer, who emphasizes the impossibility of reducing teaching to a technique and the importance of a teacher's ability to 'weave a complex web of connections among themselves, their subjects, and their students' (Palmer, 1998, p. 11). This echoes his earlier insistence on the need to 'allow the power of love to transform the very knowledge we teach, the very methods we use to teach and learn it' (Palmer, 1983, p. 10).

This does not obviate the need for careful reflection on the belief dimension of approaches to teaching discussed above. It would hardly be a responsible reaction to Stevick's example to conclude that a loving teacher is excused from seeking to improve the more formal dimensions of his or her teaching practices. A consistently lived spirituality will lead to more than adding personal warmth to whatever methods happen to be currently fashionable; it will be interwoven with reflection on the ways in which the designs adopted encourage or undermine the goals implicit in the teacher's pedagogic orientation. Belief and orientation are thus closely interrelated, and both combined may be of considerable relevance to ongoing revision of teaching practices (Smith, 1999).

CONCLUSION

This chapter began with questions concerning how spirituality and method could relate to each other. I have homed in on the tension between the ideal of a watertight, self-enclosed method and a Romantic understanding of spirituality as bound up principally with preconceptual experience, feeling and self-expression. I have explored how the method ideal has come to seem inadequate in the context of discussions by applied linguists of appropriate foreign language teaching methods. I have also expanded a model which has emerged from that discussion in order to show structurally how a particular spirituality may inform an approach to teaching a subject such as modern languages. I have done this in the present chapter in terms of the role of beliefs and orientations, leaving other avenues of investigation, such as the role of metaphor in conceptions of teaching, unexplored on this occasion.

This analysis suggests that something may need to shift on both sides of the dilemma as initially posed. On the one hand, the modern ideal of a self-enclosed method which guarantees certain results and excludes the fertile soup of particular beliefs, commitments and orientations which nourishes the pedagogic imagination is riddled with problems. The process of designing ways of teaching and learning is permeated by such commitments and orientations, and the disengaged, methodical stance with its virtues of rigour and detachment can itself be seen as rooted in a particular spirituality, a particular complex of beliefs, orientations and virtues (Schwehn, 1993). This suggests that a concern for spiritual development is not something to be simply added to teaching methods already established on other grounds, or slotted into the gaps, the pauses for reflection and admiration which are interspersed among the more solid and methodical matters of teaching. Particular beliefs about the spiritual nature of the learner and about the role of spirituality in our life in general must be allowed to function as part of the process of design if spiritual development is held to be important. I have explored how this works out in the detail of particular ways of teaching elsewhere (Smith, 1997a, 1997b, 1998, 1999; Smith and Dobson, 1999).

This suggests, on the other hand, that discussions of spiritual development need to be open about the beliefs, commitments and orientations which inform them. If they are to become more integral to discussions of subject teaching across the curriculum, and not remain an outgrowth of religious education, such discussions will need to consider not only the commonality suggested by considering all people as spiritual beings, capable of spiritual development, but also the significance for teaching of particular spiritual commitments, with their accompanying beliefs concerning (for instance) the nature of learners. An abstracted 'spirituality in general' seeking to retain its purity by abstaining from messy involvement with beliefs and commitments is likely to reap a limited degree of relevance when it comes to shaping the day-to-day design of teaching and learning.

While this chapter has focused mainly on the modifications which need to take place in the idea of teaching as method if spiritual development is to be taken seriously as a cross-curricular educational concern, the need to rethink does not lie exclusively on this side of the divide. Romantic conceptions of spirituality may also need to be reconsidered in the light of the ideas explored here. I have suggested that spirituality may operate within educational processes in ways which go beyond the inner, the mystical or the ineffable. Specific spiritual beliefs, commitments and orientations can become interwoven with the concrete practices of teaching, and discussion of spiritual development needs to take account of such specific and concrete operations of spirituality, and not merely its more intangible dimensions.

It is a consistent implication of recent literature on teaching method in foreign and second language learning that beliefs and orientations of some kind play a role in the design of sequences of teaching, and this clearly opens up for investigation the possibility that beliefs and orientations which flow from particular spiritual commitments can have specific relevance. This may be threatening to attempts to replicate one feature of modern ideals in proposals concerning spiritual development, namely the attempt to exclude from consideration the implications of particular beliefs and commitments in the name of a generic spirituality. However, if investigation of the implications of such commitments is sidestepped, then what we may be left with in many subject areas is an occasional pause for contemplation inserted periodically into a teaching process with which it has no coherent connection.

REFERENCES

Allen, R. T. (1993) Christian thinking about education. *Spectrum,* **25** (1), 17–24.

Anthony, E. M. (1963). Approach, method and technique. *English Language Teaching,* **17** (2), 63–7.

Blair, R. W. (ed.) (1982) *Innovative Approaches to Language Teaching.* Rowley, MA: Newbury House.

Brumfit, C. (1991) Problems in defining instructional methodologies. In de Bot, K., Ginsberg, R.P., and Kramsch, C. (eds), *Foreign Language Research in Cross-cultural Perspective,* pp. 133–44. Amsterdam/Philadelphia: John Benjamins.

Davies, A. (1993) Speculation and empiricism in applied linguistics. *Edinburgh Working Papers in Applied Linguistics,* **4**, 14–25.

Descartes, R. (1968) *Discourse on Method and the Meditations.* Harmondsworth: Penguin.

Dunne, J. (1993) *Back to the Rough Ground: Practical Judgement and the Lure of Technique.* Notre Dame: University of Notre Dame Press.

Feyerabend, P. (1975) *Against Method: Outline of an Anarchistic Theory of Knowledge.* London: NLB.

Gadamer, H.-G. (1989) *Truth and Method.* (2nd edn.). London: Sheed & Ward.

Gergen, K. J. (1991) *The Saturated Self: Dilemmas of Identity in Contemporary Life.* New York: Basic Books.

Kinginger, C. (1997) A discourse approach to the study of language educators' coherence systems. *Modern Language Journal,* **18** (1), 6–14.

Kumaravadivelu, B. (1994) The postmethod condition: (e)merging strategies for second/foreign language teaching. *TESOL Quarterly,* **28** (1), 27–48.

Larsen-Freeman, D. (1991) Research on language teaching methodologies: a review of the past and an agenda for the future. In de Bot, K., Ginsberg, R. P. and Kramsch, C. (eds), *Foreign Language Research in Cross-cultural Perspective,* pp. 119–32. Amsterdam/Philadelphia: John Benjamins.

Olthuis, J. H. (1985) On worldviews. *Christian Scholars Review,* **14** (2), 153–64.

Palmer, P. J. (1983) *To Know as We are Known: A Spirituality of Education.* San Francisco: Harper & Row.

Palmer, P. J. (1998) *The Courage to Teach: Exploring the Inner Landscape of a Teacher's Life.* San Francisco: Jossey Bass.

Pennycook, A. (1989) The concept of method, interested knowledge, and the politics of language teaching. *TESOL Quarterly,* **23** (4), 589–618.

Pennycook, A. (1990) Towards a critical applied linguistics for the 1990s. *Issues in Applied Linguistics,* **1** (1), 8–28.

Polanyi, M. (1958) *Personal Knowledge: Towards a Post-critical Philosophy.* London: Routledge & Kegan Paul.

Prabhu, N. S. (1987) *Second Language Pedagogy.* Oxford: Oxford University Press.

Prabhu, N. S. (1990) There is no best method – why? *TESOL Quarterly,* **24** (2), 161–76.

Richards, J. C. (1984) The secret life of methods. *TESOL Quarterly,* **18** (1), 7–23.

Richards, J. C. and Rodgers, T. S. (1982) Method: approach, design and procedure. *TESOL Quarterly,* **16** (2), 153–68.

Richards, J. C. and Rodgers, T. S. (1986) *Approaches and Methods in Language Teaching: A Description and Analysis.* Cambridge: Cambridge University Press.

Schön, D. A. (1979) Generative metaphor: a perspective on problem-setting in social policy. In Ortony, A. (ed.), *Metaphor and Thought,* pp. 254–83. Cambridge: Cambridge University Press.

Schön, D. A. (1983) *The Reflective Practitioner: How Professionals Think in Action.* New York: Basic Books.

Schwehn, M. (1993) *Exiles from Eden: Religion and the Academic Vocation in America.* New York: Oxford University Press.

Smith, D. (1997a) Communication and integrity: moral development and modern languages. *Language Learning Journal,* **15**, 31–8.

Smith, D. (1997b) In search of the whole person: critical reflections on counseling-learning. *Journal of Research on Christian Education,* **6** (2), 159–81.

Smith, D. (1997c) Power and mutuality in modern foreign language education: the possibility of a Christian orientation. Unpublished MPhilF., Institute for Christian Studies, Toronto.

Smith, D. (1998) Culture, conflict and communication: the troubled waters of modern language pedagogy. In Blomberg, D. and Lambert, I. (eds), *Reminding: Renewing the Mind in Learning*, pp. 52–76. Sydney: Centre for the Study of Australian Christianity.

Smith, D. (1999) *Making Sense of Spiritual Development*. Nottingham: The Stapleford Centre.

Smith, D. and Dobson, S. (1999) Modern languages. In Bigger, S. and Brown, E. (eds), *Spiritual, Moral, Social and Cultural Education: Exploring Values in the Curriculum*. London: David Fulton.

Stevick, E. W. (1973) Review article: Counseling–learning: a whole person model for education. *Language Learning*, **23** (2), 259–71.

Stevick, E. W. (1990) *Humanism in Language Teaching: A Critical Perspective*. Oxford: Oxford University Press.

Swaffar, J. K., Arens, K. and Morgan, M. (1982) Teacher classroom practices: redefining method as task hierarchy. *Modern Language Journal*, **66** (1), 24–33.

Taylor, C. (1989) *Sources of the Self: The Making of the Modern Identity*. Cambridge, Mass: Harvard University Press.

Tench, P. (1985) Teaching English as a foreign/second language. *Spectrum*, **17** (2), 42–4.

Weideman, A. J. (1987) Applied linguistics as a discipline of design – a foundational study. Unpublished doctoral thesis, University of the Orange Free State, Bloemfontein.

Williams, G. (1992) *Sociolinguistics: A Sociological Critique*. London: Routledge.

Wolterstorff, N. (1984) *Reason within the Bounds of Religion* (2nd edn.). Grand Rapids: Eerdmans.

Wright, A. (1997) Embodied spirituality: the place of culture and tradition in contemporary educational discourse on spirituality. *International Journal of Children's Spirituality*, **1** (2), 8–20.

Wright, A. (1998) *Spiritual Pedagogy: A Survey, Critique and Reconstruction of Contemporary Spiritual Education in England and Wales*. Abingdon: Culham College Institute.

Yoshikawa, M. (1982) Language teaching methodologies and the nature of the individual: a new definition. *Modern Language Journal*, **66** (4), 391–5.

CHAPTER 5

Common schools, good citizens: towards a public discourse model of moral education

Don Rowe

THE NATIONAL CONTEXT

In May 1999 the government announced its intention to include citizenship education as a statutory element of the revised secondary curriculum from 2000 (Qualifications and Curriculum Authority, 1999). After many unsuccessful campaigns this century to win a secure place in the curriculum for citizenship education, this represents a watershed in the history of civic, and also for moral, education in England. The orders as framed offer two distinct but interrelated rationales for citizenship education. First, it is to provide young people with essential knowledge of social and political structures enabling them to make informed choices and to develop skills of 'enquiry and communication' and 'participation and action'. This can be described as 'capacity building'. Secondly, citizenship education is to promote certain essential values or dispositions, including 'justice, respect for democracy and diversity'. Education for citizenship should also help pupils gain a disposition for reflective discussion. This second set of aims is motivational, developing the qualities and character traits essential to the democratic way of life. Knowledge, understanding and skills are not enough, a liberal democracy also requires a citizenry committed to its core values.

However, in such a society citizens, by definition, are free to accept or reject involvement in democratic activities and the state must be wary of overstepping the line which distinguishes 'empowerment' from 'propaganda'. The draft orders appear to accept the limitations of public schooling in this respect despite the claims of a small number of critics (e.g. Phillips, 1999). In discussing the values component of citizenship education the language of the document is restrained, acknowledging the fact that moral and political ideas are essentially contested. The document suggests that pupils should '*learn about* the key concepts, values or dispositions of fairness, social justice, respect for democracy and diversity' (my italics), stopping short of the suggestion that schools should promote such values in an intrusive or oppressive way. Thus the framework of values underpinning citizenship education is placed firmly within the range of public or civic virtues (White, 1996) which are non-partisan and about which schools need not be defensive. As Crewe *et al.* (1996) put it:

> a democratic society has an obligation to educate children into citizenship. This democratic principle requires the state to cultivate through the schools the capacities for civic engagement and rational deliberation. Although a liberal democratic society permits adults to lead isolated and unexamined lives if that is what they choose, it cannot support an education that is neutral between these two options, and it cannot claim that the two ways of life are equally desirable. The ideal of democratic education is at the core of commitment to democracy and it therefore falls to the professional responsibility of teachers in a liberal democracy to foster the knowledge, skills and habits of civic engagement and public discourse.

Moral education has not always been seen in this civic context. Over the years, considerable emphasis has been placed on the role of moral education in developing 'good character' where goodness has often been defined in religious terms such as having the will to 'resist evil' (NCC, 1993) or the Christian duty to sacrifice self in the service of others. This view lingers on in some interpretations of the term 'active citizenship' as *service,* which goes beyond the civic duty to play one's part in democratic life and follow a 'decent' (White, 1996), law-abiding and responsible (McLaughlin, 1996) way of life. Religious schools may promote other virtues as part of the ethical base to which parents and pupils have signed up but this is much less straightforward in the multicultural, multi-faith school where 'active citizenship', if it is to be promoted at all, must be on a basis acceptable to citizens of all persuasions. Accordingly, the government's published framework (QCA, 1999) offers a broad 'entitlement' model of citizenship – a model which even the most self-centred citizens might be expected to support on the grounds that it enables them to pursue their personal vision of society within a stable and pluralist democratic framework.

The emphasis on the skills of reflection and debate, particularly in the context of public policy, places this model of citizenship education within a range of 'critical' models. This is to distinguish it from more conservative models of moral education which tend to minimize opportunities for critical reflection and emphasize respect for tradition, shared values (QCA, 1997) and the role of personal morality in the development of 'good character' (McLaughlin and Halstead, 1999).

The new curriculum proposals suggest an approach to citizenship which is continuous and progressive throughout all the key stages, placing emphasis on conceptual development and the nurturing of the skills of analysis and debate essential to a deliberative democracy. The discussion of moral issues, including those focusing on issues of justice and fairness, rights and responsibilities, feature in each key stage, including the non-statutory primary school programme. This is seen as laying the important foundations for the secondary programmes of study.

What are the implications of this approach for the discussion of moral issues in the classroom? While moral issues arise tangentially in a number of subjects such as science or English, they emerge in their own right in religious education (RE) and personal and social education and citizenship (which, for convenience, I shall refer to as PSHCE). There are close similarities in the pedagogy of moral discussion between these two subject areas, although differences arise over issue selection. In RE, the focus is on the ethical codes of the major world religions with regard to issues such as abortion, euthanasia, genetic engineering or cloning. In PSHCE, moral problems may have a personal focus or they may be socially and politically controversial, such as the legalization of drugs or the lowering of the age of consent for homosexuals. Thus both RE and PSHCE appear to operate on separate but closely parallel lines with their focus on what can be called 'big issues'. The 'big issues' approach has come to dominate moral education as if there were no practical alternative. However, its weaknesses have been insufficiently scrutinized. Before proposing an alternative approach, I want to look in more detail at what seems to me to be the broad characteristics of the 'big issues' approach and its function in the moral curriculum.

THE 'BIG ISSUES' APPROACH TO MORAL EDUCATION

In outline, the features of this approach are as follows.

- Selection of issues is primarily on the basis of their contested nature, intrinsic interest and their ability to exemplify certain *types* of contested issue where the protagonists typically divide along predictable lines (such as religious/secular, interfaith or conservative/progressive). *Issues are not selected for their value in teaching particular moral concepts.*
- Pupils are introduced to the central arguments and relevant facts, prior to discussing the issue for themselves. Discussion, therefore, takes the form of 'rehearsal', rather than an exercise in analysis.
- This rehearsing of the arguments has the potential to offer pupils fresh perspectives against which to judge their own positions and develop new understandings. Thus this approach is felt to encourage a disposition of open-minded enquiry – one which recognizes the importance of basing arguments on reason and reflection. Pupils may even be asked to argue for positions they do not themselves hold, to promote better perspective taking.
- The active discussion of such issues is seen as encouraging pupils to develop the skills and dispositions which underpin all democratic discourse even though, because of the inexperience of the discussants, pupils might easily become more confused about the issue itself.
- Besides providing information, the teacher's role is seen as facilitating discussion. The most influential model in this respect has been that of the 'neutral chair' (Stenhouse, 1971) – neutral that is, in relation to the substantive issue, though (we would add) far from neutral in respect of the underlying democratic values.
- A successful debate would be characterized or assessed largely in terms of process (see e.g. Gurney, 1991; Foster, 1993) – the liveliness of exchanges, the involvement of a large number of pupils, arguments and

opinions being well supported, pupils showing respect for difference and demonstrating knowledge of accepted procedures such as taking turns and not interrupting.

One major weakness of this approach is that the selection of course content is determined by circumstance or the current news agenda rather than the philosophical structure of moral thought. This makes systematic coverage, including the progressive introduction of moral ideas, virtually impossible. In particular, it would not be clear on what principles one would develop a spiral curriculum for all key stages. Rendering whole areas of a subject vulnerable in this way makes little educational sense. Teachers would normally expect to work the other way round – namely, to identify what is to be learned by pupils and then to find an appropriate way to teach it.

An unfortunate side effect of issue-based discussion is the dominance of one (adversarial) methodology which means that topics not susceptible to this treatment (such as what different people mean by 'good character') tend to be overlooked. Adversarial approaches to a subject can be divisive, encouraging rhetorical devices which can do as much to obscure as to clarify. Facts can be suppressed or distorted as well as elucidated and forms of public discussion which aid the emergence of understanding or consensus can become undervalued.

Surprisingly, despite the emphasis on discussion in this model, pupils are generally assumed to be knowledgeable about the process of argumentation (Downs, 1993). Little attention is paid to debriefing debates from the point of view of the coverage or quality of the discussion itself. For example, no texts I have come across encourage students to learn how to use common forms of moral argument such as 'ends versus means' or 'slippery slope'.

The heterogeneous and conflicting elements of these 'big issues', relating both to principle and practice, produce levels of complexity which challenge many mature citizens, let alone emergent ones in school. This is not to argue that schools should not help pupils address these subjects but, rather, that they are not giving pupils the tools with which to do so adequately. One would not expect pupils to debate an economic issue without an understanding of the appropriate language. Why, then, is this commonly the case with moral issues?

TOWARDS A PUBLIC DISCOURSE MODEL OF MORAL EDUCATION

A public discourse model of moral education derives its justification from the educational imperative for democracies to induct citizens into public deliberation. Its aim is to enrich public debate in its quality, breadth and diversity at the same time as enabling citizens themselves to pursue their own purposes more effectively in the public domain. Public discourse around moral and political issues has its own values and characteristics which distinguish it from the private discourses in which like-minded citizens privately engage (Strike, 1994). Public discourse involves engaging with others with different value systems in the search for understanding, agreement or compromise. To engage in public discourse is to recognize that, while some broadly defined values and beliefs may be shared across a liberal democracy, the possibility of profound and irreconcilable disagreement also exists – a far more significant challenge for education. Some philosophers, including Strike (*ibid.*) refer to 'overlapping consensuses' around which, through deliberation and public talk, socially stable institutions can be built. Gutman and Thompson (1995) suggest that the promotion of quality public discourse is essential in a deliberative democracy if it is to be more than merely a crude form of majority rule, in which minorities are left to feel overlooked and frustrated. In the civic forum, talk is the primary form of action (*pace* those who argue that one only learns citizenship by 'doing'). It is the main vehicle by which the democratic way of life is sustained and transmitted to the next generation. However, as Andrews (1995) points out, public discourse is rich but 'the range available in schools and colleges has been much narrower than that deployed in society', leading, in effect, to the denial of an entitlement.

A highly significant feature of moral discourse is that it develops throughout childhood and into adulthood. In her study of three-year-olds, Dunn (1988) discovered children already wrestling with the same concepts which infuse adult deliberations – ideas of positive justice, responsibility, guilt, mitigation and power. It is through talk that children, in Bruner's words (1989), learn to 'calibrate the workings of their minds against one another'. But this is talk which is socially constructed and into which one has to be painstakingly inducted. Many of its features do not come naturally and its 'ground rules' (Mercer, 1995) can be difficult to learn, such as the value of giving due weight to the views of others in the search for fair solutions. The developmental nature of this process is hinted at by Mercer, who observed the development of talk in classrooms in which the earlier and more crude forms of discourse, which he calls 'disputational' and 'cumulative' (i.e. co-operative but non-critical) talk, gradually give way, under the right conditions, to a more sophisticated form of talk which he calls 'exploratory'. In exploratory talk,

> partners engage critically but constructively with each other's ideas.... Statements and suggestions are offered for joint consideration. These may be challenged and counter-challenged, but challenges are justified and alternative hypotheses offered. Compared with the other two types, in exploratory talk *knowledge is made more publicly accountable and reasoning is more visible in the talk.* (Mercer, 1995, author's italics).

Children at all stages of their education should, therefore, have an opportunity to explore ideas about right and wrong, good and bad, rights and responsibilities. Such matters permeate people's dealings with each other at a personal and public level. They are central to the challenge of constructive coexistence and, on this view, would rate as even more fundamental to human society than either literacy or numeracy. In one sense, this is to advocate a form of moral philosophy for schools. When ideas are suitably embedded (Donaldson, 1978) in terms and examples which children recognize, then complex understandings can often be expressed and directly examined even by children in Key Stage 1 (e.g. Costello, 1995). By scaffolding pupils' arguments in a supportive, stimulating and increasingly sophisticated way around a framework of concepts, children's thinking can be extended and developed in a fashion which is unlikely to occur when the curriculum is constructed haphazardly and with no reference to a clear underpinning conceptual structure. In this respect, the project described below should be seen as one manifestation of the 'thinking skills' movement in which educationists (e.g. Fisher, 1998) have claimed great benefits for pupils across a range of subject areas through increasing their capacity for critical thinking and metareflection.

THE MORAL EDUCATION IN SECONDARY SCHOOLS PROJECT

In 1996, the Moral Education in Secondary Schools Project was established by the Citizenship Foundation[1] to develop a thoroughgoing public discourse model of moral education. This followed the development of a resource, entitled *You, Me, Us!* (Rowe and Newton, 1994), which provides discussion material for Key Stages 1 and 2 around key concepts such as rights, responsibilities, justice, power and authority. This material mostly uses the medium of narrative to stimulate moral reasoning and empathic awareness in a spiral curriculum. The new project was to build on this approach, revisiting the core moral concepts at a more complex and appropriate level for secondary schools. After a developmental period and several drafts, materials were developed for Key Stages 3, 4 and post–16. The new course, called *Good Thinking*, is constructed around 15 lessons per key stage. Relatively simple definitions, ideas and issues are dealt with in Key Stage 3 using straightforward examples. The core concepts are revisited in more detail and complexity in the subsequent stages. Examples tend at first to be at an interpersonal level, progressing towards more society-centred issues in later stages.

The course is designed to introduce pupils to the following characteristics of public moral discourse:

- even the ordinary 'surface events' of daily life can be construed in moral terms which have implications for interpersonal and community life;
- moral thinking at all levels is based around a number of recurring core concepts the nature of which determines the shape and function of the discourse itself, including *rights, duties, obligations, justice, good/bad, right/ wrong;*
- moral arguments draw on different sources of moral authority, for example, religion or human reason, and on the fact that different people value things differently, in ways not susceptible to rational argument;
- moral dilemmas utilize distinctive forms of reasoning, including, for example, consequential thinking and principled reasoning;
- moral argumentation takes characteristic forms such as 'greater good' and 'lesser of evils' and employs identifiable techniques of persuasion or rhetoric (some positive, some negative);
- moral reasoning itself should be subject to tests of logic and integrity of purpose.

Each unit is constructed around a number of discursive or analytical processes, the most crucial of which are:

- analysis of events in moral terms;
- reflection on the ideas;

- learning of definitions;
- application of new ideas to novel situations;
- familiarization with different forms of argument;
- extension of thinking to more abstract or generalized contexts;
- reinforcement of vocabulary and metareflection.

How does this process of systematic introduction to moral ideas work in practice? I will illustrate with reference to one of the central concepts of the moral curriculum, *justice* (Rowe, 1993). Justice, Rawls (1972) suggests, is the highest value by which to scrutinize the quality of public life. It is, therefore, essential that students properly understand the term and use it accurately in its different applications. From a developmental viewpoint, children approach justice issues egocentrically in the early years (Kohlberg, 1984; Dunn, 1988; Eisenberg Berg and Mussen, 1975). Their understanding of justice is externally determined by authority figures such as parents and teachers (Piaget, 1932). According to Piaget and Kohlberg, children's understanding develops as the result of reflection on more complex applications and by taking the perspectives of others. During the adolescent years, given the right stimuli, young people begin to take on the perspective of society at large: the citizen's perspective. Children deprived of the appropriate stimuli, e.g. those who live in homes where talk is absent and justice is erratic and violent, do not develop these wider perspectives, staying locked into immature self-centred ways of thinking and acting (Kohlberg, 1984). Pupils, therefore, need opportunities to extend their understanding in the direction of these increasingly sophisticated and, civically speaking, essential forms of thought.

The kinds of opportunity presented by the Project are exemplified below.

Level 1, Key Stage 3

In *Good Thinking* Book 1, two units examine different forms of justice. In the first unit (called *It's So Unfair!*), the class reads a short story about Toby, who unfairly suffers a whole-class punishment of extra homework over the weekend. It takes Toby, a pupil with special needs, much longer than other students to complete the work and his weekend is badly affected. On the Monday morning, a friend, who has not done the homework, begs Toby to let her copy his work, to which he reluctantly agrees. However, the teacher realizes some children have copied and asks the culprits to own up. Toby does so, but his friend keeps quiet.

Working in pairs, pupils analyse the story in terms of different kinds of injustice. The teachers' notes list ten possible examples. Pupils are offered different categories of justice into which to group their examples, such as 'getting what you deserve' (a form of retributive justice), 'having equal rights' (distributive justice), 'having fair ways of doing things' (procedural justice), although these more complex terms are not introduced at this level. The unit continues by asking pupils to consider when justice might require people to be treated differently and when not.

The second unit at this first level (*Making Rules*) examines the idea of procedural justice as applied to decision-making. Pupils consider what happens when a gang of children builds a den and some of their friends and relations want to join in. Problems arise as to who can use the den, when and how. The gang agrees that rules are needed but on what basis should they decide who is to have a say in making the rules?

Through examining this story pupils consider fair decision-making procedures for the gang, giving reasons, and then go on to apply these ideas to other social contexts such as families, professional football clubs, religious bodies and youth clubs where factors are weighted differently according to circumstance. It is not difficult, even for this age of pupil, to go on to consider fair ways of decision-making in school, by no means a simple issue. This would be a good example of an important issue which is not helpfully approached by the adversarial discussion technique.

Level 2, Key Stage 4

At this level, the idea of social justice is introduced more directly in two further units. In *A Just Society,* pupils consider the merits of a fictitious society called Sikkal in which the people have all their material needs met, including food, health and housing. This is achieved by careful allocation of everyone to a predetermined role in life for which they are trained from the age of five. All decisions are made by a benign despot and what few dissenters there are are well looked after in secure mental institutions.

This scenario is designed to help pupils realize that there are different kinds of social justice and, while benefiting from some of its forms, the inhabitants of Sikkal are denied others, including freedom and democracy. They are asked to imagine what might happen if Sikkal became more democratic: would the benefits outweigh the disadvantages? Pupils are then asked to compare the justice available in Sikkal with aspects of our own society and consider the general question of whether it is possible to construct a society which could be fair to all its members.

A second unit on this theme is called *For the Good of the Community,* in which pupils are presented with a scenario in which a rapidly expanding community is desperately in need of a number of new facilities: but which facilities would serve it best? This raises the question 'what makes a community a good one in which to live – harmony, security, prosperity or justice?' In a further exercise, pupils reflect on justice issues in their own communities in which actions which arguably benefit the community as a whole, such as imposing curfews on troublesome young people, may be against the interests of certain groups.

Level 3, post-16

At this level, justice issues are presented in more complex social problems. One unit looks at the competing claims of different forms of government and another asks pupils to consider the difficulties of creating public policy in a society in which there are deep differences of opinion about what is 'good'. As an initial exercise, students consider an incident in an FE college where, as the result of a student council decision, condom machines are to be installed in the toilets. Not surprisingly, various local groups are deeply affronted by this proposal and protest to the principal who finds herself in a difficult position. Who should have the final say in such a situation? What weight is to be given to the democratic decision of the majority of students? To what extent should minority views be allowed to determine policy? In later units, justice issues are revisited in other contexts such as the workplace and the criminal justice system.

In the *Good Thinking* programme, other central concepts, such as rights, duties and obligations, are treated in a similar fashion to that described above for justice.

The materials also cover a number of broader topics in which the nature of public discourse itself is subject to scrutiny. In the Key Stage 3 course, for example, pupils consider the purposes of discussion both for the resolution of conflict and as the right to express oneself. Later, pupils think about why it is important to give reasons for your beliefs and why some forms of argumentation or rhetoric may be regarded as unfair or even immoral.

Having described in some detail the pedagogical model based on public moral discourse in contrast to the 'big issues' approach, we are in a position briefly to summarize the arguments and compare the main characteristics of each approach (Table 5.1)

Table 5.1 Comparison between 'Big Issues' and 'Public Discourse' Models

	Big Issues Model	Public Discourse Model
Selection	• selection of topics by virtue of controversiality and topicality	• selection of topics according to moral concepts, and the nature of public moral discourse itself
	• topic selection haphazard, coverage of types of moral thinking is uncertain and unpredictable	• topic selection planned, coverage of moral thinking is systematic
	• defines issues against a background of social science disciplines and politics	• draws on broad traditions of philosophy and religious debate
Focus of learning	• emphasis on the rules and procedural skills of debate	• emphasis on language, forms of thought, and content of moral discourse
	• induction into existing debates between communities in society	• induction into general characteristics of public discourse
	• promotes familiarity with common arguments	• promotes familiarity with common *forms* of argument
	• students choose between opposing views	• students reflect on nature of the disagreement
Progression	• moral thinking remains embedded and situation-specific	• moral thinking increasingly disembedded and generalized
	• progression determined by complexity of the substantive issue	• progression determined by sequencing of moral ideas in a spiral curriculum

One further point remains to be made about the pedagogy of moral education. It is not enough for teachers to remain 'neutral' and hope for a good quality lesson. Moral education as outlined above requires specific pedagogies *according to the task in hand.* In the primary school project referred to above (Rowe and Newton, 1994), I and my colleagues developed a model in which the teacher consciously encourages three different types of thinking, each with its own characteristic focus and forms of questioning: moral reasoning, empathic awareness and philosophical reflection. Similarly, at secondary level, we suggest teachers develop the following strategies, each of which has a clear purpose within the overall aim of promoting the moral development of the young citizen:

- encouraging logical and clear reasoning, e.g. by asking 'why?', 'what's your reason for saying that?' or 'what did you mean by that?'
- developing moral judgement, e.g. by asking 'which do you think is better?'
- generating alternative viewpoints, e.g. by asking 'can anyone think of a different idea?'
- encouraging perspective taking and empathic reasoning, e.g. by asking 'what do you think the other person would think or feel about that?'
- broadening moral perspectives, e.g. by asking 'is that best for the group as a whole?' or 'what would society be like if everyone behaved like that?'
- to encourage justice reasoning, e.g. by asking 'is that fair?'
- to establish common ground, e.g. by asking 'what things do we all agree on?'
- to summarize the discussion and draw out its main features, e.g. by asking 'what have we learnt today?' or 'what arguments were used today?'

CONCLUSION

In this chapter, I have argued that the public discussion of moral issues is an essential component of civic involvement and that schools have a duty to induct young people into the moral life of the nation in all its diversity. This is fully in line with the government's programme of study for citizenship and, in my view, will strengthen the previously precarious foothold which moral education *per se* has had in the curriculum. I have further argued that the prevailing methodology of the discussion of 'big issues' is a necessary but not sufficient element of moral education and that more is required for the education of citizens than 'moral joyriding' from one issue to another. These two approaches should be seen as complementary. Given the appropriate stimuli and support, carefully planned and delivered at each key stage, there is no reason why pupils should not become much more skilled in thinking about civic and moral issues and, as a result, develop into more aware, more sensitive and responsible citizens.

NOTE

1 The Citizenship Foundation is an educational charity working nationally and internationally. Don Rowe is director of the Moral Education in Secondary Schools Project. The project officer is Ted Huddleston, who has been jointly responsible with Don Rowe for the overall shape of the public discourse model set out here.

REFERENCES

Andrews, R. (1995) *Teaching and Learning Argument.* London: Cassell.

Bruner, J. (1989) The transactional self. In Murphy, P. and Moon, B. (eds), *Developments in Learning and Assessment.* London: Hodder and Stoughton.

Costello, P. J. M. (1995) Education, citizenship and critical thinking. In Fields, J. I. (ed.), *Young Children as Emergent Philosophers,* special edition of *Early Child Development and Care,* **107**.

Crewe, I., Searing, D. and Conover, P. (1996) *Citizenship and Civic Education.* London: The Citizenship Foundation.

Donaldson, M. (1978) *Children's Minds.* London: Fontana.

Downs, W. (1993) The values trap in personal and social education. *NAVET Papers,* **9**.

Dunn, J. (1988) *The Beginnings of Social Understanding.* Oxford: Blackwell.

Eisenberg Berg, N. and Mussen, P. (1975) The origins and development of concepts of justice. *Journal of Social Issues,* **31** (3).

Fisher, R. (1998) *Teaching Thinking: Philosophical Enquiry in the Classroom.* London, Cassell.

Foster, J. (1993) *Issues, the Cross-curricular Course for PSE.* London: Collins Educational.

Gurney, M. (1991) *Personal and Social Education, an Integrated Programme.* Cheltenham: Stanley Thornes.

Gutman, A. and Thompson, D. (1995) Moral disagreement in a democracy. In Paul, E. F., Miller Jnr., F. D. and Paul, J. (eds), *Contemporary Political and Social Philosophy.* New York: Cambridge University Press.

Kohlberg, L. (1984) *The Psychology of Moral Development Vol 2.* New York: Harper and Row.

McLaughlin, T. H., (1996) Educating responsible citizens. In Tam. H. (ed.), *Punishment, Excuses and Moral Development.* Aldershot: Avebury.

McLaughlin, T. and Halstead, J. M. (1999) Education in character and virtue. In Halstead, J. M. and McLaughlin, T. H. (eds), *Education in Morality.* London: Routledge, pp. 132–63.

Mercer, N. (1995) *The Guided Construction of Knowledge, Talk Amongst Teachers and Learners.* Clevedon: Multilingual Matters.

National Curriculum Council (NCC) (1993) *Spiritual and Moral Development – a Discussion Paper.* York: National Curriculum Council.

Phillips, M. (1999) The indoctrination of Citizen Smith Jr. *Sunday Times,* 7 March 1999.

Piaget, J. (1932) *The Moral Judgement of the Child.* London: Harmondsworth, Penguin Books.

Qualifications and Curriculum Authority (QCA) (1997) *The Promotion of Pupils' Spiritual, Moral, Social and Cultural Development.* London: QCA.

Qualifications and Curriculum Authority (QCA) (1999) *The National Curriculum: Key Stages 3 and 4.* London: QCA.

Rawls, J. (1972) *A Theory of Justice.* Oxford: Oxford University Press.

Rowe, D. (1993) The citizen as a moral agent – the development of a continuous and progressive conflict-based citizenship curriculum. *Curriculum* **13** (3).

Rowe, D. and Newton, J. (1994) *You, Me, Us! Social and Moral Responsibility for Primary Schools.* London: The Home Office.

Stenhouse, L. (1971) The Humanities Curriculum Project: the rationale. *Theory into Practice*, **10**: 154–62.

Strike, K. (1994) On the construction of public speech: pluralism and public reason. *Educational Theory*, **44** (1). Illinois: University of Illinois.

White, P. (1996) *Civic Virtues and Public Schooling: Educating Citizens for a Democratic Society.* New York and London: Teachers College Press.

CHAPTER 6

Learning by heart: the role of emotional education in raising school achievement and promoting the caring community

Kevin McCarthy

> Developing children as rounded people and active members of the community is at the heart of what schools are about.
>
> (Estelle Morris speaking to the SCAA Primary
> Curriculum Conference, June 1997)

This is a busy government with a missionary zeal – or at least much missionary rhetoric. On the one hand, we have the push towards raising achievement, improving standards of literacy and numeracy. At the same time, schools are being placed at the heart of Tony Blair's task of social regeneration. The government wants young people to become active, caring and committed citizens, stakeholders in its new modern democracy, aware of their responsibilities not just their rights, globally and environmentally conscious, geared up for the information age, developing skills through lifelong learning. It is an ambitious and taxing agenda, perceived by many as dangerously top-down in its approach and one, moreover, announced at a time when the teaching profession feels demoralized and disempowered.

Estelle Morris's best soundbite has been much quoted but never fully elaborated. How do we translate this vision of a new society into practical action? An important part of the curriculum review focuses on the Preparation for Adult Life group at QCA. Over the past seven or eight years we have seen a series of initiatives as first the NCC, then SCAA and now QCA have tried to give expression to a rationale for pupils' inner development in terms of their spiritual, moral, social and cultural education. It has not been a pure search. It has been raided and buccaneered by those who would seek a return to some Golden Age, when society supposedly held commonly agreed moral norms. It has been pressed into the service of moral rectitude. It has been blown off-course and has sometimes been completely lost sight of by the great winds of change: literacy and numeracy which, according to many, threaten the very creative, meaning-making activity which lies at the heart of education.

The whole question really stems from a deeper search for a rationale for education in the current age. We have had a generation growing up right through the 1980s and 1990s in which the implied model for education has been firmly instrumental, ultimately vocational. Really what is needed – and what QCA has tried to do for the first time in a generation – is a fundamental reappraisal of what kind of education is required by young people growing up in a complex and rapidly changing world.

Last year, the Calouste Gulbenkian Foundation commissioned Re:membering Education, a pressure group established to focus on this pressing agenda, to bring together educationists from a variety of different backgrounds and organizations: from heads and teaching unions, from pastoral care and PSE to bring together research evidence about the effects of emotional education. This chapter draws heavily on the outcome of that project in setting out the case for emotional education, which is to say education *about* emotion and education which *engages* the emotions. This is a useful and necessary reference point for addressing both the challenges of raising achievement and of creating a healthier, more caring society. We will begin by making the somewhat artificial distinction between, on the one hand, the school ethos, the whole style and culture of school including crucially how it manages all its relationships and, on the other, how its teaching and learning takes place within and outside the classroom.

PUTTING THINKING INTO FEELING: DEVELOPING EMOTIONAL SKILLS

You know the sort of thing, though, don't you? It's Monday after break. The door crashes back on its hinges and Lee sulks in to your lesson just as you've got them settled. You kind of ease him in without getting too confrontational, and then he hasn't got a pencil, a pen or anything. What you don't know is what's happened to him before he reached you . He had a row before school with his step-dad, went out with no breakfast, has already been hassled about his uniform. 'Introducing Matrices' is about the last thing on his mind. You're on to a loser before you start.

This honest gem came from a strong and experienced teacher, a national union official, no 'luvvie' or lefty. He was using it to demonstrate the importance of relationship skills in the classroom. To guess what happened next, you would need to know more about the child's background, about the personality of the teacher and so on. The most important factor, though, would obviously be the nature of their relationship. As it happens, the teacher in question was probably able both by instinct and by experience, like so many striving teachers, however powerful his/her feeling reaction, to stay cool and firmly offer the pupil some win-win opportunity, some chance to de-escalate the situation and create at least the chance of some learning taking place. For another teacher, there might have been another outcome: confrontation, loss of control, shouting, accusation.

If, quite possibly for the new purpose of deciding his or her future pay, we try to identify the particular quality of the successful teacher in such a case, what do we say? She is good with kids? To say that he has 'strong interpersonal intelligence' sounds transatlantic. To call a teacher 'emotionally literate' definitely still requires inverted commas. All this is in spite of the enormous success of both Howard Gardner (Gardner, 1985) and Daniel Goleman (Goleman, 1996), whose research and writing figure widely in so much current thinking. Gardner makes a tentative but compelling case for the theory of multiple intelligences, arguing that the commonly measured cognitive human capacities give an inadequate picture of the qualitatively different ways in which humans can show 'intelligence'. For Gardner, the inter- and intra-personal intelligences – knowing and relating well to yourself and forming good relationships with others – represent two strands of a single intelligence quite independent of other intelligences such as linguistic or mathematical capacity. Goleman expands Gardner's somewhat cognitively constrained fields to include the affective dimension. For us to thrive and develop as full human beings, he argues, we need to bring intelligence to emotion, some thinking into our feeling.

So, what about Lee – and his teacher for that matter? And there are thousands of them up and down the country: kids with low self-esteem, who get into bullying or being bullied, who truant, underachieve, do drugs and are generally to a greater or lesser extent emotionally out of control. What is the answer? Peter Salovey, the psychologist credited with coining the term 'emotional literacy' and a pioneer in this field, proves a useful basic characterization (Salovey and Mayer, 1990). Emotional intelligence, he says, has five main domains:

1. Knowing one's emotions: being self-aware.
2. Managing emotions: handling feelings in a way that is appropriate.
3. Motivating oneself: stifling impulsiveness, delaying gratification, being able to get into the 'flow' state that characterizes productive and effective people.
4. Recognizing emotions in others: empathy.
5. Handling relationships.

Goleman (1996) describes numerous practical projects in the States with well-documented evidence of significant improvement in behaviour and attitude as a result of structured programmes aimed at directly teaching emotional skills. Linda Lantieri, for instance, has a widely successful programme which tackles violence and aggression in her Resolving Conflict Creatively Programme, which is in use in hundreds of schools in the States. Other programmes with well-accredited research evaluations are the Yale–New Haven Social Competence Programme and the Fast Track Project being monitored by the University of Washington (Goleman, 1996, Appendix F). For many young people, simply to have a name to attach to the feeling they are experiencing gives them some foothold, some point of reference. Our not-so-fictional Lee, for instance, might well have benefited from the New Haven 'stoplight' poster with its six steps: stop and calm down; say the problem and how you feel; set a positive goal; think of lots of solutions; think ahead to the consequences; go ahead and try the best plan. The importance of such projects is that even surprisingly short-term interventions seem to produce long-lasting effects on all five of these fronts. What all these programmes stress, however, is the school and community-wide focus on a long-term process.

Research indicates that successful schools are characterized by a strong ethos which supports good relationships with clear, safe and secure boundaries (Sammons *et al.*, 1997). Such an ethos can be created in a number of ways both within formal structures and in the myriad of tiny interactions which take place between teacher and pupil, pupil and pupil, pupils and other staff in lessons, in the playground or corridors. Successful schools see themselves as learning communities in which both teachers and pupils are consciously working on the development of healthy relationships. Such schools create an atmosphere in which there is:

- a space for everyone to listen and be listened to,
- a time and a place for reviewing and reflecting on what has been learned,
- a shared and developing language for describing one's own and others' emotions,
- a feeling of community and responsibility.

Scale, too, is an important factor affecting school climate (Cotton, 1997). The size of both schools and individual classes is directly connected with climate and 'feel'.

Even more importantly, and this will come as no surprise to anyone who has ever been in a classroom, more learning takes place. A growing body of evidence points towards the importance of self-confidence and a feeling of well-being in the learning process (Weissberg and Greenberg, 1997). Pupils who have taken part in programmes to raise their awareness of emotions and to enhance their self-esteem achieve better scores on standardized achievement tests. As Goleman points out, 'This is not an isolated finding; it recurs again and again in such studies. In a time when too many children lack the capacity to handle their upsets, to listen or to focus, to rein in impulse, to feel responsible for their work or care about learning, anything that will buttress these skills will help in their education' (Goleman, 1996). To put it quite simply, then, the government's own targets for raising achievement are more likely to be reached if serious attention is paid to developing these skills.

We do not only have to look to America for such innovative work. A host of mainly small, often local, initiatives are flourishing in Britain chiefly in urban and disadvantaged settings.[1] The National Pyramid Trust, for example, bases its approach to nurturing self-esteem through carefully structured therapeutic activities in after-school clubs. In East London, the Circle Works seeks to create reflective spaces in which people across the school community can learn to communicate with greater clarity and depth. In Newham, Conflict and Change has been working in schools for the past ten years, offering mediation and conflict resolution training to students and staff. Their whole-school approach is based partly on the model developed by Highfield Junior School in Plymouth, which was transformed from a poorly achieving school with major behavioural problems into an award-winning school under the inspired leadership of its former head, Lorna Farington. Family Links' Nurturing Programme based in Oxfordshire also stresses a whole-school approach to creating a safe and calm environment. The challenge for all these groups is to find exactly the kind of 'joined-up solutions' which the government is seeking.

No one has better articulated this perhaps than Jenny Mosley, whose Quality Circle Time is so often recognized by Ofsted inspection as having a profound effect on the whole ethos of schools working with her model (see Chapter 14 in this volume).

From individual schools and inspirational workshop leaders, such new work is spreading to whole authorities. Bristol City Council has a pilot programme to develop pupils' emotional literacy. Liverpool and Birmingham both have local authority initiatives. Perhaps no authority has gone further and faster than Southampton in putting emotional literacy firmly on its agenda of educational priorities, placing it alongside literacy and numeracy as the primary aims of its Strategic Education Plan. Peter Sharp, the city's chief educational psychologist, is himself piloting a programme on anger management in an attempt to reduce the level of permanent exclusions in the city's schools. On a much wider scale, though, through seminars, workshops, presentations and publications, Southampton is developing an Emotional Literacy Curriculum, the core content of which is:

- Conscious awareness: building a feelings vocabulary to understand ourselves and others
- Understanding thoughts, feelings and actions so as to permit informed decision-making
- Managing feeling so as to be more effective in getting our needs met without violating the interests of other people
- Promoting self-esteem so as to feel good about ourselves and hence about others
- Managing conflict: aiming for win-win outcomes through effective anger management and better interpersonal skills
- Understanding groups so as to behave more effectively in them
- Communication skills developed so as to promote feelings and thoughts

I have spent some time characterizing these initiatives because there are a number of absolutely critical points in them. Firstly, these programmes show that the social issues of truancy, bullying, violence and disaffection are intimately and inextricably connected with the issues of emotional literacy. Secondly, it is clear that there is a direct link between emotional education and the raising of school achievement. Thirdly, they all stress the need to involve teachers, parents, carers, other agencies including psychologists and social workers and the whole community both within and beyond school. They provide, in other words, practical examples of the 'joined-up solutions' which the government is seeking. Finally, it is worth noting that the work we have described here is not the result of a government policy or a top-down intervention. These are mainly local initiatives, developed 'in the field' as a result of individuals and communities responding to their own perceptions of children's needs.

PUTTING FEELING INTO THINKING: EMPATHY AND EXPERIENCE

Delight, wonder, mystery, pity, beauty and pain are to me every bit as important to our understanding of the human experience as anything I could ever be tested on. (From an address by Lord David Putman CBE at Circle Time: the Heart of the Curriculum conference, 25 June 1998)

In the second part of this examination of emotional education, I shall argue that much central government thinking is based on an implied model of human development which is too narrowly cognitive. We will look at the ways in which the school curriculum could be enriched by taking into account feelings and relationships across the whole curriculum, in each subject and across traditional subject divides.

In spite of apparently living in a 'touchy-feely' age, we are curiously suspicious of feelings and emotions; men especially so. We use the adjective 'emotional' as a rebuke, implying some loss of control, an avalanche-like sweep towards chaos and unreason. And sometimes, it really is like that, when emotions cloud the judgement, when they are not subject to the kind of conscious management described earlier. Yet none of us, least of all little children, inhabit a crystal world of conceptual understanding, nor is it a world we should even wish to live in. Emotions shape the contours of our judgement. We form our attitudes and ultimately our morality and values not on the basis of some pure logic, but on the continuous interplay of thought and feelings which we call our reflective consciousness. Crucial, too, are the experiences we have, the things we do and encounter in a practical day-to-day way. What we are seeing – and this is reflected in a wide variety of recent writing – is an emerging picture of our full humanity as much more fluid and even chaotic. Evidence about how the brain functions, research into consciousness, theories about the bodily location of emotions, work in developmental psychology, all point towards a picture of the complex interconnectedness of our thoughts, feelings and action. With this bigger picture in mind, we can begin to look at the different phases of childhood and the qualitatively different learning experiences which nurture emotional development.

What is it to be a child now of three or four years of age? What needs does a child of this age have? How can schools address those needs? What kinds of learning experiences are appropriate? What should be the desirable outcomes of nursery education? Many teachers and parents would answer such questions in terms of the young child feeling at home with him/herself, secure and trusting in relationships, physically confident, developing well socially, able to be absorbed in practical activity, in creative play and story.

We might well heed the overwhelming body of evidence, some of it from other education systems in Europe and America, which indicates that attention should be paid to young children's cognitive, social, physical *and* emotional development (see, for instance, Bruner and Haste, 1997; Pollard and Filer, 1996). In the early years, in particular, emotional learning is promoted through:

- listening to stories and to one another;
- opportunities of forming relationships with both children and adults;
- nourishing the senses and cultivating children's feelings by working from the practical and experiential, through play and participation.

Attention needs to be paid to this research in reframing assessment criteria. To ignore these findings and to press on with baseline assessments which overemphasize cognitive indicators may be to perpetuate exactly the cycle of failure – and especially the chronic underachievement of boys – from which we seek to escape.

If we follow the child into the compulsory phase of schooling, we do not have a sudden dawning of anything remotely resembling critical dispassionate thinking. Studies of children's scientific consciousness, for example, reveal an almost animistic identification with the natural world (Osborne *et al.*, 1990). The much maligned 'awe and wonder' of spiritual education lie wholly in the feeling realm of the eight-year-old. As Rachel Carson, the great pioneer of environmental awareness, put it,

> If I had influence with the good fairy ... I should ask that her gift to each child in the world be a sense of wonder ... I sincerely believe that for the child, and for the adult seeking to guide him, it is not half so important to know as to feel. If facts are the seeds that later produce knowledge and wisdom then the emotions and impressions are the fertile soil in which the seeds must grow. (Carson, 1965)

The primary science curriculum, as I have argued at greater length elsewhere (McCarthy, 1995), has at its heart the same incomplete picture of child development, placing as it does premature and inappropriate emphasis on abstract principles and hypothesizing which are entirely alien to the young child's consciousness. We need a much greater emphasis on direct first-hand experience of the natural world; the opportunity to reflect quietly, to respond creatively, to enter imaginatively into the great processes of nature. Interestingly enough, this view, which is easily caricatured as some sort of neo-Romanticism, finds expression in the recently published Nuffield Foundation report, *Beyond 2000: Science Education for the Future* (Millar and Osborne, 1998). Noting that school science 'fails to sustain and develop the sense of wonder and curiosity of many young people about the natural world', the group's authors, who include many of our most senior science educators, argue for a recasting of the science curriculum in terms of 'explanatory stories' (Millar and Osborne, 1998, pp. 13–14). In this way, they maintain, rather than remain a mass of discrete facts like a pile of bricks, the curriculum would have meaning and relevance. More boldly, Mike Watts of Roehampton Institute is developing a model of science education which embraces the feelings, arguing not only for the use of first-person narrative and diaries, but for poetry as a way of encouraging close observation, imagination and emotional engagement (Watts and Alsop, 1997).

In the humanities, too, at Key Stages 1 and 2, it is through emotional engagement that children can begin to develop the feeling for other cultures and other people which is the very basis for a tolerant society. Understanding, say, the plight of the Victorian child-worker or the situation of the black community under apartheid is not only a question of statistics or facts, but of an imaginative entering into the lives of the people to grasp their values, prejudices, preconceptions and motivation. Here, a creative teacher will embrace the opportunities offered by song, story, dance and drama. The arts, then, far from being marginal or peripheral, are quite clearly central to children's understanding of the world, literally life-giving, an animating principle of the curriculum at this stage.

Thinking and feeling, then, are inextricably linked. The problem at the moment is that the recent introduction of literacy hour, for all its good intentions in wishing to raise achievement, puts a finger in the scales of this delicate balance. It has diverted vast amounts of time, energy and resources into a heavily cognitive, highly prescriptive and ultimately mechanistic programme of decoding. It will doubtless succeed in raising standards in the narrowest quantitative way, thereby saving David Blunkett the embarrassment of sacking himself, but at what cost in terms of the *quality* of children's experience?

As children begin to approach adolescence soon after their transfer to secondary school, they need even more to bring their feelings into their thinking in all the subjects of the curriculum. As we stressed earlier, their attitudes and values, their emerging moral principles, are strongly shaped by feeling responses. The North–South divide needs more than factual understanding. The Holocaust is not simply dealt with in statistics. All too often in science, for whatever reason, teachers fight shy of engaging in moral debate about the issues of, say, genetic engineering or skirt round any discussion of feelings about pollution. Relatively few science teachers are given either the time or the encouragement to ask the spiritual questions posed by the Big Bang and the theory of evolution. It will not be enough, though, for each subject in isolation to open up to such questions. There is an extraordinary overlap and so many opportunities for work across subject boundaries. The RE 'short course' GCSE, for example, which is finding increasing popularity in schools, has topics on medical ethics, development issues and environmental issues, human rights as well as some fundamental questions about human relationships, which quite clearly call for heartfelt, emotional engagement across PSE, science, geography, history and English.

Many would say that the future simply does not lie in subjects. John White, Del Goddard and Roy Pryke, among others in the excellent ATL publication, *Take Care, Mr Blunkett* (Dainton *et al.*, 1998) all question the appropriateness and relevance of a subject-based curriculum. In the same book and elsewhere (see, for instance, Bentley, 1998), we hear a widespread call for a much more experiential, process-based curriculum which would engage the feelings as well as challenging the understanding. Under this model, for instance, citizenship will be a question not only of understanding, but also of empathizing. It will require not only grasping the basics of the democratic processes, but also getting out to the local old people's home or working with handicapped children, developing social cohesion through direct contact with others. This is, perhaps, the nub of the matter. Our current education model relies heavily on knowledge and skills which are readily susceptible to quantification and measurement. What we are failing to tackle as yet are attitudes, motivation and values: the whole middle ground of the heart.

So we end where we began, with the task of creating a more humane and inclusive society and with the curriculum review. We have tried to show how emotional education – education *about* feelings and education *through* feelings – needs to be recognized as an essential dimension of education. Thinking about feeling, reflecting on emotions and actively working at relationships helps to create not only better schools with raised performance but more caring communities. Allowing space for feelings across the entire curriculum helps young people to develop the kind of empathic understanding which is fundamental. As Daniel Goleman puts it, 'Emotions enrich; a model of mind that leaves them out is impoverished' (Goleman, 1996, p. 41). If we want a more caring, thoughtful and responsible society, it seems increasingly likely that we will need to develop practical ways of improving emotional literacy and allowing the spiritual, moral, social and cultural life of young people to be enriched by a dynamic relationship between thinking and feeling. It is this relationship which lies at the heart of emotional education.

NOTE

1   A list of these and other UK initiatives can be found on pages 89–90.

ACKNOWLEDGEMENTS

It is fitting to finish by gratefully acknowledging the enormous contribution which the original group made to the thinking behind this chapter. While I have recast the argument of the original paper and added the illustrative example, much of the thinking and expression remains the fruit of a brief but inspiring collaboration under the auspices of Simon Richey at the Gulbenkian Foundation.

REFERENCES

Bentley, T. (1998) *Learning Beyond the Classroom: Education for a Changing World*, London: Routledge.

Bruner, J. and Haste, H. (1987) *Making Sense*. London: Methuen.

Carson, R. (1965) *The Sense of Wonder*. New York: Harper and Row.

Cotton, C. (1997) *School Size, School Climate and Performance*. US Dept. of Education.

Dainton, S. *et al.* (1998) *Take Care, Mr Blunkett*. London: Association of Teachers and Lecturers.

Gardner, H. (1985) *Frames of Mind*. London: Paladin.

Goleman, D. (1996) *Emotional Intelligence*. London: Bloomsbury.

McCarthy, K. (1995) Science: power or wisdom? *School Science Review*, **76** (Association of Science Education).

Millar, R. and Osborne, J. (1998) *Beyond 2000: Science Education for the Future*. London: King's College.

Osborne, J. *et al.* (1990) *Primary Space Project – Light*. Liverpool: Liverpool University Press.

Pollard, A. and Filer, A. (1996) *The Social World of Children's Learning*. London: Cassell.

Salovey, Peter and Mayer, John D. (1990) Emotional intelligence. *Imagination, Cognition and Personality*, **9**.

Sammons, P., Thomas, S. and Mortimore, P. (1997) *Forging Links; Effective Links and Departments*. London: Paul Chapman.

Watts, M. and Alsop, S. (1997) A feeling for learning: modeling affective learning in school science. *Curriculum Journal*, **8** (3).

Weissberg, R. and Greenberg, H. (1997) *Handbook of Child Psychology*. Chichester: John Wiley & Sons.

USEFUL ADDRESSES

Antidote
5th Floor
45 Beech Street
Barbican
London
EC2Y 8AD
Tel: 020 7588 5151

Birmingham Education Department
Health Education Unit
74 Balden Road
Birmingham B32 2EH
Tel: 0121 428 2262

Principal Educational Psychologist
Bristol City Council
Avon House
The Haymarket
Bristol BS99 7EB
Tel: 0117 903 7702

The Circle Works
2 Medway Buildings
Medway Road
London E3 5DR
Tel: 020 8983 3967

Changemakers
45 Somers Road
Welham Green
Herts AL9 7PT
Tel: 01707 263080

Conflict and Change
2a Streatfield Avenue
East Ham
E6 2LA
Tel: 020 8552 2050

Family Links
The Old Rectory
Waterstock
Oxfordshire
OX33 1JT
Tel: 01865 338409

Calouste Gulbenkian Foundation
98 Portland Place
London W1N 4ET
Tel: 020 7636 5313

Highfield Junior School
Torridge Way
Efford
Plymouth
Devon PL3 6JQ
Tel: 01752 773187

Liverpool Education and Achievement Centre
Queens Dock Commercial Centre
67/83 Norfolk Street
Liverpool
L1 0EB
Tel: 0151 233 8155

Jenny Mosley Consultancies
8 Westbourne Road
Trowbridge
Wiltshire BA14 0AJ
Tel: 01225 767157

National Coalition Building Institute
PO 411
Leicester
LE4 8ZY
Tel: 0116 260 3232

National Pyramid Trust
204 Church Road
Hanwell
London W7 3BP
Tel: 020 8579 5108

Re:membering Education
66 Beaconsfield Villas
Brighton BN1 6HE
Tel: 01273 239311

Southampton Psychology Service
5th Floor Frobisher House
Nelson Gate
Southampton SO15 1GX
Tel: 02380 833106

CHAPTER 7

Curriculum and Kierkegaard: towards creating a paradigm for discerning the spiritual dimension of education

Jack Priestley

INTRODUCTION: EDUCATION, CURRICULUM AND TEACHING

Among the very first things that I was told as a teacher trainee was that the verb 'to teach' takes two accusatives, as in the statement, 'I teach John Latin'. It was not the best of examples, as would have become immediately obvious if that simple sentence had been translated into Latin, where 'John' would then be seen quite clearly as a disguised dative expressed as, 'I teach Latin to John'.

Nevertheless, in that introductory statement to the long process of induction into the profession, I was being pointed to the great and abiding mystery of teaching. In teaching a subject, any subject, it has always to be acknowledged that I am doing something to John at the same time as I impart knowledge. To clarify the position totally it is better if I use two quite separate verbs. That is to say that in *teaching* Latin I *educate* John.

For many years that Latin, together with Greek, constituted the core curriculum of English public schools following Arnold's reforms at Rugby, but their value was seen in terms of the indirect process of educating the person, not as a direct means of acquiring employable 'useful' knowledge or skills. Arnold's primary aim was that of producing Christian Gentlemen with classical humanitarian values and well-trained disciplined minds. However, this was not to ignore what today we like to call the 'job market' when the jobs concerned were those of administering a country and an empire. Such positions required character, confidence and sound judgement.

The new and rapidly developing elementary schools were also concerned with developing character, but the key values there were somewhat different, namely loyalty, obedience and usefulness. The notion of educating was far from absent but curriculum matters were dominant – basic literacy and numeracy in the form of the three Rs, accompanied by such practical skills as woodwork, metalwork, cooking, laundry and gardening.

However, what we have seen over the past half century in both sectors has been the increasing dominance of curriculum issues over those of educating the person, to the extent that, in some quarters, the very words 'education' and 'curriculum' have come to be regarded as synonymous. When curriculum was felt not to account for all that happened in schools it was decided that, like the proverbial iceberg, its undertow was 'hidden'. Attempts to surface it have resulted in a profusion of bolt-on curriculum additions such as civics, health and moral education, PSME and, now, citizenship. Significantly, some of these have already started to become transformed from subjects into processes such as Circle Time or group tutorials.

Meanwhile, however, 'child-centredness' remains a term of abuse in certain official quarters. If in terms of substance 'education' and 'curriculum' have come to be regarded as synonyms, then this is equally true of the processes of 'teaching' and 'educating'. There is an apparent assumption that if we want a child to become computer literate and, at the same time, become moral, the processes are identical: the pupil learns what the teacher teaches!

In the midst of this scenario there has emerged to some prominence the concept of the spiritual, first incorporated into the preamble of the 1944 Education Act, after which it lay more or less dormant until the mid-1970s and then, to some exclamations of surprise, was given new prominence in the 1988 Education Reform Act. Since then it has begun to occur with increased frequency, particularly in the literature of the Quality and Curriculum Authority (QCA) and the inspectorate (Ofsted).

To date it has been largely ignored by the Teacher Training Agency (TTA) which, at the launch of its new corporate plan in 1998, was still approving clear lines of demarcation between notions of teaching as an art and as a science (a favoured examination question of the 1950s), strongly promoting the latter and endorsing the denunciation of the former as 'quaint, old-fashioned and ultimately highly damaging' (Reynolds, 1998, p. 1).

Any call for more effective teaching, especially in areas of factual transmission, is, of course, to be encouraged. That is not a point I wish to dispute. What I want to argue for in this chapter is not ineffective teaching but a recognition that there is a range and diversity within the task of teaching according to the subject matter under discussion, that the indirect effects of schooling are every bit as important as the direct and that there needs to be a far more serious discussion about the notion of child-centredness within education than the facile, soundbite, debunking polemics which have issued forth in recent years from political leaders and their agencies.

I shall attempt to do this by exploring further not only what we mean by the spiritual dimension of education but also what might be involved in any serious attempt to assess and measure it. For it is quite false to suggest that it cannot be measured. Religions the world over have made such assessments throughout their long histories in the creation of rabbis, saints and gurus and in all their varied determinations of what constitutes spiritual excellence in the religious life.

RECENT TRENDS IN RESEARCH AND ASSESSMENT METHODOLOGY IN THE HUMANITIES

Throughout the human sciences, with one notable exception, we are seeing a significant shift in methodological assumptions. The old certainties associated with positivism and its great emphasis on objectivity are in retreat under the growing influence of the counter-reaction which we have come to know as postmodernism. However, simply to use that word illustrates as well as anything why so much of our present confusion exists; the language of modernity continues to predominate even in describing the major reactions to itself. Like all 'isms' it denotes a grand theory expressed as a single over-arching abstraction – the very thing that postmodernists in all their varied forms of expression are reacting against.

The effects are most marked in those areas which we might best describe as the sciences of the disinherited, such as disability, feminist, racial and, in certain instances, childhood studies. These are all relatively new areas of academic enquiry but the reaction going on within them serves to highlight what has happened within the humanities and the arts over the past two hundred years, namely the transformation of subjects (human beings) into objects with all that that means in terms of power and control.

Mark Priestley (1999, pp. 13–15) gives numerous examples from a number of fields in his own search for an emancipatory research paradigm suitable for working with disabled people. Emancipatory models, as distinct from positivistic models, he argues, 'suggest ownership of the means of research production and distribution by the research participants rather than by the researcher.' (p. 15).

That assumed objectivity all too often conceals not only power but also a high degree of self-deception, is perfectly illustrated by Mary John's experience in her studies into racism within the Anglia Region of British Rail in the mid-1980s. It was assumed that she would employ traditional social science research staff to assist. She chose instead to recruit her team from among British Rail employees, including African-Caribbeans, Hindus, Muslims and Sikhs, mostly working in jobs well below their potential abilities. Under her leadership this group compiled the questions, ran the pilot project and then undertook the fieldwork of interviewing their fellow employees. Despite the fact that all the normal procedures were strictly adhered to in terms of social science research methods, a moment's thought might lead us to expect that the responses were likely to be very different from those which would have been given to white Anglo-Saxon middle-class, highly educated professional researchers. They were certainly very different from those anticipated by the sponsors: the report was never published.

Mary John has, however, published more recent work of the same genre following an International Conference on Research and Practice in Children's Rights. Significantly, her first volume (1996) is entitled *Children in Charge – The Child's Right to a Fair Hearing* and begins with a Foreword from the Young People's Evaluation Team (11–16-year-olds) who acted as the evaluators for all conference presentations. It continues with contents such as, 'Research and Practice with the Silenced', 'Children's Parliament in Slovenia', 'Listening to the Street Children of Mwanza' and 'Children Teaching Adults to Listen', etc.

Such examples serve to demonstrate a fact which Bosaski (1997), writing from a Canadian perspective, neatly summarizes in a recent paper when she says,

During the past decade research paradigms have shifted radically from a positivist/objective/causal view to one that is hermeneutic/subjective/interpretive. (p. 109)

I noted, however, right at the beginning of this section, that there was one exception to this trend. Jerome Bruner (1996, p. 32) pinpoints it when he states, 'this revolution in public awareness has not been accompanied by a comparable revolution in education.' In the same article he goes on to discuss children as doers, knowers and thinkers in contrast with the vocabulary of certain British government agencies, which continues to regard them only as learners.

THE STATE OF BRITISH EDUCATIONAL RESEARCH

Bruner's statement needs some modification. Participatory research (albeit in which teachers rather than children are seen as the participants) has, for quite some time, been an established practice within British educational research but, in recent years, along with other forms of research, it has come under severe attack from those same powerful agencies of government which increasingly control research funding.

Such attacks have served to exacerbate a certain lack of confidence within the profession itself. Wilfred Carr (1998), professor of Education at Sheffield University, in a recent research seminar[1] expressed concern at what he termed a 'lack of consciousness' developing within British educational research which he attributed to four factors. These he listed as:

a. A lack of historical perspective within the consciousness of many researchers.
b. The removal of what he termed 'ethical categories'.
c. The bureaucratizing of recent years resulting in educational researchers being reduced in status to technicians, employed largely to enquire into questions generated by government agencies with the results filtered through those same agencies which alone could determine whether or not any implementation took place.
d. The separation of educational research from other research areas such as social and political investigation, thus leaving it isolated and weakened to the point of powerlessness.

Carr then proceeded to argue the urgent need for three significant developments:

a. an external vantage point.
b. a broader historical perspective.
c. a greater historical self-consciousness.

In doing so he drew attention to the two distinct traditions with which I began this chapter, commenting on the fact that most British educational researchers tend to work within the context of popular education stemming from the beginning of the nineteenth century, and in consequence increasingly ignore the much broader history of educational ideas going back to Plato, with their emphasis on educating the person. British education, he argued, was in danger of becoming isolated both from its history as well as from its international and contemporary social context.

There remains, however, the religious factor which, I have argued, played a highly significant part in both educational traditions within Britain and wherever a British influence was involved in establishing educational institutions throughout the world. It is all too easily overlooked that the Free Church initiative of 1808 which began the process of elementary popular education was that of the appropriately named British and Foreign Schools Society. Joseph Lancaster, whose name is most closely associated with that initiative, went on to found schools in Canada and the USA, and his monitorial system, designed for cheap mass education, is linked to what also was known as the Madras system introduced into British-ruled India.

The separation of modern educational thinking from its historical and philosophical contexts is almost certainly a direct result of political policy during the 1980s, when both the philosophy and history of education were explicitly discouraged within University Departments of Education and Teacher Training Colleges. The separation from a wider international context is more difficult to understand except, perhaps, in terms of the withdrawal of general interest from those parts of the world with which Britain had much in common, namely the former colonies, and a new focusing on mainland Europe with which, in terms of educational history, it has had comparatively very little.

For example, it comes as a surprise to many to learn just how much of the thinking which was at the heart of the 1944 Education Act can be traced directly to the second Ecumenical International Missionary Conference held in Jerusalem in 1928. The co-ordinator of the resulting volume on education, compiled from thinkers on a truly worldwide scale, including South-East Asia and Africa as well as North America, Europe and Australia, was the relatively young Bishop of Manchester, William Temple, whose contribution to the debates from 1942 onwards (by which time he had become the Archbishop of Canterbury), was highly influential, especially in areas which have since been carried over into the 1988 Act (see J. Priestley, 1991).

EDUCATION AND THE RELIGIOUS THINKER

The major point I wish to make in all this is that religious thinking has as much to offer as political and social thinking but it continues to be ignored and excluded from almost all consideration. The fault for that lies as much within religious groups as anywhere else. It is they as much as their detractors who have, in recent times, concentrated on the narrow interests of ownership of institutions and explicit religious matters instead of on a general theory for all, which was Temple's passion and concern.

But what then do I mean by 'religious thinking'? It is important to note that I am referring to a particular style of thinking and not to a body of thought known as theology, which can be shown to have changed its *modus operandi* down the years to accommodate different forms of rationality, particularly during the last two centuries. If this seems like walking some sort of conceptual tightrope then that image has gone before and it is one I gladly embrace. For it was none other that Ludwig Wittgenstein who created it when he remarked:

> An honest religious thinker is like a tightrope walker. He almost looks as though he were walking on nothing but air. His support is the slenderest imaginable. And yet it really is possible to walk on it. (Wittgenstein, 1980, p. 73)

It is the new fascination with the spiritual dimension of education which has reopened interest in such a form of thinking within general educational discussion and not just within one semi-isolated curriculum area. The spiritual, of course, is not to be identified with the religious, but it would be as absurd to eliminate religious thinking from the exploration of it as it would be to claim that it was religion's private property. However, more needs to be said by way of clarifying what is in mind and clear examples need to be given.

It was again Ludwig Wittgenstein who once commented, 'I am not a religious man but I cannot help seeing every question from a religious point of view' (Drury, 1984, p. 79). It is, I think, a statement of the utmost importance because it helps us in the task of starting to determine what constitutes the major characteristics of the religious thinker.

We can begin with some negatives. Quite explicit in Wittgenstein's statement is the assumption that it has nothing to do with whether or not the thinker is religious in terms of personal belief in a particular form of deity. Implicit are the suggestions that religious thinking is not to be confused with theology nor to be confined to, or even primarily concerned with, thinking about God or religion. It is a process and not a static concept, a form of rationality not a body of thought, even less of doctrine.

If we then ask what it is, rather than what it is not, the short answer lies in the notion of playing God. To be more specific, I think we can isolate four major characteristics, the first two of which relate directly to Carr's demands for a longer history and a broader vantage point.

First, there is what is perhaps the furthest extremity of that external reference point to which we alluded. It is contained, as it were, in the 'cloud nine' image – the idea of an overview, what in German is called *Übersicht*. It represents the broadest generality. Such an approach lacks sharp focus. That is its major weakness but the corresponding strength is that it sees things in relation to other things and not just as isolated variables. The methods of modernity can all too easily present sharp foci without any awareness of the general panorama within which they exist. We need both, but it is the generality which is the more undervalued today.

Secondly, there is the question of historical perspective. It was the American sociologist Harvey Cox (1969, p. 14), writing in the late 1960s, who remarked,

> The religious man [*sic*] is one who grasps his own life within a larger historical and cosmic setting. He sees himself as part of a greater whole, a longer story of which he plays a part.

The process of secularization, of which Cox also wrote at length in his book *The Secular City* (1968), is itself characterized by the opposite – a huge foreshortening of the timescale in which we live our lives. In contrast with earlier times when people thought hundreds of years ahead in such activities as the planting of forests for ship building, our modern secular society seems incapable of thinking beyond the lives of our children or, at most, our grandchildren. While we talk glibly of storing substances like nuclear waste, we are proving quite incapable of conceptualizing what is involved in terms of such timescales. There are also worrying signs that we are equally beginning to detach ourselves from the past which was seen as an integral part of our existence.

The characteristic to which Cox points, however, is still to be seen in what we like to term 'developing communities', where people continue to see themselves as part of a greater whole in transit to a future they can, as individuals, never expect to see, as in black consciousness movements in the USA or throughout China and South-East Asia.

A third characteristic of this mode of thinking is contained within the phrase, 'no thought without a thinker'. It is an acknowledgement that knowledge comes through feeling and emotions as well as through the intellect. It, therefore, rejects the common notion that biography is of no importance. Wittgenstein himself is perhaps an excellent example of this. Interpretations of his work by those who saw him essentially as the Cambridge philosopher who just happened to come from Austria need to be contrasted with those which focus on a *fin-de-siècle* Austro-Hungarian who happened to end up in Cambridge (see Janik and Toulman, 1973, or Monk, 1990).

The fourth characteristic follows from this. The religious thinker is wary of reducing human beings into abstractions, such as 'humanity', 'personnel', 'the public' or, more recently, 'human resources'. Such thinkers would see in these terms the dehumanization of fellow subjects who are thereby converted into objects which can then be dealt with systematically. It is systematization which destroys the human value of the person, seen at its most extreme in the totalitarian extravagancies of the twentieth century such as Fascism and totalitarian Communism, which themselves can now be seen as products of that form of thinking which stemmed from Hegelian rationality with its passion for detachment, objectivity and the grand story.

In terms of educational thinking, figures who fit within this picture of the religious thinker would include, for example, Coleridge, Thomas and Matthew Arnold, Count Tolstoy, William James, Dewey (to some extent), Whitehead, William Temple and, of course, by his own confession, Wittgenstein himself. But it was Wittgenstein who pointed back to the Founding Father of the whole concept in recent history. 'Kierkegaard', he wrote, 'was by far and away the greatest thinker of the nineteenth century. Kierkegaard was a saint' (Drury, 1984, p. 87).

THE LEGACY OF SØREN KIERKEGAARD

This tribute, from a man whom many would regard as among the greatest thinkers of the twentieth century, has rarely been acknowledged even though it might reasonably be thought that anyone who holds a predecessor in such high esteem is likely, in some significant way, to be indebted to him for at least part of the basis of his own philosophical thought. What can possibly be the relevance of such a strange and isolated Danish figure, who died in 1855, to our contemporary British educational debate a century and a half later?

Most British comment, perhaps typifying our national obsessions, has tended to centre on his relationships, first, with his melancholic father and secondly, with Regina Olsen. It is important, too, to acknowledge that his writings were not translated into English until after the Second World War when his existentialist position, essentially focused on persons as individuals, was immediately translated into an abstract and depersonalized system of ideas – the very thing he was arguing against. It is our new interest in the character, growth and significance of the spiritual within education which now makes it germane to re-examine points of relevance of Kierkegaard's thinking. The first stems from the intellectual context in which he lived and worked.

Kierkegaard was born in 1813 and therefore grew up intellectually in the excitement of the new thinking which we call the Enlightenment. Hegel's *Phenomenology of Spirit*, propounding the view that the highest rationality is both objective and systematic, was published just six years before Kierkegaard was born. It was a thesis which Kierkegaard was to spend his short adult life attacking with every weapon at his disposal.

It is increasingly possible to look back at him now as the very first postmodernist for the ways in which he attempted to devise strategies to avoid the trap of attacking systematization without himself creating a system, of advocating the priority of the human spirit without destroying it in the process. But it would be somewhat illogical to attach that description to someone living and working while the period we know as modernity was still being born. Perhaps, therefore, it is best to talk of him as the prophet of the Enlightenment. Either way, his importance to us today lies in the fact that he appears at the parting of the ways and stands at the point to which we need to return if the excesses of both modernity and what we now call postmodern*ism*, are to be avoided.

The second major point of relevance lies in his overriding concern for the primacy of the human spirit and against the domination and control of it which he saw developing all around him. He refused to be categorized, rejecting in his own lifetime such descriptions as 'theologian' or 'philosopher' simply because both of those disciplines had themselves, in his opinion, become polluted by the new forms of thought and were eagerly embracing its methods and assumptions. This, of course, has not prevented his own work becoming categorized as yet another 'ism', namely, Existentialism.

There is deep irony in the fact that he remained largely unknown until he was introduced to the German-speaking world in 1918 through the work of Karl Barth, who was both a theologian and a systematic. It is, however, Wittgenstein, who gives us the main justification for looking again at this figure. Kierkegaard's importance to Wittgenstein was that 'he gave us new categories' (Drury, 1984, p. 88). His value to us, therefore, is dependent on whether or not those categories are today meaningful in terms of teaching and education.

CATEGORIES FOR THE INVESTIGATION OF THE SPIRITUAL

Consistency and paradox

The first and most basic requirement of any categorization of knowledge is consistency but, asks Kierkegaard, where is the consistency if, by retaining a method, we do so at the expense of changing the very nature of the thing being studied? In recent years, in British educational research, there has grown up a disturbing overconsistency in so far as courses in research methods, whether quantitative or qualitative, all too often tend to assume a static situation. The question asked by Dominic Crossan (1975) about Wittgenstein is the same question as Kierkegaard was asking a century earlier of himself: 'Is he a cartographer or an oceanographer?' The map-maker and the mariner draw exactly the same boundaries of an island, the first because he wants to walk on dry land and establish firm foundations, the second because he wants, at all costs, to avoid it in order to sail the sea, which is essentially fluid and insecure.[2]

Our contemporary problem is that of assuming that only the former is consistent but that is a misconception. Rather the consistency of the sailor simply takes a different form from that of the hiker. Both may be following a compass bearing but the former is having constantly to adjust the course to take account of wind and tide and to pit one element against the other in order to arrive in port. The route is indirect. So it is with life and with learning that affects living as distinct from factual knowledge. Kierkegaard spells out with unusual brevity what this means in educational terms.

All communication of knowledge is direct communication.
All communication of capability is indirect communication.
The communication of ethical capability is unconditionally indirect communication.

And,

The mistake of the modern period is that the ethical and the ethico-religious have been taught. People have been given information about them. (Hong and Hong, 1978, pp. 282 and 289)

The implications of such statements for the classroom teacher are profound. It is a necessary condition of the spiritual that it is in motion. Like the ballerina it can only be arrested for purposes of analysis at the cost of denying the movement which gives it meaning. This is exactly what happens, however, as soon as any aspect of living becomes systematized. It is systematization which destroys the spirit because it kills all movement and perhaps the classic examples are to be found in religions, where the movements of the spirit become ossified in static dogmas and doctrines.[3]

However, Kierkegaard's prophetic warning was not that systematization would not work in analysing human behaviour but that it would work only too well. The cost, however, would be that human beings became perceived as objects rather than as fellow subjects.

He concluded then that there should be a clear distinction between the methods used to analyse the mathematico-logical and those used for everything else. The tragedy of so much of our twentieth-century inheritance is that social and educational research and assessment, to say nothing of classroom practice, have largely failed to recognize this distinction. At the same time, the danger of extreme postmodern reactions, as seen in some New Age movements, is that they will shipwreck themselves by refusing to acknowledge the rightful constancy of objective methods where they are valid. Kierkegaard himself was never anti-scientific but his concern was for human affairs and in that he determined to be absolutely constant even though, to do so, was to encourage misunderstanding and rejection.

If his reputation, however, has been damaged because he has been too closely linked with the very systematic theology of which he was so fiercely critical, it has also been too easy to dismiss him because of the unfortunate use of the English word 'paradox' to translate a concept to which he was committed – that of the embracing of opposites. As a consequence he has frequently been dismissed as illogical and irrational.

Again, if we resort to sailing imagery, we can more clearly see his line of thinking. The sailor lives by countering one force against another, sail against keel, wind against tide. So it is, argued Kierkegaard, with life. If his own age went for images of deep foundations and solid edifices, he saw life more like that of nomads living in tents held up by opposing forces, where feeling has to be tempered by intellect, justice by mercy, pleasure by duty, thinking by being and so on. If, in the end, he remained with Christianity, despite his scathing denunciations, it was because he saw in the notion of incarnation and Trinity, not contradiction, but rationality in terms of what life (*Existenz*) is really like. Stability comes through embracing opposites and thus achieving balance.

Objectivity and subjectivity are just such a pair of opposites. For, having separated off the mathematico-logico, Kierkegaard then goes on to look at gradations within the curriculum spectrum of which these two forces mark the extremes. It is here that we finally come to the core of his contribution to curriculum study which has lain neglected for so long, namely that we tend to treat what we term 'curriculum areas' as if they were separated only by their content when, in fact, they are differentiated much more by their modes of reasoning and their use of language. Any science of teaching which does not recognize this point is doomed to disaster.

The key to this whole argument, then, is this. If we are too subjective in an area that demands a high degree of pure thinking then it is knowledge which becomes distorted. This is widely recognized. It forms the basis of scientific methodologies. What is less recognized is the opposite, namely that if we are too objective in those areas which require a high level of subjectivity then what becomes distorted is not so much detached knowledge as the pupils themselves. Abstract thought belongs to the objective end of the spectrum; the danger lies in human beings becoming abstractions. This brings us to the second of Kierkegaard's categories.

Indirect communication and the double reflection
Much contemporary discussion of the spiritual dimension of education leads to a call for some definition of what that means, showing immediately a lack of understanding of the true nature of the discussion. We maintain an assumption that language is objective and literal, or what philosophers call 'referential'.

We fail to recognize that outside of the thought forms of mathematics and formal logic words are pictures and that precise communication is only possible when a word creates in the listener's mind the same picture as that which exists in the speaker's. Mathematical terms are exact; no other language is. This is why there is such a clear distinction between direct and indirect communication.

Indirect communication requires a double reflection. That is to say, the process of communicating requires, first of all, that I summon up an image in my mind, reflect upon it and find a word or phrase which I think will transmit the image to another person's mind. He or she, upon hearing my words, then must reflect upon them in order to form a mental image which, we both must assume, will correspond with that which is in my mind. The greater the need for exactness the more we will need to refine the image. Science depends upon precise correspondence and, therefore, puts a high premium on demanding as high a degree of objectivity as possible. The social scientist is one who attempts to apply the same technique to matters of human behaviour. For Kierkegaard, this was the dangerous middle ground where the language was imprecise but where there could be pretence at precision, with the ever-present danger of dehumanizing the human.

To move further through the spectrum is to enter the world of literature and poetry. Then, of course, there is religion, that most durable of all social forms and yet the one most dependent on agreed images. It is a rarely stated and yet indisputable fact that all religions have stemmed from the personal experience, in solitude, of a lone individual who has then communicated that experience via metaphors to others, whether it was the Buddha under the tree, the Prophet in the cave, the lonely man on the Cross down to John Wesley, the founder of Methodism, having his 'heart strangely warmed'.

By this stage we have moved into a realm which is dominated by the subjective, but the demand for orthodoxy, for acceptance of agreed verbal formula in creeds and doctrine, acts as the strongest of counter-forces. The cries of protest in our own century against this objectifying of the inner experience have come not from theologians but from such people as William James and the process philosophers. Religion is not the same as the spiritual but it marks the battleground where the fiercest conflicts have taken place. It is significant that the continual argument surrounding religious education is about whether it can be taught objectively, either internally through doctrine or externally through detached phenomenology, or whether its purpose is to allow every pupil to find expression for their own deepest insights and experiences: it is why RK (Religious Knowledge), RI (Religious Instruction) and RS (Religious Studies) are not necessarily RE (Religious Education).

The spiritual is as subjective as the mathematico-logical is objective which is why the artist, the poet, the dramatist, the novelist and the prophet are the key figures in expressing it and why those who follow them are often seen as subversives. It is also why ultimately silence may be seen by some as the deepest form of its expression, whether in a figure like Thomas Merton, like Jesus before Pilate or in the logic of the final proposition in Wittgenstein's *Tractatus* (1961), 'whereof we cannot speak, thereof we must be silent' (proposition 7).

Kierkegaard, himself, it must be said, did not resort to silence. He suggested other categories such as irony and humour.

Irony, humour and parable

Much humour is created by putting the immediate and the finite into the context of the eternal and the infinite. In this way it changes the proportion of things. As one of Kierkegaard's commentators puts it, 'The humourist can never be a systematic ... He [sic] lives in the fullness of things and is, therefore, sensitive to how much is always left over. The systematic thinks he can say or include everything and that what cannot be said is erroneous and left over' (Hannay, 1982, p. 156).

Parable – literally, the throwing alongside – has the same effect, which is what makes it such a potent, if not to say, offensive, teaching technique provided it is original. It is not without significance that Kierkegaard himself used parabolic methods and that the clown figure featured in them. He was himself the clownlike figure, the innocent abroad, the one who is laughed at rather than the one who laughs. Humour often conceals suffering, offends authoritarians and can be a powerful weapon of subversion.

Stages and the leap

The final categories which Kierkegaard gives to us which are of major educational significance are those of stages and the leap.

Many of the systematic theories which have dominated educational thinking and practice in recent decades have been based on the notion of stage development first propounded by Piaget but extended in the work of such figures as Erikson, Kohlberg, Goldman and Fowler.

Kierkegaard's stages are different in one crucially important respect; progression comes not via natural development but via a leap of changed perception. Again we see Wittgenstein following his lead. 'The world of the happy man', he was to write, 'is an altogether different world from the world of the unhappy man' (1961, proposition 6.43). It is by such a leap that one moves from learning about to learning from. This is that most crucial point of education where knowing is transformed into doing and being. How does the transition take place? We simply do not know: it remains the great mystery. It is summarized best in Kierkegaard's own words,

> Nowadays everything is directed towards understanding so that the child understands but it actually has no connection with life (existence) ... and it is an enormous swindle to make it seem that if anyone were merely to understand the highest he would automatically do it. From understanding to doing there is an infinitely, infinitely greater distance than from not understanding to understanding ... a whole lifetime may be spent on understanding and living (existence) remains entirely unchanged. (quoted in Malantschuk, 1974, pp. 132f.)

This surely represents our current dilemma. Glib political statements about getting children to know the difference between right and wrong are contradicted by political action which serves to demote the moral status of the teacher. We are, in fact, moving backwards. Everything once again is directed towards understanding through the basic process of teaching and learning.

Personal education is assumed to be direct rather than indirect; the person of the teacher is widely assumed to be of little significance as teaching is reduced to the sum total of knowledge and skills; the curriculum dominates to the point where it is widely assumed that curriculum and education are synonyms. While hugely expensive recruitment campaigns pronounce that, 'No one forgets a good teacher', in practice the teacher as a person is becoming ignored, overlooked and greatly reduced in status to a mere purveyor of information.

CONCLUSION

Writing on this same subject, which he called 'a neglected aspect' in 1925, Basil Yeaxlee quotes as if it were an adage of the time, 'Spiritual things are spiritually discerned' (p. vii). We all acknowledge that those making academic assessments are themselves intellectually capable. Likewise we assume that art is judged by artists, music by musicians and so on. But what, if anything, has been done to determine that those judging the spiritual are themselves accomplished in spiritual discernment?

It was Carl Jung (1982) who reminded us that where human beings are concerned the observer has a different relationship with the observed than with any other species or range of objects. 'Only the psyche can penetrate the psyche' (p. 3), he comments and then, in the same passage, reminds us just what it is we are exploring. 'Spirit is the principle which stands in opposition to matter, an immaterial form of existence' (p. 4). It is 'the inner being, regardless of any connection with an outer being' and its determining characteristic is that it is dynamic, the 'classical antithesis of matter – the antithesis, that is, of stasis and inertia' (pp. 4–6).

The hallmarks of the spirit he then lists as:

a. spontaneous movement and activity.
b. a spontaneous capacity to produce images independently of sense perception.
c. the autonomous and sovereign manipulation of these images.

Such a list sits uneasily within a system of tick boxes and established criteria against which all have to be measured identically. Central to our problem is that education as a 'subject' has, like theology, taken to itself the 'objective' criteria necessary to give it scientific, academic respectability at the cost of losing its own essential spirit.

The answer lies in restoring the balance of arts and sciences within the whole educational debate, not just in terms of curriculum but in the total way in which we discuss all educational issues. It is right to say that we need a science of teaching but it is equally true that that science should be contained within the art of teaching.

Religious people have always faced the fact that judging the spiritual is essentially a subjective process. Norman Bull, the college tutor who began his course by talking about John and Latin, pointed me some years later to what he termed, 'one of the finest novels in the English language'. Morris West's *The Devil's Advocate* is an exploration of how one judges a saint. Significantly, the novel is a well-established form of indirect communication.

Blaise Meredith is the Promoter of the Faith or the Devil's Advocate, the prosecuting counsel sent by Rome to investigate a case for making a man a saint. He has fulfilled the task often but this will be his last case. He knows that he himself is dying of cancer. He resists the challenge but then the following exchange takes place with his Superior.

'I believe this investigation may help you. It will take you out of Rome, to one of the most depressed areas of Italy. You will rebuild the life of a dead man from the evidence of those who lived with him – the poor, the ignorant, the dispossessed. You will live and talk with simple people. Among them perhaps you will find a cure for your own sickness of spirit.'

'What is my sickness, Eminence?' The pathetic weariness of the voice, the desolate puzzlement of the question, touched the old churchman to pity. He turned back from the window to see Meredith slumped forward in his chair, his face buried in his hands. He waited a moment, weighed his answer; and then gave it, gravely.

'There is no passion in your life, my son.' (pp. 25f)

Or, as Søren Kierkegaard, once said, 'Take away passion from the thinker and what do you have? You have the university professor!'

NOTES

1 Seminar held at the University of Exeter on 4 February 1998. At the time of writing, this paper has not, to my knowledge, been published.
2 This shift in imagery can be seen among certain theologians. Paul Tillich's *Shaking of the Foundations* (1948) has led to Don Cupitt's *The Sea of Faith* (1985) and *The Long Legged Fly* (1987) (the image of a water-boatman flitting across the surface of the water). More recently Salters Sterling (1999), in dealing with higher education, has painted a verbal picture of the good (religious) teacher as a 'slightly inebriated ice-skater'.
3 Two of the most vehement denouncers of systematic theology, on the grounds that it destroyed the spiritual, have been William James and Alfred North Whitehead. In his famous 1901/2 Gifford Lectures, James compared such theologians with the 'closet naturalists' of his youth, those, 'collectors and classifiers, handlers of skeletons and skins' whose interests in the living world of nature could only be satisfied by destroying it. 'We must,' he concluded, a century ago, 'bid a definite goodbye to dogmatic theology.' (See James, 1982, pp. 428 and 430.)

REFERENCES

Bosacki, S. (1998) Is silence really golden? The role of spiritual voice in folk pedagogy and folk psychology. *International Journal of Children's Spirituality*, **3** (2), 109–21.

Bruner, J. (1996) *The Culture of Education*. Cambridge, Mass: Harvard University Press.

Cox, H. (1968) *The Secular City*. London: Pelican.

Cox, H. (1969) *The Feast of Fools*. Cambridge, Mass: Harvard University Press.

Crossan, D. (1975) *The Dark Interval*. Niles Illinois: Argus.

Cupitt, D. (1985) *The Sea of Faith*. London: BBC Publications.
Cupitt, D. (1987) *The Long Legged Fly*. London: SCM Press.
Drury, M. (1984) Some notes on conversations. In Rhees, R. (ed.), *Recollections of Wittgenstein*. Oxford: OUP.
Hannay, A. (1982) *Kierkegaard*. London: Routledge.
Hong, H. and Hong, E. (1978) *Soren Kierkegaard's Journals and Papers* Bloomington: Indiana University Press.
James, W. (1982 [originally 1902]) *The Varieties of Religious Experience*. Glasgow, Collins.
Janik, A. and Toulman, S. (1973) *Wittgenstein's Vienna*. New York: Simon & Schuster.
John, M. (1996) *Children in Charge - The Child's Right to a Fair Hearing*. London: Kingsley.
Jung, C. (1937) The phenomenology of the spirit in fairy tales. In Campbell, B. (ed.) (1982), *Spirit and Nature: Papers From The Eranos Year Books*. Princeton, NJ: Princeton University Press.
Malantschuk, G. (1974) *Kierkegaard's Thought*. Princeton, NJ: Princeton University Press.
Monk, R. (1990) *Ludwig Wittgenstein: The Duty of Genius*. London: Cape.
Priestley, J. (1991) A new ERA - beginning from Jerusalem? Some reflections from 1928 on matters pertaining to 1998. *British Journal of Religious Education*, **13** (3), 143–51.
Priestley, M. (1999) *Disability Politics and Community Care*. London: Kingsley.
Reynolds, D. (1998) Teaching effectiveness. In *Teacher Training Agency Corporate Plan Launch 1998–2001*. London: TTA.
Sterling, W. S. (1999) Making all things new: the University Teachers' Project 1966–1970. In Reeves, M. (ed.) (1999), *Christian Thinking and Social Order: Conviction Politics from the 1930s to the Present Day*. London: Cassell.
Tillich, P. (1948) *The Shaking of the Foundations*. New York: Scribner.
West, M. (1996 [originally 1959]) *The Devil's Advocate*. London: Mandarin.
Wittgenstein, L. (1961 [originally 1921]) *Tractatus Logico-Philosophicus*. London: Routledge.
Wittgenstein, L. (1980 ed. G. Von Wright) *Culture and Value*. Oxford: Blackwell.
Yeaxlee, B. (1925) *Spiritual Values in Adult Education: A Study of a Neglected Aspect*. Oxford: OUP.

CHAPTER 8

The contribution of the act of collective worship to spiritual and moral development

Jeannette Gill

Although there is no suggestion that the act of collective worship has sole responsibility for the spiritual and moral development of pupils, it is nevertheless expected to 'play a major part in promoting the spiritual and moral dimension in schools' (DfE, 1992, Para. 8.2). However, societal changes which have occurred since reference to the spiritual element was first included in the Education Act of 1944 have resulted in differing perceptions of its relationship to worship. Alongside calls for the abolition of collective worship in the schools of a society which is perceived to be secular by some groups, but Christian or pluralist by others, there are also vocal demands for its retention. These insist that educators have a responsibility to transmit the country's traditional Christian faith to future generations and, by the provision of worship, to develop 'proper values and proper morals' (Thurlow, House of Lords, 12 May 1988, Hansard, Vol. 496, col. 1348).

However, there seems to be little agreement either on 'what morality and moral education actually are' (Wilson, 1996, p. 90) or on what constitutes an 'understanding of spirituality which is appropriate for the common school' (Halstead, 1996, p. 2). Numerous attempts to define the nature of spirituality can be found which emphasize variously the transcendent, the relational, the creative, the mystical and the reflective. In this discussion, because of their familiarity to teachers, I shall include as elements of this dimension those aspects which are identified by the National Curriculum Council (1993) and SCAA (1996) as fundamental to human experience such as identity, meaning and purpose, reflection, relationships with others and, for some, with God.

Moral education, values education and character education are currently the focus of much debate (see, for example, the twenty-fifth-anniversary issue of the *Journal of Moral Education*, 1996). In this chapter, moral development is identified as the acquisition and application of guiding principles which influence ethical judgements and behaviours in ways which seek to contribute to the maintenance of that which is of worth and to the well-being of the individual and of society. However, the close and interactive relationship between facets of the spiritual and the moral which, under some circumstances, may appear symbiotic means that, although it is possible to isolate them for the purpose of analysis, in practice their separation is often difficult.

THE PROVISION OF COLLECTIVE WORSHIP IN SCHOOLS

Schools' responses to the legal requirements which are incorporated in the Education Act of 1988 are not uniform, and are influenced by their social context, the backgrounds of their pupils and personal belief, as well as by practical constraints of accommodation and time. While some schools provide acts of worship which are wholly Christian, others conduct assemblies which are wholly secular. Between these extremes, however, most schools claim to make a regular provision for their pupils which, taken over a year, incorporates a broadly religious dimension. Secondary schools, however, often claim that inadequate accommodation renders impossible the provision of collective worship for all registered pupils on every day; for most students in this sector, therefore, meeting occurs weekly, usually within the year group, and any inclusion of worship is often minimal.

Evidence from Ofsted, confirmed by my own findings, indicates that in most acts the emphasis is on moral and social development (Ofsted, 1994). However, a distinction can be drawn between what the teachers consider assemblies to contribute to pupil development and what young people believe they acquire. While it is clear that students learn from the content of assembly, it is apparent that they learn also from the experiences which they encounter there, in ways which may not easily be recognized by their teachers. I shall also, therefore, examine the extent to which moral values and spiritual awareness are acquired not only from the intended curriculum of collective worship but also from pupils' experiences during this period.

BACKGROUND TO THE RESEARCH

The discussion which follows is compiled from data on the place of the act of collective worship in schools and was acquired by means of questionnaire, observation and interviews with teachers and pupils. A national questionnaire was distributed to 1:100 primary schools and 1:50 secondary schools in England and Wales during 1996, and replies were received from 81.8 per cent of the 340 schools contacted. During the same period, 65 visits for the purpose of observation were made to 35 schools situated mainly in the south-west of England and in the Midlands. Thirty-three headteachers or their representatives were interviewed, and discussions were held with 12 groups of pupils across the full age range.

In the report below, schools which responded to the questionnaire are identified by type and status as follows:

CI	county infant	CJ	county junior
CP	country primary	CS	county secondary
GMS	grant-maintained secondary	SS	special school
RCP	Roman Catholic primary	RCS	Roman Catholic secondary
CEP	Church of England primary	CES	Church of England secondary

Institutions which were visited for the purpose of observation and interview are identified as: primary schools, A–D; secondary schools, E–M. Pupils are also identified by year group, and teachers by initials.

FINDINGS OF THE QUESTIONNAIRE

Nearly all respondents claim that their institutions contribute to the moral development of pupils, although an examination of the figures for primary schools (88.6 per cent) and secondary schools (74.7 per cent) indicates a difference of emphasis between the sectors which is also apparent in respect of spiritual awareness, with 58.7 per cent of secondary institutions claiming to contribute frequently to this dimension compared with 78.9 per cent of primary schools. An examination of 956 assembly themes identified in the questionnaire provides further detail: in addition to references which are religious, curricular or administrative (any of which may also incorporate an ethical or spiritual element), 42 per cent of the titles refer specifically to elements of moral, social and personal guidance and 58 per cent of schools claim to provide at least occasional opportunities for participation in silent reflection, although such provision was seldom observed during visits.

Social and moral guidance

The majority of the themes relating to personal development are devoted to the encouragement of various kinds of interaction in social contexts and are concerned with the application of moral principles, such as truth, tolerance, justice, respect, trust and wisdom. Attitudes and behaviours which are discouraged include prejudice, selfishness, greed, racism and theft. Bullying is, however, the theme which is cited most frequently by both primary and secondary schools, while caring, sharing and helping are virtues which are commonly promoted, although only one reference is made to caring for property. Qualities such as kindliness, consideration and thoughtfulness are encouraged alongside capacities for gratitude and forgiveness. Responsibility for those in need is often met by practical action through fund-raising for charitable organizations, and the value of friendship and the importance of commitment are also stressed. Only one school, however, reports challenging moral expectations, and the conformist approach of much content may be what a young pupil meant when he claimed that the moral teaching in assembly only encourages uniformity.

> the sort of ones, like, they all want you to be really similar and not be different. (Year 6, school C)

The spiritual dimension

In seeking to identify themes which contribute to this element of pupil development, it is important to recognize the existence of both religious and non-religious interpretations of the term, and to acknowledge that for some teachers spirituality is necessarily religious. Themes which are overtly religious account for 26 per cent of the titles identified by teachers and come mostly from primary and denominational schools: overwhelmingly, the content relates to aspects of Christianity and includes material from the

Old and New Testaments, the celebration of festivals, discipleship and doctrine. There is little information available, however, to indicate how the subject matter is handled, except for occasional descriptions such as: *Noah – God's love for us* (CP) and *Elijah – fear, fatigue, how God gives us what we want* (CEP). Observation indicates that where county secondary schools incorporate a religious element it is integrated with non-religious material under a general title. Only 16 per cent of the themes identified as religious include material from traditions other than Christianity (4 per cent of the total).

In addition, many titles refer to those aspects of personhood which are identified in the NCC and SCAA definitions as facets of the spiritual dimension. For example, teachers seek to contribute to the development of a sense of self-worth in pupils by the celebration of success and the recognition of individual and group achievement. Concern for pupils' welfare is also evident, and themes refer to different aspects of personal development, incorporating guidance on emotions such as love, anger, sorrow, happiness and depression. Especially in primary schools, a sense of awe and wonder is encouraged in themes which are closely related to the natural environment, such as *nature's beauty* (CP), *our wonderful world* (CEP) and *the beauty of creation* (CJ). Other themes also give pupils cause for reflection. Remembrance Day provides an annual opportunity for a consideration of human experience and self-sacrifice; and when a death occurs in the school community or a national disaster takes place, young people are given the opportunity to reflect together on deeper issues in a meaningful way.

What do teachers think pupils gain from assembly?
While recognizing that teachers' perceptions of their pupils' learning is a subjective assessment, an open question elicited 212 responses. From these, it is clear that teachers are aware of the presence of a measure of implicit learning, describing this in terms such as 'experience', 'sense' and 'feeling'. Membership of the community is regarded as a distinctive feature which enables pupils to gain a deeper understanding of society's values and 'how they ought to lead their lives in relation to others' (GMS). A sense of mutual respect and responsibility, of shared purpose and 'a feeling of being unique yet part of a whole' (CP) are identified, and it becomes difficult to separate the development of a sense of identity, personal worth and belonging from the exercise of moral responsibility to other members of the community of which each pupil is part. 'A sense of belonging' (CS) and 'togetherness' (CS) is accompanied by the 'sharing of problems and worries' (CP) as well as 'mutual support in difficult times, e.g. bereavement' (RCS).

In county primary, denominational and independent schools, assembly is also regarded as an opportunity for pupils (and sometimes teachers too) to encounter the possibility of religious commitment. Teachers claim that pupils have an opportunity to reflect on the 'possibility of more to life than is apparent' (CP; CS), to experience God's goodness and love (CP; RCP; CEP) and to acquire a 'deepening understanding of God through Jesus Christ and relationships with others' (RCS). In denominational schools, pupils are able to observe the example of committed adults (RCS) and to share in the practice of faith (GMS).

However, it is important to note that not all provision is a positive experience for pupils. Some teachers claim that assembly is of little benefit except for providing an opportunity for students to meet together on a regular basis; and criticism of content features clearly. 'Very little spiritually and morally due to content' (SS). The gap between intention and achievement is also recognized. 'What I *hope* they receive and what they do receive is a big question' (CEP). Another teacher states forcefully that pupils gain nothing: 'they hate assemblies. Our assemblies are very very boring' (CS).

FINDINGS FROM OBSERVATION

Observation of school assemblies reinforces the picture established by the questionnaire. The main feature is a strong didactic element: rarely is the material allowed to speak for itself. Religious themes account for 28 per cent of observed assemblies (a figure very close to the 26 per cent noted in the questionnaire), but usually material is adapted to suit a purpose which is moral and social, reflecting the leader's interests and values as well as her perceptions of the needs of the school and of the pupils.

Transecting the content, however, is a range of approaches and attitudes adopted by leaders which adds another layer of influence. In some institutions, an authoritarian approach can be identified in demands for certain standards of behaviour and responsibility, accompanied by warnings of consequences and threats of punishment. Elsewhere, however, a more open approach is adopted which invites reflection and consideration, but this is not extensive and most leaders present material in a manner which is expository. Even when prayer is replaced by an invitation to reflect silently, it is rare that time is made available for this to occur.

INTERVIEWS WITH TEACHERS

While accepting their role as contributors to the personal development of pupils, teachers' attitudes to assembly are closely related to their responses to the legal requirements in respect of collective worship, and for some this demand itself raises questions of moral legitimacy. Although it is not my intention here to examine the arguments surrounding the compulsory provision of collective worship, it is nevertheless important to recognize the existence and influence of strong opposition to its provision on the part of some individuals. For some teachers, the leadership of collective worship constitutes a personal dilemma, in the conflict they experience between their desire to be seen by pupils to uphold the law in respect of a religious activity in which they feel unable to participate, while retaining their standing with pupils as individuals of personal and professional integrity. As one head teacher explained:

> I can't set myself up as someone who means what he says and says what he means and keeps promises and so on and so forth, if I act as the mouthpiece of something that I clearly don't believe. I think it would undermine my credibility with the pupils, which is important. Even more important, it would undermine my own intellectual credibility with myself. (TL, school I)

Several teachers expressed the suspicion that the legal requirements for collective worship were reinforced in the Education Act 1988 to serve as a channel by which government can exert an influence on the development of certain behaviours in young people. For example:

> It isn't the school's place to right society's ills, by telling parents, 'Well, you're not going to do it so we will.' It's not really what schools are about and the government shouldn't be trying to get a message across through schools because they think they're failing to get it across in other ways – use the schools as a vehicle for it, especially when there's so much else that schools are supposed to be duty-bound to be doing – put society's ills right by getting to the kids through the schools. (JN, school J)

Nevertheless, teachers accept their responsibility to contribute to the moral development of their pupils, although some argue that such education arises most naturally and effectively when it permeates the curriculum and is experienced in the daily routines of school life.

> Indeed, unless this happens, inside and outside the classrooms, and unless the school is founded upon recognized principles and values, no amount of moral theorizing or preaching – in assemblies or elsewhere – is going to make one ha'p'orth of difference to the actual lives of pupils or staff. (RT, school M)

At the same time, however, some teachers are committed to providing opportunities for their pupils to encounter both the moral and the spiritual dimensions through an act of worship which is regarded as a central and distinctive feature of their school's provision, and which is perceived to be influential even in the absence of personal belief:

> if you are in contact with believers and in contact with worship and in contact with Christian teaching then it has an effect upon people's conduct, and a restraining effect ... you can't divorce moral conduct from spiritual matters; the two are interrelated. (JE, school G)

> However, pupils learn also from the experiences they encounter in assembly, some of which are at variance with the intended learning objectives. In particular, what is very clear is the counter-productive nature of compulsion and stricture. Teachers recognize that, especially in adolescence, young people commonly reject adult pressure to conform:

> What you're in danger of doing is making it worse, not better, by producing the wrong kind of atmosphere altogether which will have an anti-effect (AI, school H)

Some argue therefore that the compulsory requirement for pupils to participate in the worship of a deity in whom they have no belief deprives them of their 'rights of choice and diversity' (AR, school K). It might be argued therefore that, where the law is implemented, pupils are expected to reflect on the moral dimension of life in a compulsory act of worship which itself does not take into account questions of pupils' autonomy.

Some schools choose to emphasize a dimension which is broadly spiritual and which places an emphasis on quiet thoughtfulness. It is claimed that the opportunity to participate in periods of calm reflection which are significantly different from the remainder of the day has an accumulative effect, enabling pupils to come together 'into a simple pool of ... tranquillity and stillness and silence' (AM, school B). Although this description could not be applied to many of the assemblies observed, at least one secondary school was planning to add to its provision by the inclusion of a period which would be more spiritually reflective.

The absence of such opportunities can be ascribed, at least in some schools, to problems with inadequate and inappropriate accommodation. Even where teachers feel at ease with the spiritual dimension, several hundred pupils sitting on a cold floor at 8.30 or 9 a.m. is not conducive to an atmosphere of reflection or contemplation.

> What I'm not good at ... is having contemplative silences in assembly. I can see it with 30 or 60 or 100, but I can't see it when you're dealing with larger numbers unless the richness of what you're giving can produce the mood, but what I'm saying is that very often the atmosphere is a damned wind blowing, the kids are sat on the floor and it doesn't produce that kind of atmosphere. (AI, school H)

Nevertheless, certain circumstances can produce an impact on both teachers and pupils. Many schools had meaningful and solemn assemblies after the tragedy at Dunblane, and the death of a teacher or a pupil is an occasion for remembrance and mutual comfort when all present reflect on the deeper issues of life:

> We had, sadly, a year or so ago, a lad who died from meningitis and we had some very meaningful assemblies with those youngsters, his year group. Call them acts of worship? No – but were they thoughtful? Yes. Were they prayerful? Yes, and for quite a lot of individuals present they were – spiritual? Yes, in that people stopped, stepped aside from the daily concerns, thought a bit more deeply about themselves and mortality and the world in which they lived and that particular lad ... For us all to get together and share that together with a few words and some thoughtful silences, I think is worthwhile. (RT, school M)

One further point which is rarely identified is the influence of the spiritual qualities which pupils bring into the school, which can have a noticeable and profound effect on all its members. In a secondary school which serves a largely Hindu population, three teachers commented, independently, on the spiritual influence of the pupils. A typical comment was as follows:

> The nature of living faith and commitment and spirituality – they have faith and you can see the way it leads their lives, following a strict code ... the nature of faith and spirituality evident in a school like this is very strong, but you can't put your finger on it. (AR, school K)

As we have seen, the concept of the spiritual is not without obfuscation and controversy. Some teachers express exasperation at the absence of any common definition of the term and its adoption by secular groups to the exclusion of any religious elements, while others cannot accept that the spiritual dimension might exist outside religion. Finally, one teacher was very unhappy with its inclusion in education at all:

A lot of people object to that kind of self-investigation because some people find it (a) quite difficult, (b) some people actually find it disturbing. You do not know what you are doing when you play with these things. . . . If it is as deep and subtle as people who use the word say, then how have you got a handle on this to know what it is in order to explore it safely with children of all sorts of ages and susceptibilities? (KV, school M)

INTERVIEWS WITH PUPILS

What is significant about pupils' comments is that their learning is influenced by affective experiences which are additional to the cognitive content of the material they encounter. In particular, the opportunity which assembly provides to feel part of a community, to be valued and to build a sense of personal and corporate identity are important elements:

It's good to get the year group together at least one time in a week, because otherwise you're just lots of people walking around the school. You're not a school because you don't know each other; you're not aware of the other people. (Year 10, school J)

It is also evident that pupils acquire an increasing knowledge of moral principles and their application. In some schools, however, such learning is largely restricted to the observation of a code of conduct which is rehearsed in assembly. Although the children recite these rules by rote (e.g. 'Keep hands and feet to yourselves', Year 5, school D), they complain that inappropriate behaviours continue. 'Doesn't make no difference. They just carry on' (Year 5, school D). Where pupils are encouraged instead to reflect on moral dilemmas, often through story, they claim that a consideration of consequences serves to influence behaviour. 'It's like you heard what happened so you avoid doing it' (Year 4, school C). This feature is also identified by pupils in secondary schools. However, the widely varying social contexts in which children live and are educated, and the conflicts and difficulties which some face, are themselves influential in pupils' ability to respond positively to the material they encounter.

One of the key moral values which pupils acquire from a variety of sources is an awareness of justice. Although this principle features in planned themes, it is internalized and reinforced by the experiences which pupils encounter in assembly, where they are largely passive observers of the wider group and where the circumstances which they experience sometimes serve as a catalyst for the application of a sense of justice and injustice. These situations range from teachers' insistence on petty and unexplained rules to unfair reprimands and punishments:

The wrong people get into trouble. I don't like it. It's not really fair. (Year 5, school A)

I don't reckon that's fair, because none of us were talking that time. He [the headteacher] was! (Year 4, school C)

Young people are often very supportive of their peers especially, perhaps, where they are in a minority, and the experience of regular acts of religious worship in multi-faith schools can also lead to a perception of injustice. Thus:

if you did it [acts of worship] in assemblies then I don't think that would be right, because at my old school we had it and we were always doing Christian songs and everything and I could see a lot of Hindus and Muslims. They didn't really enjoy it and we didn't do anything to do with their religion and I don't think it was fair on them. (Year 9, school I)

Other factors affecting pupil learning include the manner in which material is presented and the personal stance adopted by the leader. The influence of curriculum subjects, particularly material studied in religious education and science, raises various questions; and from about the age of ten years, pupils begin to reject any pressure by adults to believe or to conform:

The assemblies make you try and believe in it ... They teach us about religious faiths [i.e. in religious education] but they try and relate you [sic] into Christians when you don't really want to be. (Year 6, school C)

From this age, young people are in a process of transition. Teenage pupils themselves recognize that there is a conflict between their sometimes troubled search for a sense of personal identity and independence, and their need for adult support and guidance:

It's difficult because, it's like with teenagers, they are always – you know – you are growing up, you are trying to find out what kind of suits you, you've got people sort of pushing Christianity across. I think you tend to get people then rebelling against it because that's expected of you. (Year 10, school L)

In this search, however, what young people value most is sincerity and relevance. When a message is well presented and meets their needs, they are prepared to listen and to reflect on the material:

In the 'thought for the day' you really feel that the teachers practise and believe in it themselves, so they are better able to teach it to the pupils. (Year 10, school K)

All too often, however, students in secondary schools complain that, although teachers have their interests at heart, they live in a different world from the one inhabited by their pupils:

I think it's another thing, like in assemblies and morals and stuff, everyone tries to put over a perfect world, but we are here now and that's not the way it is. (Year 10, school L)

Nevertheless, young people also recognize the importance of the inclusion of the moral dimension. Although some claim that this is no longer necessary in the secondary school (Year 13, school F), others argue for its continued provision. For example:

I think that morals should be mentioned in assemblies because they – because I know a lot of people will forget those sort of things. I mean they will get told them, or they will get told off and then while they are getting told off, the morals will come out and then they will be good, and then after a while they will forget, and if they forget they will carry on. You would constantly need being told in assembly.

Yes, they would be reminded so then there's a faint chance of them trying harder, but you have got to take that chance otherwise it will just be chaos. (Year 9, school I)

Many young people are themselves troubled by the society of which they are a part. One observed assembly was led by a group of Year 10 pupils who acted out a series of sketches which warned against what they described 'serious issues' in their inner-city neighbourhood. These included theft, mugging, graffiti, drug taking and joyriding; and the students argued that more time should be devoted to assembly in order to develop their moral crusade further (Year 10, school E).

The picture which is beginning to emerge is one where young people are actively engaged in a search for purpose and meaning. Underneath an apparent façade of boredom and indifference, they value teachers' concern for them and acknowledge the underlying influences which, although subtle and hidden, are cumulative and effective (Year 10, school J):

I'm sure we all have learned but we've forgotten when, where and why. (Year 9, school I)

If they put across something very well, then it can really make you change your ideas about things and think about things in a new light. (Year 13, school F)

Nevertheless, it would be foolish not to recognize the criticisms which are also part of pupils' comments. Two implicit messages need much deeper consideration by all those responsible for the moral and spiritual development of pupils. The first is that there is a gulf between what pupils perceive that they need and their teachers' understanding of those needs:

They think they are helping us and you have got to give them credit for that but they just need to work out what we want, really, for it to work. (Year 11, school M)

Contemporary issues, current affairs and a wider discussion about the problems which confront the young in an imperfect world, they argue, should receive a much greater emphasis.

The second is that many young people express a state of growing confusion in respect of the religious and spiritual elements of their education:

a lot of people don't really want to get into any belief in particular because it can change your mind so much and you don't really want to commit yourself because, and I don't know about anybody else, but it seems pointless believing in something when you don't even know if it's true or not. You don't know the difference between one and the other. You can't prove about God and you can't prove that Muslim whatever beliefs are true either. You don't know which is right or if any of them are right. (Year 11, school M)

The difficulty which teachers face is that they, too, often share the same confusions!

CONCLUSIONS

It is of considerable significance that, even where teachers are wholly opposed to the provision of collective worship, strong support is nevertheless expressed in favour of the regular assembling of large groups of pupils. However, it seems clear that, although assembly makes a contribution to the social and moral development of pupils, this is not as consistent or as effective as it might be, nor is it wide-reaching, with many schools preferring to concentrate on a particular cluster of values rather than the application of moral principles to a range of dilemmas. It may be that one way forward is to adopt an approach which allows for more pupil participation and involvement, in order to explore the concerns of the young people themselves and to relate more effectively to the reality of their daily lives. This may need to involve some expansion into the timetable (e.g. tutor group periods) in order to do justice to the depth of some of the issues raised.

It is also clear that primary and denominational schools make a particular contribution to pupils' spiritual development as defined in its religious sense. However, it is generally argued by teachers that this does not lead to commitment unless the child comes from a faith background. A wider spirituality has yet to be satisfactorily defined for the ordinary teacher; unless it incorporates a reflective element, its current identification with relationships, individual identity and values is likely to render it indistinguishable from personal and social education. In their discussions, no pupils referred to the spiritual dimension as a feature of assemblies, except in its religious sense, and this is a matter which requires further consideration. It may be the case that the gathering of very large groups of pupils is not, except in rare instances, conducive to an exploration of the spiritual dimension.

REFERENCES

DfE (1992) *Religious Education and Collective Worship: Proposed Regulation for Inclusion in the Forthcoming Education Bill, Consultation Paper.* London: DfE.

DfE (1994) *Religious Education and Collective Worship: Circular 1/94.* London: DfE.

Halstead J. M. (1996) Editorial. *SPES,* **4** (May). Faculty of Arts and Education, Exmouth: University of Plymouth.

NCC (1993) *Spiritual and Moral Development: A Discussion Paper.* York: National Curriculum Council.

Ofsted (1994) *Religious Education and Collective Worship 1992–3.* London: HMSO.

SCAA (1996) *Education for Adult Life: The Spiritual and Moral Development of Young People.* London: SCAA.

Wilson, J. (1996) First steps in moral education. *Journal of Moral Education,* **25** (1).

CHAPTER 9

Rediscovering the personal in education

Bridget Cooper

CONTEXT

This chapter is based on the early findings from a research project into values in education, which looks in particular at the role of empathy in teacher/pupil relationships and the modelling of moral values. This qualitative research project, now in its later stages, began in an exploratory way with meetings with groups of teachers and discussions with teacher trainers. This was followed by a pilot study, which involved interviews with teachers and pupils and observations in a city centre primary school. The findings from the exploratory work led to the main study, in which a number of empathic teachers and student teachers were interviewed and observed. This chapter draws on the exploratory work and pilot study, coupled with some analysis of the early interviews and observations in the main project. The findings are illuminated by some discussion of values revealed in contemporary comedy and politics. A more detailed description of the early research can be found in Cooper, 1997.

COMEDIANS AND POLITICIANS: WORDS AND DEEDS

And there's Basil Fawlty leaping up and down, his body bent double, his hands tightly fisted and his face distorted with anguish, screaming out with frustration: 'I *am* calm!' We cannot help but laugh. The sharp contrast between his words and his appearance and actions provide instant entertainment. The manic obsessive lurks beneath a thin veneer of civility, the racist escapes from a pretence of liberalism and the misogynist violently attacks from the guise and veiled words of a loving husband, 'Yes, dear, anything you say, dear.' Classic comedy at its best. It is a tried and tested technique; say one thing and do another or mean another and the audience spots the anomaly immediately. They have no need to analyse. Our senses are naturally alert to facial expression and body movement, especially if those messages contrast with spoken words.

Other comedy uses similar techniques. The *Alan Partridge Show* initially suggests a personal interest in people. Its title and the Partridge catchphrase, 'Knowing me, knowing you', suggests we are here to learn about each other and discover some new and exciting revelations – 'Aha!' The show then proves to be the exact opposite, as the personal exchange withers away with each guest, until the catchphrase itself eventually balks on the host's tongue even as he utters it. Far from having the time and interest in other people to listen to them, Alan Partridge is mainly interested in himself and, just like Basil Fawlty, eventually his real feelings emerge and out slips the bigot, the sexist, the racist, the xenophobe, the self-centred individual, unleashing his profound prejudices against his guests and fellow professionals show after show. His mind is closed to anything which does not affirm his own ideas and opinions.

Of course the humour lies not only in the contrast between saying and doing and the mounting amusement when a slight ambiguity develops into downright deceit and charlatanism, but because we know there is a hint of this behaviour in all of us, as individuals. The skills we utilize in benign diplomacy also give us the capacity to use our language and non-verbal responses to ignore, deceive or belittle others. Co-ordinating our words and intentions with our appearance and actions is not always easy. People, throughout time, have aspired to the concept of 'loving their neighbour' in church and then have found themselves able to attack those same neighbours with words in other forms and at times more violently.

When this divergence between voiced and unvoiced beliefs and values emerges in people whom we are meant to rely on or trust or who act as role models for others, or have responsibilities which affect the lives of others, it is more likely to cause unease and anxiety than amusement. We might be amused at Neil Hamilton's appearance on the BBC's *Have I Got News for You*, after his defeat in the general election of May 1997, but we are also left feeling ill at ease and anxious. Can someone really profess his innocence and laugh at the jokes made about his own allegedly dubious behaviour? Ambiguity is much more disconcerting in people with positions of power or responsibility and engenders mistrust and alienation.

THE VALUES DEBATE

The previous Conservative government fuelled the debate on values in education. Cynics might believe it to be a distraction technique, turning the eye and the blame on schools rather than focusing on the last days of a dying government. However, the fear of an increasingly corrupt and immoral society was not restricted to the politics of the Right. Violent events associated with schools, such as the Dunblane massacre and the death of head teacher, Philip Lawrence, left many people shocked and stunned. What kind of society produces such heartless events?

The debate about values in the press and to a certain extent in the academic and educational world has centred around lists: lists of values which we ought to have, share, abide by and act upon. The implication is that if we decide which values we agree on and then voice these loud enough and long enough, post them on the classroom walls and in the corridors and reiterate them in assembly and in lessons, then our children will automatically become paragons of virtue. As time-honoured lists go, the Ten Commandments figure prominently in the debate, as do the teachings of all major religions. The

National Forum for Values in Education and the Community eventually produced its own definitive list, separating the values into four areas: society, relationships, the self and the environment. These were accompanied by principles to help translate the values into action (SCAA, 1996b).

Few people would find problems with the values emerging from these sources. Most would see them as admirable and worthy. However, lists on their own are not enough; it is what we *do* that matters. If our deeds belie our stated values then we are open to mockery and cries of hypocrisy. It is safe to laugh at the duality of Alan Partridge; we know he is fictional and his guests are actors. What happens when the people we really need to trust cannot walk as well as talk their actions? How do we turn the catchphrase into reality, the words into action, the list of values into valuable deeds?

It seems that to be consistent in our deeds we must *want* to hold the values on our lists and understand why they are important. We need to see others modelling and acting out the same values around us to understand how they work in reality. If we are able to tune into the feelings of others and value them, we can always be more aware of the consequences of our deeds and the nurturing of empathy plays a key role in this regard.

MORAL DEVELOPMENT – THE ROLE OF EMPATHY

Research into the moral development of children points to the development of empathy as a key factor in moral growth (Hoffman and Saltzstein, 1967; Piaget and Kohlberg in Hersch *et al.*, 1979; Rogers, 1975; McPhail *et al.*, 1978; Straughan, 1989; Bottery, 1990; and, more recently, Koseki and Berghammer, 1992). In order to acquire this quality children have to be shown empathy by other significant people in their lives, parents, carers, teachers, spouses. From birth, mothers and babies share emotional responses with each other through close physical, verbal and non-verbal contact. This 'attunement' is the root of empathy, according to Daniel Goleman.The works of Damasio (1994) and Goleman (1996) are summaries of some of the recent research into brain development and link the emotional, the cognitive and physical as never before. They show how our abilities to make judgements and so-called 'rational' decisions are inextricably linked to our inner feelings and physical processes, each feeding back to the other in different ways. From babyhood our brains grow and develop when we feel nurtured and cared for (Winkley, 1996). The impressions left on our brains by powerful sensory and emotional experience have long-lasting effects, as Pat Barker vividly describes in her trilogy of books on the First World War (Barker, 1992, 1994, 1996). Children's personal and emotional needs have to be met and they have to be encouraged to understand other people's emotions and needs and to take them into account when they speak and act. Feeling as others do enables us to know the consequences of our actions for others. Seeing the world from the perspective of the other allows us to share with, to learn from and consider others.

The people who commit violent and immoral acts are frequently those who have missed out on early emotional provision (Docker-Drysdale, 1990). There is considerable evidence to show that lack of empathy is a key characteristic of the psychopath and the abuser (Goleman, 1996; Rosenstein, 1995). Though the key to attunement and healthy emotional development is rooted in early upbringing, there is evidence to suggest that the effect of bad early experience can be ameliorated later in life (Docker-Drysdale, 1990; Rutter, 1981) and that schools can help in this regard (Koseki and Berghammer, 1992; Rutter *et al.*, 1979).

'Scratch a teacher and you will find a moral purpose,' says Fullan (1993, p. 10), and, despite the pessimistic views of Nicholas Tate (1997) and Chris Woodhead (1997), there is evidence to suggest schools are already our most moral places and teachers our most moral models. The 1996 SCAA paper (SCAA, 1996b) gives clear evidence that young people do regard teachers as setting the best moral example and the previous government acknowledged the good work of schools in relation to the promotion of moral values (DfE, 1992). Ofsted's evidence confirms this (Taylor, 1997). If this is so, then we need to consider how best to evaluate, improve and extend that already beneficial but intangible influence, since the 'good' work of teachers in schools does not seem to be alleviating the perceived moral crisis in society at large.

To enhance further the 'moral' ethos in schools, we may need to model empathy even more clearly to our children, not only as individual teachers but as organizations and systems which have the power and capacity to meet emotional and personal need more effectively. Some people and some systems seem better than others at understanding, recognizing and meeting the needs. We can function better academically if we are nurtured and valued as people and this can apply in higher education as well as in schools. Research into empathy links it to excellence in teaching and learning (Aspy, 1972), as well as to moral development.

Many British educationists imply or touch on the significance of empathy either in relation to the values debate or more generally in reference to effective teaching, teacher/pupil relationships, school ethos and the 'hidden curriculum' (Pring, 1984; Kyriacou, 1986; Straughan, 1989, 1994; Bell and Harrison, 1995; Mulgan, 1996). Managers in both business and education are beginning to look afresh at the importance of such qualities in creating more human firms with higher standards of ethics (Martin, 1993; Dobson and White, 1995; Bell and Harrison, 1995; Bottery, 1992). Daniel Goleman (1996) linked empathy to morality and Koseki and Berghammer's research (1992) into the role of empathy in the motivational structure of school children emphasizes the relationship with morality. They explain how they see empathy developing through different stages, with the most advanced stage being moral or adaptive empathy. They believe this quality can be enhanced by both parents and schools as children mature.

In its simplest form, empathy is a quality which enables people to feel and see the world from the perspective of others. Kyriacou speaks of: 'the importance of teachers being able to see the lesson from the pupils' perspective' and explains it is a significant contributory factor in all eight of the characteristics which are seen in the effective teacher (Kyriacou, 1986). The groups of teachers I first talked to in this research believed an ability to see things from the child's perspective was one of the most important skills a teacher could have (Cooper, 1997). However, in order to see things from the perspective of others, an individual has first to accept others as they are. Carl Rogers describes it like this: 'To be with another in this way (empathic) means that for the time being you lay aside the views and values you hold for yourself in order to enter another's world without prejudice' (Rogers, 1975, p. 4).

The 'moral or adaptive' empathy decribed by Koseki and Berghammer (1992) finds its strength in a long-term view of the other's perspective. It is not sufficient to be aware of the other's feelings when it suits you, for example, to beat an opponent or to close a sale. The empathy involved in competition is less mature in nature. Moral empathy is of a different order where concern for and understanding of the other has to be a long-term phenomenon, where the aim is to bring about a positive long-term result for that person, to continue to be aware of their past and to envisage their future. It involves taking responsibility for others.

CAN EMPATHIC TEACHERS BE MORAL MODELS?

In the context of the research reported here the following operational definition of empathy evolved:

A quality shown by individuals, which enables them to accept others for who they are, to feel and perceive situations from their perspective and to take a constructive and long-term attitude towards the advancement of their situation, by searching for solutions to meet their needs.

The importance of a long-term view emerged in conversations with the teachers I began to interview. To help them teach children, they found out about their families, houses, cultures, holidays, pets, worries, problems, pleasures, interests, aspirations and ambitions. Teachers saw this as central to valuing and teaching the child. Asked whether they ever thought about their pupils' pasts or futures, one teacher, Mary, said:

because of the backgrounds they come from, because they come from such totally different backgrounds to the majority of children in the school and my life, I think its important to keep that on board otherwise you can't really understand a lot of the things that happen within the lesson.

Maggie, responding to the same question, described how the personal and the learning intertwine:

I suppose [when I say things] like 'Remember when you did this' and you can link it back to their, *their* history ... their own personal history and ... quite often we'll talk about ... if we're doing a topic ... Doctors or whatever, 'Would you like to ...? What do you think about ...? Would you like to be a ...? Somebody who works in a hospital ...?' – so I suppose you throw them backwards and forwards all the time in a conversation. It gives them them a feeling of ... there's a future to look forward to and I've also got a past and ... these things happened to me and that's something we can share ... and it can be conquered or whatever.

Teachers, like these, use empathy in their teaching but it should not only be the responsibility of individuals. If long-term needs are to be properly addressed, an empathic approach needs to be embedded in the strategic planning and organizational processes of large organizations and institutions. Ultimately, however, interpersonal relations are at the heart of this quality, the complexity of which is challenging, hard to define and in the classroom has its heart in the split-second interactions between people.

SEEING AND HEARING IS BELIEVING

Comedians, who utilize lack of empathy as a source of humour, are clearly aware of the powerful effect of the visual and the importance of voice tone. The lack of 'attunement' between Basil Fawlty and Sybil as they each carry on their individual conversations without listening or even looking at each other seems to be the reverse of empathy. When Alan Partridge's guests talk about their lives, his face may register nothing. The non-committal tone of voice and the 'Oh' without further comment is more deflating than a genuine look of displeasure. He is more concerned about his own next comment than he is about his guest. Children seem very attuned to visual clues and to voice tone. They read the non-verbal language which reveals our true feelings long before they understand the words with which we try to express or conceal them. In my pilot study, the 'expressionless' face or 'false smiles' (of feigned interest) came over clearly in the pupils' responses as the mark of someone who does not understand you (Cooper, 1997).

The visual, smiles and laughter
The smile, by contrast, was seen as the key sign of someone who did understand (Cooper, 1997). The teachers in the main project echoed this and frequently mentioned the importance of the smile and humour. For one teacher, Anna, they were a key tool: 'I rely on smiles a heck of a lot.' Humour and laughter seemed to be important elements in the whole area of relationships and shared understanding. The children voiced this in the pilot study (Cooper, 1997) and several teachers in the main project echoed this view. For example, Anna explained how the initial work with a special needs child is all about forming relationships, and her teaching programme begins with lots of games and 'anything that makes them laugh really ... I really feel that I've got to get them totally relaxed.'

Pupils in the pilot study considered the 'grim' or 'straight' expressionless face denoted lack of understanding and teachers in the main project also described this as a characteristic of someone who is less empathic. Charlotte described unempathic teachers like this: 'I suppose they probably don't show a lot of emotional ... expressions in their face ... sort of not understanding a problem ... people aren't very patient. They've got something to put across and you're going to take it in regardless.'

Although it can be effective as a means of control because it induces an element of fear, the grim face produces a feeling in the child that the teacher does not understand them. According to my pupil interviewees, they would feel 'bored', 'fed-up' and 'didn't take as much notice if the teacher was grumpy'. The delicate balance between control and encouragement is an important factor in classrooms but perhaps our facial expressions are more significant than we think. The teachers in the main project thought that children who suffer too much 'control' with both non-verbal and verbal communication are less able to communicate, less able to get close to the teacher, to form positive relationships and exchange information. In large classes, with more needy children and teachers having to work harder at classroom management, there must be a considerable negative effect on self-esteem and personal development as children are likely to feel less valued and therefore less able to value others. As Mary said:

> the compliant ones in the classrooms ... seem to be the ones ... the class teachers speak more normally and nicely to ... the children who are problems in the classrooms, they can never ... get very close to the teacher because the teacher's ... keeping them in their place all the time. ... it must just snowball, mustn't it? ... the more well-behaved [they are], the nicer response they get and the naughtier they are, the more they ... get barked at.

Another teacher (Karen) in the pilot, recognized this same problem in her own classroom:

> Sometimes you can be so tied up with the control if you have got a bad behaviour problem but you have to say to yourself – 'Now, stop' and say, 'What will really improve this situation?' Rather than just controlling the behaviour ... what can really motivate this child to be able to concentrate? Find out what he's interested in.

The implication for children with particular needs of different kinds is quite significant here. In overusing control with some children we may be producing the exact opposite of what is needed. If we stop smiling, stop accepting, then the child may simply feel misunderstood and rejected. Ironically, these children are likely to need more time and effort to understand them fully and their life experience may be far removed from those of the teachers.

Human and fair

According to Aspy (1972), children seem to form better relationships with people who do not behave 'like teachers'. In the pilot one child echoed this idea and the teachers in the main project talked frequently of just 'being themselves' in the classroom. Anna said: 'I think I'm lucky in that, I don't feel that I have to put on an act' and later she described empathy as: 'being sensitive towards the needs of the child – trying to treat each one of them as a little human being as opposed to a pupil'. The skill of listening seemed particularly significant to get to know pupils and to treat them as 'little human beings'. The pupils appreciated teachers who listened to them and in the observations teachers could be seen to be listening closely to children. In her interview, Maggie gave a detailed description of her own gradual development into a more 'listening' teacher.

In the pilot the children felt understood by teachers who were personal, warm, friendly and jokey, but they also ran 'fair' classrooms (Cooper, 1997). These characteristics have also been echoed in the ideas of several teachers in the main project. Here is a typical example of the 'fairness' described by Anna, which emerged both through voicing simple rules and modelling positive behaviour in the small groups in which she worked:

We're small and we're focused and we all have to get on together, so we have basic rules: you're polite, you don't knock somebody else's work; but I do say 'Don't you think they did really well on that?' (*very positive voice tone*) and a child who has maybe thumped somebody in the playground will say, 'Oh yes, that's good, in'it, really'

Children in the pilot study did not like teachers who give mixed messages, who say one thing and do another, leaving them confused and unsure. This was echoed by teachers in the main project. Charlotte connected empathy to honesty and lack of empathy to these mixed messages:

I mean if you are showing empathy for a child you're trying to be honest, aren't you? ... So I think there's the link of honesty there that goes through with it. You know if you create a false impression ... a child soon sees through that ... and I suppose somebody who is immoral really is showing a falseness ... if they say ... something like 'Oh I'll do that for you' ... promises that aren't kept ... that comes through in adults as well ... You know they said they'd do so and so and they didn't.

Following through your promises with actions shows honesty and builds trust, allowing openness and growth; the reverse builds disrespect and mistrust.

Attunement

Daniel Goleman's concept of 'attunement' was highly visible in the main project. Teachers working in small groups and one-to-one situations were observed to have very close relationships with pupils. These teachers scanned pupils' faces for signs of anxiety, understanding, pleasure, dismay, confusion or boredom and were able to respond rapidly to signals. Teachers and pupils work in pairs, building up ideas, words and sentences together and the conversations waltz along, with pupil and teacher often speaking in unison, echoing each other's thoughts and ideas, laughing together and sharing jokes. The body language and tone of voice of one constantly echoes that of the other, bending, now forwards, now backwards, coming physically very close and then falling apart in laughter. The relationships were very positive with much mutual pleasure involved. The messages relayed by these teachers through their conversation and interpersonal skills were clearly and constantly reiterated: I like you; I enjoy your company; you are important as a person and so is your family, your culture, your health and welfare, your school work, your literacy, your success and your happiness; good manners are important as is good behaviour; we need to be considerate to other people and recognize other people's achievements; it is important to listen and to understand other people, to value other pupils, to care about each other but also to enjoy what we do.

In these very close relationships, good behaviour and positive modelling were the norm. There was no need for overt disciplining because both teacher and child were so engaged in working and learning and sharing. Moral lessons were modelled and voiced naturally in the course of events and were well accepted. These children felt 'good' and were 'good', with no attention brought to their possible 'badness'. The teacher's sensitivity to the child's perspective requires awareness of and empathy with the individual and forms the basis of relationships. When asked how relationships played a part in her teaching, one teacher (Maggie) explained how she relates differently to different children:

Because, with each child's needs and personalities being so different, then you've to adjust your way of teaching ... to bring out the best in them. So if a child's extremely shy you're going to spend time giving them a sense of their own self-esteem and self-worth ... so really the child is the dictator in that and you've got to alter too ... so you've got to know your child pretty well and what makes them tick and what their likes and dislikes are so you can ... just go forward really.

IMPLICATIONS

From my work to date, the evidence suggests that the path to moral growth is through personal development engendered through positive human relationships. Such relationships are fostered by teachers who try to find time to get to know and understand their pupils on a personal and emotional level as well as on an academic level and whose concern for 'the other' reaches into the out-of-school lives of their pupils. These teachers are face-scanners, listeners and responders, who laugh and smile a lot. They know when to intervene and when not to because they watch their pupils very carefully and respond to what they see.

Lists of values might clarify or encapsulate complex ideas and may provide an excellent point of reference by which to weigh decisions, but if they are not also seen in action then they can create that phenomenon in the emotional and moral sphere that in the academic sphere Piaget once described as 'empty' tricks (cited in Wood, 1988, p. 24) and which Howard Gardner's daughter encapsulates when she says about her physics course 'I have never understood it' (Gardner, 1991, p. 5). Lists of values may have limited use if they are not internalized, applied to real world situations and modelled in action. A conflict of word and deed might also create confusion, mixed messages, lost trust and missed opportunities for development for needy individuals.

Though we can seek to enhance this aspect of school provision, it is not enough to see values in action in schools, delivered through empathic teachers. Such values must be modelled by other influential people, nurtured by families and exemplified in the wider world of politics, the economy and the media, in the systems, organizations and institutions which we initiate, develop and venerate. If we see selfishness and coldness flourish and succeed in the outside world, while selflessness is abused or left unrecognized, what can we aspire to? Shen Te, Brecht's 'Good Person of Setzuan' has to create a more selfish alter ego to survive in a ruthless and turbulent world, while she herself struggles with moral precepts which condemn her to poverty and abuse. The values she is asked to sustain are not echoed or valued in the world around her.

Our own sense of self-worth is founded in our emotional relationships with others. There seems to be a mutual and reciprocal characteristic in human beings to value and to feel valued, to open up and to respond to each other. We need to appreciate this characteristic alongside others and be prepared to allocate time and resources to nurturing this very human ability. At any point in our lives we can lose or regain self-esteem through relationships or lack of relationships with others. Although his actions belie his commitment, Alan Partridge is right. It really is about 'knowing me – knowing you', but in the real world, it is not funny; it is deadly serious. It requires us to take time with people, to work at understanding, accepting and valuing them and for teachers it is about developing children in their personal relationships, not just enabling them to progress to the next level in the National Curriculum. Ironically, those who are preoccupied with the curriculum overlook the fact that the latter may be much more easily achieved if the former is as keenly addressed. The teachers in this research were desperate for more time with pupils in order to know them better and thereby teach them more effectively.

These teachers tried to make time for the personal. Maggie expressed it in this way:

> the most important thing that you can ever give anybody in life is time – is *your* time for them. . . . you're giving people time. You're giving people time because you feel everybody is important and as such they then should feel that others are worthy – *for the greater good of mankind!* [laughs]. *This is it* – that we are all important individuals, aren't we? And we all need time and we should give each other time. (teacher's emphasis)

She also linked empathy to morality. Maggie again:

> this was told to me a long time ago, over many glasses of wine: 'Love thy neighbour as thyself' and then no other crimes will be committed . . . because you wouldn't do it to yourself . . . you wouldn't so . . . that's empathy and . . . to my mind that's morality as well. I think . . . if your doctor feels that . . . you know his ultimate care is for you. If a teacher feels that . . . yes . . . they are caring about you . . . yes, you feel trusted . . . then . . . it's reciprocated . . . it's . . . morality . . . it's really thinking . . . that the other person is more important or . . . as important as yourself . . . isn't it?

CONCLUSION

From the preliminary findings of this research it is clear that even small children were alert to the visual, the personal, the moral and the caring qualities in their teachers, and that this is important to them. They feel they know when people care, by their actions, their faces, their body language and voice tone.They are alert to the discrepancy between word and deed, to the discrepancy between what is said and how it is said. There is more to empathy than imagining another's experience. It involves demonstrating consistency in our words, deeds and mannerisms. It incorporates the personal and the human at the most basic level of personal interaction when we react as concerned people, who are interested in others for their own sake. The teachers in this research were able to demonstrate this clearly in one-to-one situations and in small groups. Yet in schools, in large classes, this may happen often only as an added extra, as a passing chance in a crowded corridor or between lessons. The Elton Report, SCAA, even Ofsted, stress the importance of relationships and of school ethos, but how is the significance of relationships recognized in pupil/teacher ratios, in quality time with individuals in schools, in special time for needy pupils and in the time pressure on education generally? If our values are in part shown by the effort and time we devote to them in practice, then education as a whole reveals a failure to value the significance of the personal, the informal and human relationships by not recognizing and allocating sufficient time to these issues.

When teachers scarcely pause to draw breath in a school day, when they no longer reach the staffroom at breaks and lunchtimes, when nights and weekends are filled with marking and bureaucracy and when exam results for the minority drive the curriculum, what values do we really demonstrate? Alienated and exhausted teachers will not be able to find time to take a personal interest in children. If conditions prevent teachers from modelling a caring and personal approach, it is difficult to envisage who else might have the opportunity. It becomes increasingly difficult for teacher training courses to model or discuss the significance of relationships, given the increasingly subject-oriented and technicist curriculum and ever-larger student groups. The shift towards school-based training may exacerbate the problem because mentoring has to be squeezed in among the real business of educating pupils. Trainee teachers, like pupils, may be lucky even to get individual 'corridor' time. Mentors endeavour to find time, but often at their own expense. Caring schools try to create time for staff, student teachers and parents as well as for pupils, but time is a finite resource.

If we want concerned and caring people to emerge from our education system, then we need the time and resources to treat all students, at whatever educational level, in a concerned and caring way, as people, not as academic products. We need to allocate time thoughtfully and create systems which nourish the personal and which value the kind of personal interactions seen in this research. Teachers also need to be valued and nourished. Schools and other educational institutions should form a part of what it involves to be human, where academic and personal development are interdependent for both staff and students. When teachers repeatedly ask for recognition and support from government, the TTA or Ofsted, perhaps they are seeking that valuing which they need to feel as people, to enable them to model human, other-centred sensitivity to their students.

REFERENCES

Aspy, D. (1972) *Towards a Technology for Humanising Education*. Champaign, Illinois: Research Press.

Barker, P. (1992) *Regeneration*. London: Penguin.

Barker, P. (1994) *The Eye in the Door*. London: Penguin.

Barker, P. (1996) *The Ghost Road*. London: Penguin.

Bell, J. and Harrison, B. T. (1995) *Vision and Values in Managing Education*. London: David Fulton.

Bottery, Mike (1990) *The Morality of the School*. London: Cassell.

Bottery, Mike (1992) *The Ethics of Educational Management, Personal, Social and Political Perspectives on School Organization*. London: Cassell.

Brecht, B. [originally 1953] *The Good Person of Setzuan*. Harmondsworth: Penguin Plays.

Cooper, B. (1997) Communicating values via the 'Hidden curriculum' – messages from the teacher (Conference, *Education, Spirituality and the Whole Child*, London, June 1997).

Damasio, A. R. (1994) *Descartes Error*. London: Macmillan.

DfE Circular (1992) *Choice and Diversity (a New Framework for Schools)*. London: HMSO.

Dobson, J. and White, J. (1995) Towards the feminist firm. *Business Ethics Quarterly*, **5** (III), 463.

Docker-Drysdale, Barbara (1990) *The Provision of Primary Experience*. London: Free Association Books.

Fullan, M. (1993) *Change Forces: Probing the Depths of Educational Reform*. London: Falmer Press.

Gardner, H. (1991) *The Unschooled Mind*. London: Fontana.

Gilligan, C. (1982) *In a Different Voice – Psychological Theory and Women's Development*. Harvard, Cambridge, Mass, and London: Harvard University Press.

Goleman, D. (1996) *Emotional Intelligence*. London: Bloomsbury.

Hersch, R., Paolitto, D. and Reimer, J. (1979) *Promoting Moral Growth: Piaget to Kohlberg*. NY and London: Longman.

Hoffman, M. L. (1970) Moral development. In Mussen, P. H. (ed.), *Carmichael's Manual of Child Psychology*. New York: Wiley.

Hoffman, Martin. L. and Saltzstein, Herbert (1967) Parent discipline and the child's moral development. *Journal of Personality and Social Psychology*, **5** (1), 45–57.

Kozeki, B. and Berghammer, R. (1992) The role of empathy in the motivational structure of school children. *Personality and Individual Difference*, **13** (2).

Kyriacou, C. (1986) *Effective Teaching in Schools*. London: Simon & Schuster.

McPhail, P., Middleton, D. and Ingram, D. (1978) *Startline Moral Education in the Middle Years*. London: Longman.

Martin, C. (1993) Feelings, emotional empathy and decision making: listening to the voices of the heart. *Journal of Management Development*, **12** (5), 93.

Mulgan, G. (1996) Rights and wrongs. *Guardian*, 30 Oct. 1996.

Noddings, N. (1984) *Caring – A Feminine Approach to Ethics and Moral Education*. Berkeley, LA, and London: University of California Press.

Ofsted Inspection Report. *12/1/1996 School No 927/4063*.

Pring, R. (1984) *PSE in Curriculum*. Sevenoaks: Hodder & Stoughton.

Rogers, C. R. (1975) Empathic: an unappreciated way of being. *The Counselling Psychologist*, **5** (2), 2.

Rosenstein P. (1995) Parental levels of empathy as related to risk assessment in child protective services, *Child Abuse and Neglect*, **19** (11), 1349–60.

Rutter, M. (1981) *Maternal Deprivation Reassessed*. London: Penguin.

Rutter, M., Maughan, B., Mortimore, P. and Ouston, J. (1979) *15000 Hours*. Somerset: Open Books Publishing Ltd.

SCAA (1996a) *Consultation on Values in Education and the Community*. SCAA: Com/96/608.

SCAA (1996b) *Discussion papers NO6: Education for Adult Life: The Spiritual and Moral Development of Young People*. London: SCAA.

Straughan, R. (1989) *Beliefs, Behaviours and Education*. London: Cassell Educational.

Straughan, R. (1994) Are values under-valued? A reply to Christopher Ormell. *Journal of Moral Education*, **22** (1).

Tate, N. (1997) National identity and the school curriculum. *CPSE News,* Univ. of Leeds, No. 11, Summer 1997.

Taylor, M. (1997) How can research into values education help school practice? (Conference, *Values in the Curriculum,* London: Institute of Education, 10 April 1997).

Winkley, D. (1996) Towards the human school. (Conference, *Beyond Market Forces – Creating the Human School,* Birmingham: Westhill, 8 Feb. 1996).

Woodhead, C. (1997) Reported by John Carvel, *Guardian,* 26 Feb. 1997.

Wood, D. (1998) *How Children Think and Learn.* Oxford: Blackwell.

CHAPTER 10

Vocational education and SMSC

Stephen Bigger

INTRODUCTION

Today, there is widespread concern about gene manipulation, cloning and the use of human embryos in tissue culture as 'playing God'. These are difficult debates which show that work is not values-free, and that many of the issues arising are complex. The issue I discuss in this chapter is whether vocational education courses, and in particular GNVQs, currently give sufficient attention to values and moral behaviour in ways which encourage students to develop informed views on issues they are likely to meet in their working lives.

Current vocational courses have not traditionally explored values: yet the workplace is an area of values conflict, comprising a confusing array of expectations. Ambition is more favoured than selflessness, survival and competition stronger than principle. Social values such as teamwork are favoured, within an imperative not to 'rock the boat' by raising objections that might damage profitability. Customer satisfaction is driven by a fear of legislation, which can define its limits: the occasional unsatisfied customer without a legal complaint, while not desirable, is ultimately not a problem. The imposition of corporate social responsibility has been attacked (for example, and most notably by Milton Friedman) on the basis that business should be concerned only to make profits within the law (Mullins, 1996, pp. 315–18). Implicit values may differ from explicit ones: an institution's rhetoric may favour collaboration, honesty and efficiency, but reward those who through self-publicity falsely claim credit for other people's effective actions. Implicit values – like the hidden curriculum in school – are powerful. These revolve around the maintenance of personal power (or the illusion of power), the need to succeed and the desire for respect and recognition. All are self-centred values, promoting personal status. These provide the 'killer instinct' which may be seen as promotion potential.

Nevertheless, companies can and do have a degree of altruism beyond strict concerns of self-interest, giving in cash and kind to community projects such as *Business in the Community* (BITC) and the *Prince's Trust*, and to education–business partnerships (see Bigger, 1996, 2000b). Such companies do not aim for maximum profit at any cost but can go out of their way to contribute to the community in time, kind and even cash. Values at work do not feature in depth in business management, although there is a growing interest in business ethics. It is important for most companies that teams work effectively, and quality standards such as Investors in People emphasize the personal development of staff. Although difficult to achieve, business explores ideas such as that of 'learning companies' which encourage reflective practice.

Pupils need to be 'literate' in values, to question processes and to challenge abuses. This needs careful handling. If key values are about personal status and ambition, personal advancement will inevitably become the goal, rather than the well-being of the company. If however values are negotiated within the group, this can provide an agreed agenda for action. If, as individuals, we disagree with these values, we may experience personal tension and find it difficult to thrive. The less the tension between personal and professional aspects, the less the stress and the greater the motivation. Understanding these issues will help students choose careers which offer them a degree of fulfilment. They need *knowledge* (to be informed and to be aware of the potential consequences of attitudes and actions); *understanding of the issues* (through involvement in debate); and the personal and social *skills* to deal with difficult circumstances.

VOCATIONAL EDUCATION AND QUALIFICATIONS

Vocational education refers to the range of courses preparing students for general vocational areas or for specific careers. I am not here considering higher level National Vocational Qualifications (NVQs) at levels 4 or 5 (which have been slower to develop) or professional training (e.g. medical, legal or teacher training), as these fields demand separate treatment. Higher level courses tend to put greater emphasis on issues.

The vocational curriculum for school leavers and young people has fundamentally changed over the past decade. Up to the end of the 1980s, students either took academic courses (GCSE, or Advanced Level) or trained for specific occupations through BTEC, RSA or City & Guilds courses. Generally these had to be taken in Further Education (FE) Colleges and were not offered in schools. Provision was 'incoherent and confused' (Tomlinson, 1997, p. 5). The recession in job opportunities for 16-year-old school leavers in the late 1980s led to greater numbers entering FE and an urgent need to provide suitable courses. GNVQs (General National Vocational Qualifications) were piloted in three areas – Business, Art and Design, and Health and Social Care. These were rapidly extended to include a larger range of vocational areas. Unlike previous vocational courses, GNVQs were designed to be general within a vocational sector, not designed to prepare students for one particular career. Unlike NVQs, designed to accredit competence in the workplace in real work tasks, GNVQs were for use in the classroom. NVQs operate at different levels, level 1 being the most basic; GNVQs were similarly designed, although levels 1–3 were eventually named 'foundation', 'intermediate' and 'advanced'. Today, these three GNVQ levels constitute a sizeable proportion of the work of FE Colleges and increasingly of sixth forms, as my evaluation of GNVQs in Oxfordshire revealed (Bigger, 1997).

From these early stages, NVQs and GNVQs were regarded as equivalent to academic qualifications, and a chart of equivalences offered in official literature (reproduced in Tomlinson, 1997, p. 2). In particular, establishing the advanced GNVQ as equivalent to two A levels was given high government priority with university admissions for successful advanced GNVQ students officially encouraged. Annual reports since that time indicate that this has been generally successful, with the new universities taking the majority of students onto vocational courses. (See Bigger, 1996; and 2000b on vocational initiatives in Birmingham). GNVQs are by no means a marginal sector, and offer real opportunities for progression. The educational experience of students within it deserves rigorous scrutiny.

The GNVQ assessment model was imported from NVQs, largely because the task of developing GNVQs was given to the National Council for Vocational Qualifications (NCVQ) which used its already established NVQ competency assessment model. There are complications and implications in this. The assessment model was designed to record evidence of competence as demonstrated in the workplace; but GNVQs are for the most part delivered in the classroom with few opportunities for on-the-job assessment. Using projects and simulations does not strictly match workplace assessment. Secondly, assessment determines the syllabus, so only aspects which offer assessment opportunities are strictly relevant. Assessment of performance shapes content. Thirdly, a GNVQ syllabus does not have a body of knowledge which needs to be known and understood, such as might raise issues and values. Smithers (1997, p. 57) complains that the GNVQ approach 'lacks precision, is fragmentary, does not prioritise, and devalues knowledge and understanding'. In general, he contends, 'the flaw runs so deep that it will require a radical re-think to get us back on track' (p. 56). Such a rethink is helped by the merger between NCVQ and SCAA (the School Curriculum and Assessment Authority, representing the academic curriculum) into the Qualifications and Curriculum Authority (QCA) from 1 October 1997.

Much of the potential of GNVQ for motivating students through active learning was not realized in practice through problematic delivery based both on inexperience and on lack of clear central guidance. Criticism was severe (Smithers, 1997; Tomlinson, 1997; Hyland, 1997), both of policy and performance. The assessment system for vocational qualifications involves Performance Criteria (PCs) which measure how people perform rather than what they know. Each PC has to be demonstrated, assessed and signed off by an assessor before the qualification can be awarded. Teachers inexperienced with PCs found the system inscrutable and infuriating as there is no real place for professional judgement. GNVQs are explicit assessment regimes, revolving around performance criteria, not courses revolving around content. Nevertheless, assessment can be creatively planned and delivered in line with sound educational principles, with skills (measured by PCs) placed alongside knowledge, understanding and attitudes to form a coherent integrated whole which encourages analysis and reflection. Official policy needs to learn from and incorporate good practice into routine procedures.

REFLECTING ON WORK

This chapter contends that in considering a way forward for GNVQs, QCA should encourage and require students to consider issues in a rigorous way and come to some understanding of the values which operate in the workplace, and also of their own developing values. Vocational education is more than skills training. It should raise questions of what kind of workforce we have and need, whether it is socially responsible and morally aware, proactive or merely compliant, knowing where to draw the line in terms of probity and acceptability. Business ethics need to consider the pressures upon companies in a complex economic world, for companies have to compete and survive; however an education which explores values and choices can develop building blocks of commercial ethics which, as these students advance in their careers, could influence future policy and strategy.

Preparing young people for work engages questions of how we regard work what values are implied within work and what analysis of values can be addressed to work situations. Work can be viewed as a chore, a necessary evil for money or as a pleasure which brings its own rewards. Classroom activities and discussion might focus on the following different types of issue:

- the notion of a worthwhile job (viz., philosophical);
- doing a job as well as we are able (viz., spiritual);
- beneficial and predatory jobs (viz., ethical, moral);
- working with and relating to others (viz., social);
- jobs which expand people's minds and experiences (viz., cultural).

Such discussions closely relate to the SMSC agenda. They engage students, as future employees, in asking fundamental questions about what we do in work and why. Rigorous debate will challenge attitudes and develop a range of sensitivities to the perspectives of others, raising questions of race, cultural identity, gender and disability, for example. Young people have to balance the need for employment and money (even if the job is not ideal) with their ideal career choices which may require further study and training. Student employment can be helpfully analysed using the questions above: these are not their final career choices and their main motivation for doing them is the money they earn, so they can be critical without destroying their motivation. The lessons they learn in this will in due course be applied to their major career choices. Thereafter, the sensitivities they develop will affect the way they behave in employment and contribute to the corporate ethos. If they become managers and decision-makers, their habit of personal reflection will influence the nature of the institution in which they work. Our question, then, of what kind of workforce we need cannot be taken lightly. Compliant employees who do not think for themselves will not ultimately provide their companies with initiative and ideas. QCA, in developing vocational syllabuses, needs to allow students to ask penetrating questions of policy and practice, and of objectives and outcomes.

A PERSON-CENTRED MODEL OF SMSC

Within QCA, GNVQ planners can gain great benefit from cross-fertilization of ideas originally associated with SCAA and academic subjects. We are primarily concerned here with SMSC, promoted by Ofsted (1994) after initiatives by NCC (1993) and SCAA (1996). We seek here to determine whether spiritual, moral, social and cultural issues can provide an agenda for action for GNVQ courses. Thomas (in Bigger and Thomas, 1999) suggested four simple questions as a key to experiential learning relating to SMSC. Each question provides a stimulus for ideas, choices and issues. Each relates primarily to one SMSC area, offering together coverage of all four. Each is developed in detail below. These questions are:

- *Who am I?* Students need to become aware of self-image, self-worth, issues of identity and self-realization. What kind of person am I? What kind of person do I want to become? These are identified as *spiritual* issues.
- *How do I relate?* How can I define and develop my relationships? What value do I give to others and how does this affect my behaviour to them? How should I behave towards others? These are *moral* questions which raise issues of responsibility, people orientation and business ethics.
- *How do I fit in?* How does my life fit alongside other people's lives? How do I gain approval? What groups do I relate to? What social rules and expectations do I need to take account of? And what kind of response is proper to these? These provide a *social* agenda.
- *How do I live?* How can my way of life be defined, described and analysed? Can we come to appreciate what is positive in our background and culture? Can we learn to appreciate other cultures and lifestyles that we encounter? This offers a *cultural* dimension.

In the following sections, we consider each of these in turn to determine their potential to enrich vocational education.

'WHO AM I?' – SPIRITUAL ASPECTS

A central issue here is the distinction between 'spiritual' and 'religious'. In exploring the contribution of religious education to the world of work (Bigger, 1990, 1992a, 1992b) I argued for a broad view of religious education which recognized religious pluralism and personal experience of life. I take a similar broad view of spirituality also (Bigger and Brown, 1999, pp. 3–15): that the 'spiritual' refers to our contemplation of ourselves, our emotions and personality, our commitments, our place in the cosmos and the meaning we ascribe to our experiences. The contrary view is that the traditional links between spirituality and religion are so close that spirituality can only assume religious belief. However, not all who attend church, mosque or temple can be said to be 'spiritual' – motives and understandings are many and varied. Traditionally, the spiritual path was a personal quest for truth, holistic in its desire to take account of all personal experiences and insights. In today's plural world we seek to express inner truth and personal vision in a variety of ways, which may draw on secular as well as religious insights as we contemplate who and what kind of people we are, and how we relate to the rest of the world. Not all religious people reflect in this way: religion might involve uncritical obedience, strengthened by social conformity. If religious people need not be spiritual, and atheists can be spiritual, these two terms are clearly not interchangeable (see McKenzie, 1998, for a critique of Carr,

1996). The difference between them is crucial to our definition of the spiritual: that is, personal reflection on life in ways that transform and inspire everyday existence.

It is religious 'vocations' ('vocation', meaning 'calling') which have given us the term 'vocational' in secular contexts. 'Vocation' as a metaphor for the inner drive to succeed in a field can be helpful in secular employment if it promotes the view of a job as a commitment, involving motivation, enjoyment, fulfilment and self-esteem. Not all jobs manage this. Religions sometimes regard work as a form of prayerfulness, that people worship through what they do and give it highest value. In a secular context, work can similarly be viewed as self-expression, a service to others, a quality activity which transforms the lives of those involved and those benefiting, and is viewed as having great value. Buddhists might refer to this as *right-mindfulness*. Handy (1997, p. 127) describes the possibility of a worker being 'an instrument of the sublime', stimulating imagination and bringing out the best in people. Quality in work is an inner drive to do a job well, for its own sake and for the sake of people involved, with commitment and motivation. Reflection on the nature and purpose of work and its effects is close to what a Buddhist might call *right livelihood*.

Vocational education needs to address how meaningfully we view our work exploring concepts such as commitment, motivation, value, worth, relationships, respect, esteem, job satisfaction, personal fulfilment and self-realization. This features more strongly in higher level work, which explores issues relating to the individual (including individual differences, personality and perception) and on organizational processes (including the nature of work motivation and job satisfaction) (see Mullins, 1996, parts 2 and 6). It draws on Maslow's hierarchy of needs (Maslow, 1968) which placed freedom, justice, orderliness, challenge and stimulation as preconditions for need satisfaction; and above this in rising order, love and a sense of belonging, self-esteem and, at the top, self-actualization (involving meaningfulness, truth, goodness, beauty and self-sufficiency). White (1997) linked work with personal well-being; Fisher (1999) uses the concept of spiritual health. Work can be fulfilling, undertaken with dignity, providing personal commitment to a job worth doing and personal growth which is at the same time intellectual, emotional, social and ethical. This is an ideal not reached by many jobs today, but this gives all the more reason for GNVQs to tackle it.

'HOW DO I RELATE?' – MORAL ASPECTS

From a secure understanding of our identity and ideals – who we are and what we want to become – the employee relates to a range of other people – colleagues, senior managers, trainees, customers and other stakeholders. The web of relationships and responsibilities within which an employee functions raises moral issues that need resolving individually, which implies understanding of principles and experience of their practical application. Mullins (1996, p. 320), for higher level (HND) students, lists a range of areas for discussion including personal ethics, organizational responsibilities, workers' rights and responsibilities, staff relationships, consumer safety, age/race/sex discrimination, codes of conduct, accounting practices, energy utilization, animal rights and corrupt practices. These could be summarized as rights, responsibilities, honesty, accountability and fair dealing. GNVQ students also would benefit from working out the implications of these within their own sector. If a decision made on ethical grounds makes a company less competitive it could endanger it; yet ethical policies need not be a financial liability, particularly in the longer term where new opportunities may be found by creative managers trained and experienced in ethical business strategies. Some companies, such as Bodyshop and the Co-operative Bank, use their ethical policies as helpful public relations.

Business ethics has global implications. We might question whether trade with the developing world is fair, whether policies are environmentally friendly and sustainable, whether sales techniques are fair and advertisements true, and whether a product is safe. These are matters of company policy, with senior managers and directors held accountable both in law and public opinion; they have to tread an uncertain path between profitability and public pressure (which might ultimately affect profits and even survival). To study values in international settings, the Lasswell Value Dictionary (see Montgomery, 1997) organizes critique of international development around the terms power, enlightenment, wealth, well-being, skill, affection, respect, rectitude. Analysis is never simple, since measures are imprecise, but affection (that is, loyalty and commitment), respect (between ethnic communities) and rectitude (i.e., agreed moral standards) are particularly interesting.

Including a moral dimension in vocational courses is complex and problematic. Some see moral behaviour in terms of 'virtues' (Carr, 1991; Skillen, 1997; Ridley, 1996). Moral standards presented as absolutes (i.e. deontological) make clear what is considered to be right and wrong, what *ought* to be done, lose credibility where circumstances are more grey than black and white, and where not all agree on the standards. Training courses might rather look to the *consequences* of particular actions (teleological), to judge issues of fairness (justice), honesty and positive relationships. Here, moral action may be seen as a matter of judgement with pro and anti points being balanced against each other. Tensions and differences of opinion could occur when a line manager makes demands that a subordinate finds unacceptable. Another view that might be taken is one of moral relativism – that morals are based on what society at large feels acceptable, whatever the personal sensitivities of individuals. Society at large is not always morally sensitive, and there have been in recent history political systems where discrimination (for example racism or sexism) has been accepted as the norm. Case studies could enable students to analyse ethical issues from different standpoints, to examine moral principles and society's expectations, including concepts such as justice, honesty, trust and truthfulness, and the possible consequences of actions and prejudices.

Encouraging employee empowerment to create a motivated workforce can be explored through role play and simulation in vocational courses. These could set up situations in which consultation and collaboration are valued, people are involved in decisions, individual potential is developed and a sense of belonging is promoted. GNVQs were designed to use active learning strategies. This 'learning by doing' adds to experience as they work out problems, work with fellow students and develop skills, competence and confidence. Role play and simulations can confirm stereotypes and prejudices and if uncontrolled can give opportunity to the bully and do psychological harm to others. Teachers can turn this around into effective learning, and help students to become more reflective. Much of our view of life is based on superficial stereotypes. We may be locked into a phoney world-view in which our attitudes to race, gender, class, occupations, age and so on are unreflectively fossilized. To break through such stereotypes, students need to humanize and personalize situations. By developing imaginary scenarios, they put flesh on the bones of employers, employees and customers in the simulation so the characters appear as real people. This builds up respect for other people and a sense of their worth and value. We have seen the opposite too often – depersonalizing people, identifying them as groups and not as individuals who might then be subject to inhuman treatment. GNVQ needs teachers who facilitate, guide, explain and challenge.

'HOW DO I FIT IN?' – SOCIAL ASPECTS

If reflection on how we relate to others is essential to moral understanding, balancing our individual ambitions with the aspirations and needs of others is part of what we mean by society. In employment, individual talent and ambition is normally harnessed to group or team success for the benefit of people as a whole – promoting the health, safety, comfort or potential of others within the community. How we fit into this network is considered next.

Society is socially constructed. Our view of it will depend on our assumptions of membership, of who we regard to be 'in' and 'out'. Society is made up of a range of different communities and constituencies, some local, some ethnic, some religious. The local community may contain a mix of generations, religions, backgrounds and ethnic groups. It may work well together, with community activities and self-help groups, or it may be dislocated and full of tension. The locality is a network of jobs, career opportunities and training schemes. Employers may have close links with the community, working with schools and supporting community projects. Ethnic minority students on vocational courses may require support not only in English but also in social assumptions and practices, whether they be Punjabi, Polish or Persian speakers. Whether employees or customers, they may need support to fit in, with others understanding their point of view and able to help them resolve problems. For religious communities, religious observance and festivals are substantial issues in the workplace; and with so many shades of opinion in all religions, enough information is needed to avoid stereotyping people as all having the same or extreme views. Misunderstandings of attitudes, body language and way of life can happen: a consideration of multicultural issues is needed in GNVQ to shed new light on relationships and stereotypes which would otherwise hamper effective work relationships.

The term 'society' is problematic: xenophobic as well as inclusive pluralist views of society can be found. Equal opportunities raise issues such as prejudice and justice, bigotry and respect, fairness and inequality, hostility and friendship, segregation and communication, betrayal and trust, fear of strangeness and appreciation of difference, ignorance and awareness.

Education fosters tolerance but this is a troublesome word (Burwood and Wyeth, 1998): I tolerate someone who is 'out' rather than 'in'; 'I am tolerant' has come to suggest open-mindedness, but still has an edge of accepting what is not enthusiastically embraced. In other words, tolerance is a negative value and not a celebration of difference. Business, as it is legally required to do, has adopted equal opportunities policies and its monitoring forms, although some ethnic minority groups experience high unemployment rates, and women tend to dominate lower-paid jobs. The discourses of feminism and anti-racism are now powerful and well articulated (Griffiths and Troyna, 1995; Ashcroft, Bigger and Coates, 1996). Recognition that work needs to be balanced with family life (as opposed to workaholic cultures) removes undesirable social pressures but cannot be taken for granted. Yet these issues are barely covered in GNVQ.

Career choice is a serious task, requiring information and experience, with aspiration needing to be balanced with realism, with personal strategies which encourage adaptability and flexibility encouraged. The current thrust towards lifelong learning creates second chances for people without qualifications. How to develop job satisfaction and motivation should be high on an employer's agenda: as Winch notes (1998, p. 377) this 'touches on the heart of what any society is about'. Particular jobs offer status: 'a good job' assumes a reasonable salary, enjoyable work and a degree of tenure. People are ambitious to aspire to a 'fitting' job but being unemployed carries stigma. Vocational education needs some discussion of why people work, their views on work and what they regard as 'fitting' long before they begin to make choices at 16. Career choices, to be informed, require realistic research about the nature of the work, about entry requirements and competition for jobs, and about job satisfaction. There are more business studies students than jobs they can progress to. Many aspire to be doctors, vets, barristers and media stars, but few make it. For young people, this is a crucial discussion.

HOW DO I LIVE? – CULTURAL ASPECTS

There are two rather different concepts of culture, each of which has implications for the role of vocational education in SMSC. Culture can refer to the arts (e.g. theatre, art galleries, dance and music) and heritage industries (museums, castles and stately homes) – and there are vocational implications in these. The arts are much less Eurocentric than they once were, with contributions the world over highly valued (although concepts such as 'primitive' art still survive, and it may not always be the artist who benefits financially). Heritage is essentially political, with conflicts seen from the winner's point of view, resulting in history from a Western viewpoint with underlying colonial values. Historical interpretation is an expression of ideology, leaving a very thin line between history and propaganda. Potential workers in the heritage industries need the skills to understand that historical claims are rarely objective and values-free. A vocational course such as leisure and tourism could offer a critique of such issues: the students, as they become heritage workers, will face a range of questions and of situations which require sensitivity that they will only have if they are informed of the issues through their training.

Culture can refer also to a group's whole way of life with its distinctive belief system and world-view, and we speak of ethnic minority cultures, youth culture and so on. All employees benefit if they have an understanding of cultural differences, since this helps them relate to colleagues and customers, so these should be strongly represented in GNVQ programmes. There is some literature growing on intercultural understanding in business. Lewis (1996) speaks of faulty information, cultural myopia and bias, commenting: 'Managers must have multinational skills. They will have to work shoulder to shoulder with many nationalities in the global village of the twenty-first century. They must understand them, speak to them, co-operate with them, handle them, not lose out to them, yet like and praise them. These are our cultural challenges' (pp. 310–11). Specific jobs such as the travel industry and the caring professions deal routinely with people from many backgrounds. An understanding of religion ensures awareness of high days and holidays, food preferences and dress codes (Bigger, 1995). Much embarrassment can be saved if we are aware of and respect other people's customs and expectations. Other people's cultures contain a story: of past events, of heroes, prophets and villains, perhaps expressed through song, drama, dance, music and festivals. Sharing these stories is one of the delights of intercultural understanding.

How to prepare people has proved problematic. Confrontation, accusing people of being racist or prejudiced, sets up resistance but has featured in the past in racism awareness courses. Gradual 'permeation' of these issues takes time and can be lost in the face of competing agendas. Superficial learning in students disappears when social expectations change and new buzzwords appear. Finding out about other cultures is important, for people need to be informed, but does not change racist attitudes (Bigger, 2000a). Anti-racists stress that the dominant culture (in our case the white middle class) marginalizes others to maintain its own advantage. Kincheloe and Steinberg (1997) in a US context, prefer the term 'critical multiculturalism'. Boyd (1996) argues that moral responsibility needs to encourage the dominant 'to acknowledge their embeddedness in a culture that oppresses others'. Applebaum (1997) argues that our moral responsibility is not absolved by our claim to not have racist intentions, if we at the same time wish to enjoy the benefits of dominance. Discrimination can, in other words, be a product of a system even if individuals are not conscious of its existence, with minorities let down by policies, procedures and accountability processes as well as by individuals. Eradicating discrimination from the workplace may demand deep-rooted and structural changes.

GNVQ courses need to develop an awareness that culture enriches life through history and the arts, but cannot be simplistically presented. Students need to understand that behind heritage lies a political ideology, and that the movement from Eurocentric (and mainly male) art to more representative forms has consequent issues of stereotype and status. Above all, GNVQ students need to understand the cultural perspectives and expectations of different ethnic, national and religious groups around the world, as these will impact on their professional lives at many points. Multicultural and anti-racist studies, not currently found in GNVQs, are essential. Although course handbooks can help to some extent, appreciation of other cultures comes through meeting a wide range of people from different backgrounds and engaging in non-threatening discussions using visits and visiting speakers.

CONCLUSION

We urgently need to recognize that vocational education is more than skills training and enable GNVQ students to have a broader educational experience. Students need to be critical about the values, policies and procedures used in employment and in their sector in particular. The concept of SMSC, currently in use by QCA in relation to academic courses including the National Curriculum, provides a helpful starting point for future curriculum review which is widely viewed as urgent. The revised courses need to incorporate issues of personal motivation, enrichment and meaningful work; of responsibility, moral behaviour, ethics, positive relationships and an empowering ethos; of respect for others, with particular regard to those of different social and ethnic backgrounds, enabling students to develop a sound understanding of equal opportunities; and open, appreciative but critically aware understanding of cultural events and artefacts and the ability to both promote and interpret these.

This implies that GNVQs will become more than assessment frameworks. They need to develop clearly articulated syllabuses which emphasize knowledge and understanding relevant to the vocational sector but which also encourage and enable students to be challenged by issues focusing on their attitudes to work and their careers, on their responsibilities to others, on their handling of the social networks they will encounter and on developing respect for other people and their lifestyles.

REFERENCES

Applebaum, B. (1997) Good liberal intentions are not enough! Racism, intentions and moral responsibility. *Journal of Moral Education*, **26** (4), 409–21.

Ashcroft, K., Bigger, S. and Coates, D. (1996) *Researching into Equal Opportunities in Colleges and Universities*. London: Kogan Page.

Bigger, S. F. (1990) Religious education and economic awareness: a TVEI project. *Journal of Beliefs and Values*, **11** (1), 15–17.

Bigger, S. F. (1992a) Religious education for today's world: RE and TVEI. *Journal of Beliefs and Values*, **13** (1).

Bigger, S. F. (1992b) Work-related religious education. *Resource*, **15** (1), 6–8.

Bigger, S. F. (1995) Challenging religious education in a multicultural world. *Journal of Beliefs and Values*, **16** (2), 11–18.

Bigger, S. F. (1996) Post-16 Compact in Birmingham. In Abraham, M., Bird, J. and Stennett, A. (eds), *Further and Higher Education Partnerships: The Future for Collaboration*. Buckingham: Open University Press.

Bigger, S. F. (1997) *GNVQ in Oxfordshire*. Abingdon: Heart of England TEC.

Bigger, S. F. (2000a) Spiritual and religious education and antiracism. In Leicester, M., Mogdil, S. and Mogdil, C. (eds), *Education, Culture and Values*, Vol. V. London: Falmer, pp. 15–24.

Bigger, S. F. (2000b) Motivating students to succeed. In Leicester, M.,

Mogdil, S. and Mogdil, C. (eds), *Education, Culture and Values*, Vol. III. London: Falmer, pp. 85–95.

Bigger, S. F. and Brown, E. (1999) *Spiritual, Moral, Social and Cultural Education*. London: David Fulton.

Bigger, S. F. and Thomas, D. (1999) Drama. In S. Bigger and E. Brown (1999) *Spiritual, Moral, Social and Cultural Education*. London: David Fulton, pp. 26–35.

Boyd, D. (1996) A question of adequate aims. *Journal of Moral Education*, **25** (1), 21–9.

Burwood, L. and Wyeth, R. (1998) Should schools promote toleration?, *Journal of Moral Education*, **27** (4), 465–73.

Carr, D. (1991) *Educating the Virtues: An Essay on the Philosophical Psychology of Moral Development and Education*. London/NY: Routledge.

Carr, D. (1996) Rival conceptions of spiritual education, *Journal of Philosophy of Education*. **30** (2), 159–78.

Fisher, J.W. (1999) Helps to fostering students' spiritual health. *International Journal of Children's Spirituality*, **4** (1), 29–49.

Griffiths, M. and Troyna, B. (1995) *Anti-racism, Culture and Social Justice in Education*. Stoke-on-Trent: Trentham.

Handy, C. (1997) *The Hungry Spirit: Beyond Capitalism – A Quest for Purpose in the Modern World*. London: Hutchinson.

Hyland, T. (1997) Reconsidering competence. *Journal of Philosophy of Education*, **31** (3), 491–503.

Kincheloe, J. L. and Steinberg, S. R. (1997) *Changing Multiculturalism*. Buckingham/Philadelphia: Open University Press.

Lewis, R. D. (1996) *When Cultures Collide: Managing Successfully Across Cultures*. London: Nicholas Brealey.

McKenzie, J. (1998) David Carr on religious knowledge and spiritual education. *Journal of Philosophy of Education*, **32** (3), 409–27.

Maslow, A. (1968) *Towards a Psychology of Being* (2nd edn.), New York: Van Nostrand Reinhold.

Montgomery, J. D. (1997) *Values in Education: Social Capital Formation in Asia and the Pacific*. Hollis, NH: Hollis Publishing.

Mullins, L. J. (1996) *Management and Organisational Behaviour* (4th edn.), London: Pitman.

NCC (1993) *Spiritual and Moral Development* (Discussion Paper 3). London: SCAA.

Ofsted (1994) *Spiritual, Moral, Social and Cultural Development*. London: Ofsted.

Ridley, M. (1996) *The Origins of Virtue*. London: Viking/Penguin.

SCAA (1996) *Education for Adult Life: The Spiritual and Moral Development of Young People*. London: SCAA.

Skillen, T. (1997) Can virtue be taught – especially these days? *Journal of Philosophy of Education*, **31** (3), 375–93.

Smithers, A. (1997) A critique of NVQs and GNVQs. In Tomlinson, S. (ed.) (1997), *Education 14–19: Critical Perspectives*. London: Athlone Press, pp. 55–70.

Tomlinson, S. (ed.) (1997) *Education 14–19: Critical Perspectives*. London: Athlone Press.

White, J. (1997) Education, work and well-being. *Journal of Philosophy of Education*, **31** (2), 233–47.

Winch, C. (1998) Two rival conceptions of vocational education: Adam Smith and Friedrich List. *Oxford Review of Education*, **24** (3), 365–78.

CHAPTER 11

For richer? For poorer? For worker? – For citizen!

Bill Law

This chapter sets out principles for careers education in schools. But it does so to emphasize their common ground with other areas of spiritual, moral, social and cultural education (SMSC). It means touching on ideological, curriculum and theoretical issues; they are set out in the first half of the chapter. The second half sets out curriculum-management frameworks developed in response to those issues.

The chapter does not assume that careers education should be given more resources and importance; instead, it argues that careers educators and their colleagues – not least in SMSC work – should work more closely together.

IDEOLOGIES FOR CAREERS EDUCATION

I was once, long ago, a religious education teacher. I have never quite lost the feeling that careers education is the same thing! In both roles I talked with students about facing up to dilemmas, making choices and wondering why one course of action might be more worthwhile than another.

Both hats have ideological feathers. Careers education has at least three.

A humanist ideology

In talking about work, it seems to me that students and their families are speaking of what they value: making money from work, feeling safe in it, maintaining friends through it, getting respect by it, being interested in it and feeling important because of it. In one way or another, work is about personal well-being, self-realization and finding value in its rewards. But taking available employment is – sometimes – how *not* to get what you most value. Then, people may turn to alternative lifestyles – enterprising or downshifting – as rich dude, poor woman, beggar-man ... or thief. It is all work.

Times change; but careers education has been driven, from its beginning, by a commitment to help individuals to make such choices in a personally rewarding way (Bates, 1989).

A liberal ideology
Work is a social act; a worker is not just an individual, he or she is a
participant in a community. Work makes a difference to other people:
dependants, colleagues, paymasters and 'customers'. Your choice of work is
influenced by people you know; it introduces you to new people with new
interests; and it influences the well-being of people you will never meet and
whose interests you may never even consider.

Career is, then, not just a lifestyle choice; consciously or unconsciously, it
is a series of social, moral and even political acts.

It is not hard, then, to find among careers educators an ideology, which
seeks to alert and enable students for participation in social change (Law,
1996b).

A vocational ideology
Careers work is about who gets to do what in the labour market. It therefore
raises issues for economic performance. Careers educators are asked to
attend to national competitiveness and to the 'skills' needed to promote it.

A consequence is that careers education can now be seen as a branch of
vocational education. An important contribution to society is sometimes
claimed to be its economic benefits. The business world, though capable of
spinning a humanist web around its case, exerts much economically
significant and skill-driven influence on careers education (Law, 1999a).

WHAT IS CAREERS EDUCATION FOR?

Until recently, thoughtful careers educators were fairly free to explore the
practical usefulness of all this. There is a range of ways for thinking about
outcomes (though there is no *exact* correspondence between the following
types of outcome and the foregoing ideologies).

Procedural learning
There are some nuts-and-bolts career-management procedures which should
not be neglected. Students need to:

- get hold of career information
- identify their own preferences
- implement a choice in making applications for education, training and work
- effectively present themselves for selection
- manage the ensuing transition.

There are big questions here – about what constitutes 'information',
'preference' and 'choice'! Leaving that aside, the list describes procedural
learning for career management.

In schools this work is often squeezed into specialized careers education or
made part of the already mercilessly overloaded personal, social and health
education programme.

Underpinning learning
Schools can enable a more extensive structure of knowledge, helping students
to:

- say why they pursue one preference rather than others
- appreciate who else has an interest in what they do
- anticipate the probable consequences of their action – for themselves and for other people
- know whether they are ready to live with those risks and to deal with them
- understand how working roles and other roles are interdependent
- consider what might persuade them to change their mind
- know what else they might do.

This is knowledge called up by open questions, such as: 'What gave you the idea of doing that?' or 'Is there anything that you would like to ask me?' It underpins career management by developing an understanding of how the world works; this includes knowing something about what people do – and why; and an appreciation of what I do – and why. It will not come through worksheet-driven lessons, squeezed to the edge of the timetable.

It can come from reflective engagement in the National Curriculum. Some students would be surprised to hear that the National Curriculum can be useful to them in this way. But its stories give us each a clue to our own, its concepts help us understand how things work and its values fertilize in each of us the growth of an inner life.

Enabling such learning is subtle, layered and dynamic, calling on high orders of teaching ability. And so, even students who do well in exams and SATS – or who may be able to paste up a plausible application and fake a convincing interview – can still be at a loss when asked a question about what gave them the idea and why it is so important to them.

Meta-learning

If education does not help students to transfer knowledge, from the inside to outside 'the classroom', then it is not working! In order to transfer knowledge, students need to know where in their lives they can use it (Law, 1999b). For example, to use biological knowledge in order to work on risks to the environment, people need to be able to imagine being 'there', doing 'this' with some 'Friends of the Earth'. Biology is useful knowledge; but you would need to know in what sorts of *settings*, on what sorts of *tasks*, with what sorts of *relationships* its knowledge can be used. Then a person can:

- scan the knowledge for relevant information, skill and concepts, and work out what more they need to know
- organize what they know, so that it applies to the matter in hand – this usually means moving across 'subject' boundaries (no subject, not even biology, is ever enough)
- focus on what is important, often by appreciating the differences between my own and other people's points of view
- then work out how the knowledge can be used – trying it out, receiving feedback, understanding the meaning and use of both 'success' and 'failure'.

To make these gains is to transfer learning out of the classroom and laboratory; and it is to learn how to learn. It is called meta-learning because, once acquired, it can change what a person sees, feels and does – about everything.

LIFE-ROLE RELEVANCE IN A CHANGING WORLD

We have moved from focused to expanded conceptions of careers work. It is at the expanded level that boundaries between careers and other learning break down. This is learning, for both enjoyment and effectiveness, in *any* life role:

- In its *settings* – not just in employment but in voluntary work, active citizenship and having fun.
- In its *tasks* – not just for being competitive but for solving all kinds of problems and making all kinds of decisions.
- In its *relationships* – not just with colleagues and customers but with friends and partners.

In careers education much of this learning is gained in work experience, in design-and-make and mini-enterprise projects. There are many more opportunities – relevant to contemporary working life – in theatre and media activity, in leisure and sports activity as well as in environmental, social and other voluntary work. A lot of this relates to SMSC. All need strong links with mainstream curriculum.

Table 11.1 lists possible topics for life-role relevance. Teachers use such topics to enliven interest, engage motivation and embed learning. Where they can establish links between subjects – assigned long blocks of time, with community involvement and real-time engagement – then, and only then, students move from underpinning learning to meta-learning.

Table 11.1 Topics for life-role relevance

Global economy	Why should you care who in the world makes your trainers?
Deregulation	Suppose Rupert Murdoch's satellite TV company made a bid for Ourtown United?
Environment	Suppose you could live near Walt Disney World in Florida or a slate mine in N. Wales. Which?
Third World	How much would it cost to give your pet better food than Bangladeshis get?
Technology	Which work in Ourtown employs most people? ... pays most wages? ... makes most profit?
Markets	Why is Ronald McDonald such a good friend? And what is he feeding you?
Pensions	Why are some grandmothers able to afford such a good time? And what about the others?
Present and future	What do you want to remember to tell your grandchildren about your life now?
Health risks	Who lives longest? Why? Is it fair? What can anybody do about it?
The labour economy	Which work do you most depend on? Is it high paid? What is coolest in Britannia?
Communication	How do you find friends worth having on the net? How would you know?
Recruitment	What kind of people get to be bosses in business? Who decides? Does it matter?
Techniques of persuasion	What can you find out from advertising? Does anybody pay any attention?
The media	Does it matter what newspapers say about rock musicians, soap stars and politicians?
Equal opportunities	What are your rights on where you live and what you do? Who else has those rights?

Table 11.1 *cont.*

Past and present	Who do you know who can tell you what really happened in the 1960s?
Lifelong learning	You are compelled to come to school, but you cannot stay forever! Who says so? Any why?
Substance use and abuse	Who should be able to get hold of any drug, if they are convinced it does good?

To summarize:

- There is much common ground between SMSC and an expanded concept of careers education.
- It is not learning to add to the National Curriculum; it is the National Curriculum looked at in another way.
- It depends on being able freely to explore and use subject learning.
- Effectiveness depends on making links – subject to subject, curriculum to community and learning to life.
- Then what students learn at school reminds them of life, and what they meet in life reminds them of school.
- With such links knowledge can be transferred and continuously reapplied – as worker, friend, consumer, partner, parent and citizen.
- Learning for one role enables action in others.
- Without such links, even successful procedural learning is shallow and deceptive – at worst *self*-deceptive.

The life-role relevant claims of citizenship are currently being asserted (QCA, 1999). But it is an open question where people can make most difference to the quality of life: in politics? in employment? in the family? ... or in the mall? We will come back to citizenship, at the end of the chapter.

CHANGING POLICY FOR A CHANGING WORLD

Here is a nice irony: if all of the health, lifestyle and environmental learning we seek to enable pays off, we will soon be welcoming students into our schools, whose active working lives will extend into the *twenty-second* century. Who knows now what they will need to know then?

We know about the trends. Technological change means that, whatever new thing you want to do, the probability is that you need to learn something new. Social change means that the expectations, feedback, modelling and other influences that shape you are no longer primarily family and neighbourhood based. Change is also biographic; and what we mean by 'self' must make coherent sense of increasingly fragmentary experience. That is the case for meta-learning – learning how to learn, as a basis for lifelong learning.

In this respect, curriculum development has not been going well. The first decade of the National Curriculum has been dominated by the question: 'What shall we teach?' It is a question for content, and has led to the formulation of learning as lists of subjects and targets. In this situation, it has called upon a deep professionalism to link subject to subject, learning to community or anything to life-role relevance. A subject-based, target-driven curriculum pulls the other way – fragmenting learning. What curriculum puts asunder students must somehow join together.

Assigning careers education special statutory status further fragments learning (Law, 1997), as will making citizenship a separate entitlement (DfEE, 1998). We must hope that other legitimate interests do not pursue counter-claims. Tussling for special interests is not good long-term thinking and – ultimately – pits everybody against everybody. That way lies madness.

But things are looking up. The QCA is now concerned with the more fundamental question: 'Why should we try to help anybody to learn anything?' Its response is 'a new agenda', which seeks to relate the curriculum to personal, social and health education, citizenship, careers and to SMSC (QCA, 1998).

There is a wide and overlapping range of concerns including:

- career development
- citizenship
- consumer roles
- creative and cultural roles
- domestic, family, parent and partner roles
- enterprise
- environmental matters
- equal opportunity
- finance, tax, debt and welfare
- health – including exercise, diet and the use and abuse of substances
- leisure
- media pressures
- race, racism and ethnicity
- relationships
- sex and love life
- thinking, studying, learning and learning to learn
- values and beliefs.

This is an agenda for life-role relevance in education. The question now is one for curriculum management in schools: 'Where is the framework for integrating the diversity?'

The second half of this chapter sets out theory-based management frameworks for career learning. It would be a big step forward if such analyses proved to be useful to other life-role-relevant concerns. Let us see.

REVIEWING CURRICULUM CONTENT

A tool used by careers co-ordinators, for reviewing the content of their programmes, is called the DOTS analysis (Law and Watts, 1977). It represents people's need to get to grips with: (D) decisions, (O) opportunities, (T) transitions and (S) selfhood.

The framework poses key questions: 'Have we given enough attention to the opportunities available to our students?', '... to what they can know of their own motivations and abilities?', '... to how they deal with their decisions?' and, as they move on, '... to how they can anticipate and manage their lives?'. These categories add nothing to the National Curriculum; rather, they reframe its content.

That reframing readily transposes into first-person questions:

- 'Where am I?'   opportunity awareness
- 'Who am I?'   self-awareness
- 'What will I do?'   decision learning
- 'How will I cope?'   transition learning

These are not just career questions; they are life's issues. And there is no subject on the National Curriculum which is incapable of helping students get a grip on some part of it all. Some people think that is what curriculum is for.

Table 11.2 tests this wider usefulness of DOTS. That would mean successfully applying it to any lesson or scheme, focused on any topic (like those in Table 11.1), for any area of curriculum concern (listed on page 148). In the chart the focus is called 'this'. 'This' could be, for example, 'the use and abuse of substances'.

Use the columns on the right to mark up, and then to compare and discuss with colleagues, how your scheme helps your students in 'this' respect.

The review identifies bases for a curriculum action, to change:

- Where in their lives students can use this learning – in what life roles.
- Helping students to answer questions most useful to their needs.

Table 11.2 Planning chart on content

SMSC concern (see p. 148):   ... so that they can manage their *role* as a ...

... and focus for this:

On *opportunities*: students learn ...	friend	consumer	partner	worker	parent	householder	citizen
who is involved in this, and what they do							
what it is like for them							
how it is changing							
what this would need or demand of me							
what I might get from it							

On *self*: students learn ...	friend	consumer	partner	worker	parent	householder	citizen
what I do best about things like this							
what I like best							
what people let me know about what I do							
what makes me feel uneasy about this, and why							
when it comes to this, what I admire in people							

Table 11.2 *cont.*

SMSC concern (see p. 148): ... so that they can manage their *role* as a ..

... and focus for this

	friend	consumer	partner	worker	parent	householder	citizen
On *decisions*: students learn ...							
possible ways forward for myself							
what other people say to me about this							
what my decision is							
what others might say about my decision							
what I say about my decision							

	friend	consumer	partner	worker	parent	householder	citizen
On *transitions*: students learn ...							
what to expect as I move on from this decision							
what new people I will then be with							
what new challenges that could involve							
what others' needs and expectations might be							
why I feel good about doing what I am doing							

If the DOTS-based checklist is any good, it will provide a framework for clarifying what is needed and organize it into a basis for curriculum development.

That is what theory is for!

REVIEWING METHOD

We turn from content to process, concerned with how people learn. It is written in learning verbs, such as: 'enquire', 'express', 'classify', 'probe', 'appreciate', 'explain' and 'anticipate'. The National Curriculum is full of such verbs. But, in order to help students use them, we should help them to keep them in mind.

If students can be helped to do that, they are not just being helped with 'this' knowledge, they are also being helped to work out how to get more knowledge – about other matters.

Process is progressive: basic learning is engaged first, preparing the way for more developed learning. In career learning (Law, 1996a) progression is said to be from sensing to understanding:

- sensing   getting enough to go on – by enquiring, searching and observing
- sifting   putting information into useful order – by comparing, classifying and conceptualizing
- focusing   knowing who and what to pay attention to – by considering, prioritizing and probing
- understanding   knowing what action to take – by trying out, explaining, anticipating and checking.

It is what, as a species, we do. We make mental representations of what we must deal with. These become the models from which we work out where the main causes and probable effects of action lie. On that basis we act; and, unless we mean only to use rote learning, we need good mental models for effective action. It is our fingerhold on survival.

Sometimes the mental model is bad: people sometimes think they have learned what the probable effects of being a woman – or black or working class – are. But they have learned stereotypes – a prematurely formed understanding of how things work. Stereotyping – particularly self-stereotyping – is more damaging to life chances than any procedural deficit. Indeed, the more skilful people are in using the procedure, the more damaging the stereotype becomes.

We are adding an important dimension to the DOTS analysis; and, in so doing, we are creating a learning space (see Figure 11.1).

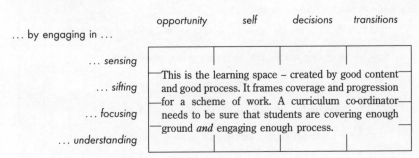

Students find out about . . .

	opportunity	self	decisions	transitions
. . . by engaging in . . .				

. . . sensing				
. . . sifting				
. . . focusing				
. . . understanding				

This is the learning space – created by good content and good process. It frames coverage and progression for a scheme of work. A curriculum co-ordinator needs to be sure that students are covering enough ground *and* engaging enough process.

Figure 11.1 Learning space for contemporary curriculum

Table 11.3 provides a curriculum-management framework based on the vertical dimension in Figure 11.1. Like Table 11.2 , it works best for a specific focus (again called 'this'). It could be, for example, about learning on equal opportunities. In the planning chart (see Table 11.3) use the columns on the right to say if, and at what stage, the scheme helps students in each of these respects.

As before, the review suggests curriculum-management action:

- Students need to be enabled to move in due order through the processes – if action is not to be a shot in the dark.
- Students need to know not just what, but *how* they learn – so that they can use these processes on other matters.

Due processes offer students alternatives to gullibility, impulse, superstition and just switching off. Understanding how to help them means understanding where, along the line of progression, they get stuck.

A good theory should help us to do that.

Table 11.3 Planning chart on process

SMSC concern (see p. 148):

… at this stage
in the scheme

… and focus for this

For *sensing*: students need to know how to …

	begin	develop	resolve
go into this – asking questions and finding the facts			
make contacts with people who know first-hand about this			
find out what happens and how it feels to be in this position			
get some new ideas for action – things I've never considered before			
say what I feel, I want to do, and I can do about this			

For *sifting*: students need to know how to …

	begin	develop	resolve
find how different people say and do different things about this			
say how my views and actions are like, and not like, other people's			
say how changes in this will make a difference to me			
use useful 'teachers' words' to think and talk about it			
sort the information into useful order, putting 'like with like'			

For *focusing*: students need to know how to …

	begin	develop	resolve
say what are my own hopes, anxieties and other feelings about this			
appreciate how other people have a different point of view			
appreciate the important ways in which points of view are different			
work out who and what is important to me in making a decision about this			
probe for answers to the questions that are now important to me			

Table 11.3 *cont.*

SMSC concern (see p. 148):

SMSC concern (see p. 148):

... at this stage
in the scheme

... and focus for this

	begin	develop	resolve
For *understanding*: students need to know how to ...			
work out how this got the way it is			
work out why I deal with it in the way that I do			
say why I pay attention to some people, more than others			
work out what I mean to do now, and how I think it will work out			
be ready for where my plan could take me – so that I am sure I can deal with it			

AN EXPANDED CONCEPT OF CITIZENSHIP

When people make up their minds about work they may be realizing their personal values and they are certainly negotiating their economic life chances. But what is also certain is that they are influencing the life chances of others, including the people who will one day depend upon them. More than that: they are aligning themselves with systems for getting and spending both personal and collective wealth. More even than that: their work will impact the built and natural environment and will change the quality of their community and of the social fabric.

Career management is, at the same time, an intellectual and an emotional process, and an individual and a social one – both self-seeking and moral, both personal and political. It links to all the interests alphabetically listed on page 148.

Students sense much of this; in voicing work preferences they refer – often quite explicitly – to whom they will pay attention, whose respect they seek and whose interests they will support. All of the environmental, social and economic issues listed in Table 11.1 can figure in this process. The more diverse the world of work becomes, the more such links become visible.

But careers educators would be unwise to argue that 'worker' is the basic role here; indeed, the way things are now, it is an open question which role has most influence on anything – 'worker', 'citizen', 'householder' or 'consumer'.

But the much strengthened position of citizenship in the curriculum may yet prove to be critical. Narrow conceptions of citizenship will not serve, because, in contemporary society, there are more ways of being an effective and responsible citizen than through conventionally understood politics. A person's *work* has a collective dimension. A work choice is, very substantially, a choice of how rich a *consumer* you would like to be. And consumer roles are increasingly understood for their *political* significance.

In any event, students are more likely to welcome learning for citizenship if they can recognize its relevance to life roles with which they identify. The concept of citizenship is capable of considerable expansion, so that 'the institutions of democracy, its rights and responsibilities' include a citizenship that can be exercised in social, domestic, consumer and working roles.

There is a basis, in such an expanded conception of citizenship, for finding meaning and purpose in education. Careers work is only part of that expansion. You will have other ideas. There is also a basis for school-based development that might, one day, show government what it wants to do next. Such things happen!

Final words to Richard Hoggart (1995):

Some people want children to be literate enough to be handed over to the persuaders, not literate enough to blow the gaff on them!

Now there *is* a conception for citizenship!

REFERENCES

Bates, Inge (1989) Versions of vocationalism: an analysis of some social and political influences on curriculum policy and practice. *British Journal of Sociology of Education*, **10** (2).

Department for Education and Employment (DfEE) (1998) *Education for Citizenship and the Teaching of Democracy in Schools*. London: Qualifications and Curriculum Authority.

Hoggart, Richard (1995) *The Way We Live Now*. London: Chatto and Windus.

Law, Bill (1996a). A career-learning theory. In Watts, A. G., Law, Bill, Killeen, John, Kidd, Jennifer M. and Hawthorn, Ruth, *Rethinking Careers Education and Guidance: Theory, Policy and Practice*. London: Routledge.

Law, Bill (1996b) Careers education in a curriculum. In Watts, A. G., Law, Bill, Killeen, John, Kidd, Jennifer M. and Hawthorn, Ruth, *Rethinking Careers Education and Guidance: Theory, Policy and Practice*. London: Routledge.

Law, Bill (1997) Revolution in schools – for liberté, accountabilité and futilité? *NICEC Careers Education and Guidance Bulletin*, No. 47.

Law, Bill (1999a) Learning for work: global causes, national standards and human relevance. In Collin, A. and Young, R., *The Future of Career*. Cambridge: Cambridge University Press.

Law, Bill (1999b) Career learning space: new-DOTS thinking for careers education. *The British Journal of Guidance and Counselling*, **27** (1).

Law, Bill and Watts, A. G. (1977) *schools, Careers and Community*. London: Church Information Office.

London Enterprise Agency (1997) *Pathways Toward Adult Life*. London: Kogan Page.

Qualifications and Curriculum Authority (QCA) (1998) *Developing the School Curriculum*. London: QCA.

Qualifications and Curriculum Authority (QCA) (1999) *The Review of the National Curriculum in England – The Secretary of State's Proposals*. London: QCA.

CHAPTER 12

Cultural development: its relationship to school improvement and the role of religious education

Vanessa Ogden

Culture may be thought of as a causal agent that affects the evolutionary process by uniquely human means. For it permits the self-conscious evaluation of human possibilities in the light of a system of values that reflect previous ideals about what human life ought to be. Culture is thus an indispensable device for increasing human control over the direction in which our species changes.

(Honderich, 1995, p. 172)

INTRODUCTION

In September 1997, a nationwide consultation on the draft guidance for spiritual, moral, social and cultural development was commissioned by the Qualifications and Curriculum Authority. It was conducted through a cross-section of representative teachers drawn from each curriculum subject area at primary and secondary level across the country. In this process, cultural development was separated from the others and dealt with apart, throwing it into relief against the spiritual, moral and social. This focused attention on a dimension of the curriculum which has been overshadowed by the others to some extent in the more recent 'SMSC' debate; much academic consideration has been given to questions of spiritual and moral development at conferences and in research projects, particularly in the field of religious education, and social development has been included in research and development work on personal, social and health education (PSHE). Cultural development has received less attention.

Opportunities for cultural development within the curriculum seem to have been generally confined to the celebration of ethnic roots and music, art or literature which, although obviously valuable and enriching, fall short of a full appreciation of the nature of culture. Culture is pervasive, with transformative power; it influences human choice and self-determination. It is a 'causal agent' and thus, it must be fundamentally and intricately linked with education, which seeks to enable, enrich and enfranchise. It is possible that cultural development has more consequence in the educational process than has yet been attributed to it in the research and discussion so far undertaken in spiritual, moral, social and cultural development.

This chapter seeks to explore aspects of the importance of cultural development within schools and its potential to impact upon society. The discussion attempts a definition of cultural development before considering how opportunities for cultural development might be provided within one subject area: religious education. An example is provided of a scheme of work written to promote opportunities for cultural development. The importance of cultural development for preparing young people in the UK to take their place within a diverse, multicultural, multi-faith and multi-ethnic society is argued before a second aspect is considered: the role of cultural development in school effectiveness and improvement in urban education.

It is argued that the provision of opportunities for cultural development is a significant factor in pupils' achievement. The significant contribution of the 'learning culture' to school effectiveness is well documented, and since 'schools make a difference' to future adult achievement (Stoll and Myers, 1998) in urban environments, it is possible to argue that cultural development has more importance than has been formerly recognized. Ultimately, this chapter addresses the proposition that cultural development is worthy of much more attention than it has previously been afforded, particularly in inner-city education, and it concludes with the suggestion that cultural development in education has the power to promote urban regeneration through recognition of the value of enrichment, diversity and self-worth.

CULTURAL DEVELOPMENT: ATTEMPTING A DEFINITION

Defining cultural development engages the classroom practitioner in a twofold process: first, the isolation of the phenomenon of cultural development and then the decision about methodology, or how this phenomenon might be promoted through education. The first is complex. Culture is multifarious and dynamic; a living, changing, moving force, subject to many influences that may be generational, ethnic, material, spiritual and so on. It can be vibrant, stimulating, even provocative; it can be elusive in essence, subtle or refined. It is pervasive and it fundamentally sways community and social structures.

Culture seems to be popularly understood on several levels. It is recognized as a set of social mores characterizing a generational or ethnic group; it is perceived to be a creative force, which inspires a particular artistic movement such as Impressionism or pop art; it is seen to represent ideologies, philosophies and other inherited belief systems which influence public life; and it is used to describe a general ethos.

What is distinctive about culture is that it is shared collectively by a group of individuals, a fact recognized in anthropology and sociology. Although seminal sociologists Weber and Durkheim each have a fundamentally different approach in defining culture, nevertheless they both agree that culture must be shared. While Durkheim refers to culture as the 'collective conscience' of a social unity (Thompson, 1982, p. 83), Weber emphasizes the individual as the significant agent in the development of culture, arguing that 'collectivities cannot think, feel, perceive; only people can' (Parkin, 1982, p. 184). For both however, culture is the shared expression of a collection of individuals, whether they come to their shared cultural understanding through a collective or individual consciousness.

Culture can also be used to exclude socially. Cultural language that is used can be heavily loaded; the word 'cultured' itself can be used to mean 'enlightened' in some way, such as in the contrast sometimes made between 'high' and 'low' culture (QCA, 1997), contrasts which are often subjective and value-laden. As Wittgenstein argues in his work on language-games (Hacker, 1997), non-verbal and verbal languages themselves operate subjectively and culturally among groups of people:

> Language use is a form of human rule-governed activity, integrated into human transactions and social behaviour, context-dependent and purpose relative. (Honderich, 1995, p. 461)

Among social groups, language-games are constantly in play and include the use of 'instruments' (*ibid.*) such as gesture, word patterns, word correlation, idioms and so on. An 'in-joke' is one example of an instrument sometimes used in a language-game.

Language is a part of the shared expression of culture resulting from a particular way of making sense of human experience, and precisely because of this subjectivity, it can lead to conflict and misunderstanding between different cultural groups. Language is a meter of cultural priorities, as those involved in combating racism and sexism have often pointed out.

Culture expresses how a society perceives itself spiritually, morally and socially. It pursues, explores or exposes dimensions of that vision through expressions of human belief about purpose. These expressions are manifested in the arts, the media, political and philosophical discourse, education and community organization. Religion powerfully inspires much of cultural expression because it is closely connected with the spiritual and moral, and central to the social structure of many ethnic groups. It is for these reasons that one could argue the importance of religious education in the provision of opportunities for cultural development in the school curriculum, and it is to the consideration of this argument that this chapter now turns.

CULTURAL DEVELOPMENT AND RELIGIOUS EDUCATION

Religious education has a vital part to play in supporting and promoting cultural development. Because religion is so central to the structure of many social groups, it provides a key with which to unlock the language-games which provide barriers to communication and common sympathy between those of differing cultures. Understanding the language of religion provides a means for bridge-building; learning the skills of interfaith dialogue enables ambassadorship between cultural groups that might otherwise be in conflict. Fragmentation in multicultural, multi-ethnic and multi-faith societies is a very real concern; as Hulmes writes,

In many parts of the world ... – not least in Britain and the USA – it is the integrity of society which is at stake. By the word 'integrity' I mean the organic unity of society, a unity that may as certainly be disrupted as enriched by religious and cultural diversity, especially if the educational implications are not understood, or if understood, simply ignored. (Hulmes, in Watson, 1992)

Aiming to prevent social fragmentation requires a genuine appreciation of deeply felt sensitivities in belief, both theistic and non-theistic, and an understanding of potential areas of conflict. It also demands that members of our society be equipped with these tools of language, knowledge, understanding and sensitivity of the kind that I would argue good religious education promotes. It is unlikely that citizenship education alone could provide enough specialism to enable society to achieve this. How then can religious education contribute to this? What kind of opportunities exist for religious education to promote this kind of cultural development?

In an educational context

[p]upils' cultural development consists both of a deepening understanding of their own cultural roots and of a broadening of their cultural horizons and aspirations. (Ofsted, 1994)

Religious education promotes opportunities for cultural development on both these levels. Pupils on many occasions will have explicit opportunities for cultural development through learning in RE. Religious education is intricately connected with cultural development since religious frameworks are important to, or underpin, many cultural institutions. Pupils have immediate access to cultural frameworks through the theoretical study of religion and they also explore culture experientially as a result of engagement in AT 2 of the Model Syllabuses for RE – 'Learning from religion'. Pupils will broaden and deepen their cultural understanding via exposure to a variety of cultural experiences connected to the study of religion, so the use of the expressive arts is a significant tool in the repertoire of the RE teacher, as is the involvement of pupils (with teachers) in interfaith dialogue through work with faith communities. These tools enable pupils to be immersed in the experience of what it means for a particular believer to practise such a commitment, and therefore for such a person to be part of a collective religious and cultural group. This is by no means to equate religious education with cultural development, but it does provide a rich diversity of opportunities for cultural development which could be made more explicit. An example of how this might be achieved is set out below:

BUDDHIST MEDITATION – Key Stage 3, Year 8
Aims:

1. To understand the centrality of meditation in Buddhism as a means to enlightenment.
2. In so doing, to learn about and understand the Eightfold Path, symbol in meditation and the process of meditation in two different types of Buddhism – Theravada and Zen.

3. To explain and evaluate the principles that have been learnt at the end of the course.
4. To provide opportunities for cultural development.

Attainment targets (from SCAA model syllabuses):
1. Learning about religion
2. Learning from religion

Activities:	Approach:
1. Build a shrine with pupils in the classroom using artefacts which pupils can see, touch, smell and hear. Explain their symbolic significance. Pupils to record and explain their significance, evaluating their use in worship.	AT 1 and AT 2
2. Visit a shrine to see Buddhism in practice and engage in dialogue with believers. See 'sitting' and 'standing' images of Buddha. Pupils conduct study of what it means to be a member of this faith community and to live out this faith daily through religious dialogue.	AT 2
3. Use Buddha image. Explain centrality of statue in meditation – not worship but inspiration. Draw wheel and explain Eightfold Path. Pupils to record and give examples of the practice of aspects of the Eightfold Path in daily life.	AT 1
4. Pupils to experience meditation through simple relaxation techniques. May opt out. Use of bell and incense. Explain kasina meditation and metta bhavana meditation in Theravada Buddhism.	AT 2
5. Examine Zen meditation, particularly 'working' meditation in gardens. See photographs. Discuss principles of working meditation, record, pupils to design own miniature meditation garden.	AT 1 and AT 2
6. Pupils to make miniature gardens and present and explain them to the class.	AT 2
7. Class to make a display which reinforces all knowledge gained both visually and in written form through discursive and analytical writing.	AT 1 and AT 2

Aside from the religious education taking place, this particular unit provides explicit opportunities for cultural development at every stage. The interconnection of experiential learning with conceptual understanding permeates this course. It both broadens pupils' cultural horizons through theory and deepens their understanding through experiential learning, using both the expressive arts and work with a living faith community.

This kind of opportunity for cultural development can be common to many programmes of study in religious education. Other opportunities for cultural development could take place through the exploration of democracy and Christian belief about democracy; religious foundations for passive resistance and civil disobedience through the lives and works of Gandhi and Martin Luther King; Judaism and the Holocaust; Sikhism and commitment to the Five Ks in daily life.

RE, CULTURAL DEVELOPMENT AND THE GENERAL LEARNING CULTURE

It is a straightforward matter to expose the connections between religious education and cultural development; there are obvious links between religion, values and collective action that can be explored in the classroom. However, religious education has more to offer. RE provides a sensitive meter for informing a school about how effective its programme of cultural development is. Cultural development influences the success, or otherwise, of pupils' learning in religious education.

Since culture derives from many intricately interconnected and often conflicting aspects of human life, which continuously impact upon the affective and cognitive faculties of children as they develop, pupils enter a classroom bringing with them a wealth of cultural perceptions, some of which an adult will be unfamiliar with. It is these with which an RE teacher has to work, sensitively and intelligently, valuing the cultural roots of individuals while at the same time extending their horizons by providing genuine opportunities for cultural and religious experience with which pupils might not ordinarily come into contact. If the prevailing culture is hostile either towards other cultures or to exposure to alternative world-views to their own, pupils will present much more of a challenge to the RE teacher; inevitably, initial progress in achievement in RE will be affected.

Religious education of the kind which informs the relationship between pupils' performance and the promotion of a culture of achievement in a multicultural school community, which is supportive of diverse individuals, should be a focus for consideration. Bridge-building, gaining a critical sense of personal identity and belonging and feeling recognized and valued as an individual achiever are some of the hallmarks of success in raising standards of pupils' attainment. RE supports this process. It should be of profound interest that a culture which is opposed to learning has a fundamental impact upon levels of achievement. It seems to suggest that culture, and the development of a learning culture within schools, are of key significance in their effectiveness. It suggests that pupils learn best when they relate to the school and the school relates to them.

CULTURAL DEVELOPMENT AND SCHOOL EFFECTIVENESS

'Changing the culture' in struggling or 'failing' schools is a common theme of school improvement literature. Sammons *et al.* (1995) cite the establishment of a shared set of values as one of the key characteristics of effective schools. Barber (Barber and Dann, 1996) discusses changing the culture at some length as part of his framework for creating a successful school. Among the other points that he makes in the same article, he mentions self-belief, creating an atmosphere of pressure and support (a concept originally applied to education by Michael Fullan) and transforming the school into a learning institution for both staff and pupils by encouraging critical reflection, evaluation and self-development. Stoll and Myers (1998) recognize that in some few cases exterior cultural influences prevent schools from succeeding despite all efforts to raise standards. Brighouse (in Barber and Dann, 1996) argues that one reason why standards are held back in urban schools is because of pupils' low self-esteem. Interestingly, both Barber and Myers note that there is a common language of school improvement that is typical of schools in which the culture is geared towards raising achievement. Cultural factors which either promote or impede school effectiveness are commonly discussed.

Ofsted too has an interest. The Chief Inspector's annual report for 1996–97 included references to the strong performance of Catholic schools in relation to others, which was attributed to ethos. Professor Gerald Grace at the Institute of Education has undertaken research on the relationship of ethos to school effectiveness and argues that mission statements should be examined closely as a crucial factor in school effectiveness, because, 'Mission statements have many catholic virtues. They constitute a principled and comprehensive articulation of what a school claims to be its distinctive educational, social and moral purposes' (Grace, 1997). Mission statements are expressions of shared expectations and values, normally produced by consultation with the whole-school community. They are therefore expressions of common cultural aspirations.

Research suggests that changing the culture of the school from failure to success over a short space of time has involved many of these cultural aspects of school improvement work. Establishing a clear focus on work, and extending and enriching pupils' educational experiences through an out-of-hours enrichment programme, succeed in changing the peer-group culture among pupils to one of challenge and increased self-esteem. There is enough evidence to suggest that cultural development has a much greater role to play in school improvement than has been previously allowed.

In urban education, certainly, there is a good case for further research into this. Cultural development invests in social capital. It works to help prevent social fragmentation in a diverse society. It also helps to raise standards in schools and supports school effectiveness, particularly in the inner-city and urban outer-ring estate schools, where there are pressing concerns about the rise of an urban culture of low achievement. Brighouse writes:

> At ten, eleven, twelve, and thirteen these already disadvantaged children are into adolescence – no longer children and yet not sure what sort of adults they will become. They are surrounded by a commercial culture, by drugs, drink, crime and despair. The bravado of the developmental stage camouflages the lack of self-esteem. (Barber and Dann, 1996)

This description of the problems faced by pupils in urban schools rings very true, as does his description of inner-city desolation:

> Nowadays the permanent modest unskilled jobs have gone. Your neighbour speaks a different language and worships another God. Your mind is far away with images of elsewhere – hill villages in a warmer climate for some, suburban tree-lined comfort for others. Or you are old and on a vandalized grey concrete damp estate remembering street parties as you cower nervously at the first sounds from the approaching shouts of the local gang, desperately hoping that they are off to the 'hotters' display of stolen cars and that they will not pause to vandalize your home. (Barber and Dann, 1996)

Such a bleak picture of urban degeneration leads to the realization that, with the breakdown of community in such areas, schools and other educational institutions take on a much more significant role as providers of opportunities for, in this case, cultural development. If 'schools make a difference' in urban areas, and cultural development is to be recognized as a factor that significantly contributes to successful schools, then cultural development needs to be afforded a more proper consideration both in research into spiritual, moral, social and cultural development and in school effectiveness research.

CONCLUSION

Unless we start in the classroom and the school there is no hope for our cities and our society. (Tim Brighouse, 'Urban Deserts or Fine Cities?', in Barber and Dann, 1996, p. 118)

It is Brighouse's argument for the centrality of effective inner-city and urban outer-ring estate schools in any programme of urban regeneration that I wish to take up as a final point. Brighouse contends that schools are pivotal means of transformation in these areas. They should be central to any strategy for change in such communities precisely because those people most affected by the disempowerment caused by inner-city problems should most actively participate in the process of change. He writes:

To reverse that trend requires local, not national decisions, and the involvement as participants as far as possible of those affected. The communities themselves have to be empowered to find their own solutions if our cities are to be regenerated. A sense of powerlessness is the enemy of democracy. (Barber and Dann, 1996, p. 121)

If, as I argue, cultural development in schools does make a powerful contribution towards investment in social capital, then the combination of Brighouse's argument with that of Helena Kennedy in *Learning Works* (1997) is particularly potent. Both assert the central importance of institutions of education in promoting a culture of creative change and generation of social wealth. Kennedy states;

It is this 'social capital' which has a large and measurable economic value. A nation's well-being, as well as its ability to compete, is conditioned by a single pervasive cultural characteristic – the level of social capital inherent in the society. (Kennedy, 1997, pp. 5–6)

Changing the culture of low self-esteem in learning to a culture which recognizes the richness of variety in achievement, and which values the diversity of contribution in a multifaceted society, helps schools to provide effective learning and enables schools to play a central role in inner-city regeneration. In addition, cultural development which acknowledges difference and diversity, which enables sensitive interpersonal interaction, which takes account of the relationship between private belief and public life, contributes further to the establishment of human capital within our society. It helps to prevent social fragmentation in a multi-faith, multi-ethnic and multicultural society, and to this aspect of cultural development there is no doubt that religious education is a significant contributor.

It is tenable that Britain must become culturally and socially rich to ensure unsuperficial economic success. Institutions of education such as schools hold the key to this transformation within the inner cities and other areas of urban concern. As focal points for the communities, and as providers of opportunities for cultural development, these institutions could offer the disenfranchised the power to change their vision and bring about their active participation socially, economically, democratically and culturally. Education is teleological: if common social wealth is part of our 'telos', then the contribution of sensitive cultural development through religious education and in school effectiveness projects has been significantly overlooked. Beyond the school, we will pay the price of this at the expense of social capital.

REFERENCES

Barber, M. and Dann, R. (eds) (1996) *Raising Educational Standards in the Inner Cities*. London: Cassell.

Grace, G. (1997) Realising the mission. In Slee, Tomlinson and Weiner (eds), *Effective for Whom*. London: Falmer Press.

Hacker, P. M. S. (1997) *Wittgenstein*. London: Phoenix.

Honderich, T. (ed.) (1995) *The Oxford Companion to Philosophy*. Oxford: Oxford University Press.

Kennedy, H. (1997) *Learning Works*. Coventry: FEFC.

Ofsted (1994) *Spiritual, Moral, Social and Cultural Development*. London: HMSO.

Parkin, F. (1982) *Max Weber*. London: Tavistock Publishers and Ellis Horwood Ltd.

QCA (1997) *Draft Guidance on Cultural Development*. London: QCA.

Sammons, P., Hillman, J. and Mortimore, P. (1995) *Key Characteristics of Effective Schools*. London: Institute of Education.

Stoll, L. and Myers, K. (eds) (1998) *No Quick Fixes: Perspectives on Schools in Difficulties*. London: Falmer.

Thompson, K. (1982) *Emile Durkheim*. London: Tavistock Publishers and Ellis Horwood Ltd.

Watson, B. (1992) *Priorities in RE*. London: Falmer Press.

CHAPTER 13

Developing an understanding of worth

Raywen Ford

INTRODUCTION

Objects and material culture exist alongside language as the means whereby human groups construct themselves and children are socialized (Miller, 1994), artefacts being one of the main outputs of social action. Young children recognize the routines of the context in which they live, and become orientated to and by the spaces and objects of their world. Children experience an object through direct contact using all senses, in turn and simultaneously, to understand the nature of it, and then through language interpret it in terms of function and meaning. In this context, the process of 'becoming' (Miller, 1994), in terms of our cultural identity, is in one sense defined by objects, and is enriched, modified and developed by the school curriculum.

The terms 'worth' and 'value' are at first glance synonymous. An object's value, the term more widely used by economists, can be defined as utility value (value in use), or its purchasing power (value in exchange) (Roll, 1973). However, through acts of handcrafting and giving, objects achieve value to an individual way beyond either their defined function or value in trade; they become worth a great deal more. Understanding an object's worth, in this sense, is embodied in an appreciation of craft skills and a developed affinity with kinship, and has little to do with use or exchange. Indeed such objects often stop being used, to prevent damage, and suggestions of selling would not be entertained. The term 'worth' is preferred here because of its connection with the notion of worthiness and deserving. The implication is of a recognition of the inherent, intrinsic qualities of an object, rather than external, functional properties. To apportion a price in the open market, the determining factor is what the object might mean to others, rather than to the present owner.

Each individual can reflect on the nature of the objects that had significance in their own childhood, identify those objects that have been kept and treasured when others have long since been discarded and ask why this is the case. Some objects will have, for whatever reason, become significant and personally valuable.

Traditional economic theory has taken objects (commodities) out of their cultural context (Appadurai, 1986) and in so doing deprived them of cultural meaning. It could be argued, interestingly, that collectors unintentionally achieve the same effect when objects, particularly religious objects, are 'displaced' in museums. In so doing such objects lose their 'identity' and cultural context. But, as Forty (1995) points out, objects do not have a life of their own; they are determined by people and relationships in society. Objects have a social context, reflecting society's ideas and ideals. They are made by people, for people; they give an insight into how people cope with their world. A role of spiritual, moral, social and cultural (SMSC) education would seem to be to reunite objects with people and their cultural context, and in so doing enable children to develop understandings of worth beyond monetary value.

This chapter will examine the notion of objects as entities and expressions of aesthetic understanding and the part they play, through gift giving, in developing human relationships. In addition, a suggestion will be made as to the contribution the school curriculum can make, through developing an understanding and appreciation of objects, to children's growing conception of themselves and their worlds with particular reference to notions of worth.

THE NATURE OF OBJECTS

Objects, as transmitters of culture, differ from other media by virtue of their sheer physicality. They are known and understood through sight, smell, touch and taste. Words are often used as the vehicle for sharing knowledge and understanding of objects, but invariably fall short of adequate description. Similarly, photographs of objects cannot portray the reality. All the crucial aspects of the physicality of an object, size, weight, smell, surface texture, space and three-dimensionality, are lost in a photograph. The interpretation made of these properties through the senses prompts an aesthetic response, positive or negative. In addition, objects exist physically in place. They affect the space and environment in which they are placed, and exist in relation to it. Where and how objects are kept are, in themselves, indications of the worth and meaning attributed to them. A vase stored in a cupboard would not appear to be held in the same light as one permanently on show whether it holds flowers or not.

Miller (1994) described the 'humility' of objects; existing things that do not necessarily explain themselves or demand attention. Objects are not involved in an interchange of perceptions and ideas. The relationship is not, in any usual sense, mutual or dialectic. Any investment made or interpretation drawn cannot be challenged directly. Equally, many objects become invisible through overexposure and routine contact. Familiarity can breed disinterest, if not contempt, and objects, being passive in the relationship, cannot address the situation.

Objects have histories (Weiner, 1985), they outlast people and can be the vehicle for bringing the past into the present, reinforcing cultural values, offering stability and shedding light on lost worlds. Memories of relatives, friends, places or situations can be rekindled through significant objects. 'Souvenirs' are bought for that express purpose, and heirlooms, of whatever financial value, strengthen understandings of family histories, forge continuity between generations and develop notions of roots.

Cultural understandings expressed through objects, language or indeed any other form, are not separate; however, they are 'mutually reflexive' (Guss, 1989, p. 162), interacting and enabling meaning to be developed and created. Through this interaction culture is dynamic rather than static; knowledge is reinterpreted and redefined. Handmade craft objects, perhaps more than any other, define cultural identity as they embody personal intention and are particular, a point developed later in the chapter.

However, the sheer volume of artefacts made available through mass production in contemporary society is threatening, precipitating a need for choice and selection. Questions about whether the world has become less meaningful as a result of the objects becoming increasingly meaningless need to be asked. In surrounding ourselves with objects that can be bought by anyone else, and with an expectation that they can be replaced at any time, investing objects with meaning becomes increasingly difficult. Mass consumption has resulted in a homogenization of culture, in terms of both objects and of places. Internationalization of architectural styles together with monopolies in shopping centres and chain stores generate places felt to be bereft of identity. One High Street looks very similar to any other. According to Miller (1992),

> Contemporary society has seen a massive increase in objective culture, but this has not been matched by subjective investment, instead people see the world of goods as separate and alien. The spread of objective culture has outstripped the capacity of the subject to absorb it. (p. 77)

Selection is, therefore, inevitable, and some criteria for choice and selection need to be established in the mind of the individual. What is of concern here is how those criteria and priorities are developed, and what influences the nature of the criteria chosen. Simmel (1968) suggested that culture exists when the 'subjective soul' interacts with the 'objective spiritual product' (p. 30). Culture involves the relationship between people and the objects they invest with particular meanings. Formal education clearly has a role to play in this development. Educators need to enable children to select in an informed way, and offer strategies for engaging with objects in order that they can understand them, and in turn, invest them with meaning.

MAKING

Cultural objects are made. They result from the interaction of human intention, spiritual, aesthetic and functional, and the nature of material. Handmade objects are skilful, unique and expressive, but these qualities are not necessarily reflected in price. The skills of the craft maker are undervalued in monetary terms in contemporary society. The public's perception of a craft fair is often that items can be bought more cheaply than the mass-produced equivalent, despite the fact that it is the handmade, labour intensive, unique quality that is sought. Perversely, it would seem at times that the mass-produced and disposable is chosen precisely because it can be discarded and replaced with the fashionable equivalent at any time, and that buying handmade objects in some way obliges the purchaser to take care of the object.

The question of why people continue to make objects, when mass-produced equivalents are available more cheaply is, superficially, perplexing. In one sense, 'handmade' also quite often means 'imperfect'. Hand-knitted garments have particularly suffered from a widely held assumption of inferiority. On this matter Metcalf (1997) cites the work of Dissanayake (1988) who suggests that art/craft springs from a human desire to 'make special' (p. 92), to go beyond the immediate functional need and to invest something more. Why dance, she argues, if walking or running will suffice? Why sing, if talking can get the same message across? Clearly, walking and running are not sufficient, because dancing is not concerned with getting from one place to another. It is about celebration, joy, expression and the feelings engendered within relationships between people. The combination of music and word to create song and the act of singing, and indeed poetry, are quite distinct from talk. Forms of expression have evolved that can to some degree describe and transmit the diverse range of human emotions and understandings, and inherent in these forms is a requirement to do them well.

Equally, people, throughout time and place, have exhibited a fundamental need to make with material, that goes beyond functional needs such as keeping warm or cooking food, to invest the made objects with 'special' qualities. Metcalf (1997) draws on current biological/anthropological research to present an argument for 'pan-cultural human nature' (p. 72), challenging postmodern relativism, and suggesting that certain behaviours and practices are inherent in the condition of being human. The kind of making described above is the pre-eminent example.

Making as an occupation cum way of life, often goes undescribed. Some artists pen explanations of individual pieces of work, but craftspeople less so; talk and the object itself are the preferred channels. However, the exhibition catalogue of 'Making Weaves' held in the Museum of Scotland in Edinburgh (Summer 1998) suggests:

> For some people the key function for a basket as a container for holding or transporting goods is still the initial criteria for evaluating a basket ... [but] This exhibition shows a basket being more than the intrinsic value of the material and function.

Contributors to the exhibition expressed their understandings of and relationship with their work, each explaining a spiritual dimension to the act of basket-making. Kay Anderson wrote:

> the art of basket making goes so far back into the early life of humankind that the chain of handed-down knowledge is immensely long. Sometimes a new pupil starts and, at once, one can see their fingers remembering.

Lise Bech first became involved in basket-making in Northern Ireland and wrote:

> Weaving different identities into an organic whole, mirrored the creative tension in society for the reconciliation of Catholics and Protestants, where change, tension and integrity were daily issues.

Lise uses the basket as a metaphor for society, and basket weaving for integration and reconciliation. Anna King creates baskets as containers for ideas and personal secrets rather than objects. Each craftsperson expressed a spiritual dimension to their work. Their baskets were more than functional objects (although functional they were); they were beautiful, extraordinarily skilfully executed and tangible expressions of spiritual understandings.

With the changing nature of society, particularly with regard to the role of women, the opportunity to learn a craft skill has moved out of the family and into formal education. The shift from the home to school as the location for learning craft skills might imply greater access, but, in fact, the reverse would seem to be the case. Western education favours linguistic and mathematical skills, Metcalf suggests, because they are the most useful in 'business, war-making, politics and academic careerism' (1997, p. 79). The Crafts Council report (1998) showed clearly that there has been a steady decline in craft teaching since the introduction of the National Curriculum, especially within art. The possibilities afforded by 'learning through making' are well documented, particularly through the work of the Crafts Council, and arguments for the importance of developing all intelligences (Gardner, 1985) have been well made. However, emphasis on the core curriculum, 'league tables' and open enrolment policies have compounded to effect a decline in both resourcing and opportunity in craft areas, particularly in ceramics and textiles.

Craftmaking is more than learning practical skills to make functional objects, it is a medium for personal expression. The process of making is therapeutic and creatively productive at one and the same time. It provides for the resolution of problems and the expression of possibilities in tangible form; a form that, as has been said, exists over time to allow for further refinement or contemplation.

Children certainly enjoy making. The first key finding identified by the Crafts Council report (1998) states clearly that that is the case. It goes on to say that children make at home and that they enjoy and value developing craft skills.

In addition, craft teachers recognize that, while making, children have an opportunity to talk to each other about what is important to them in a way that is not possible in other subjects. It is perfectly possible to be working hard while interspersing making with conversation. It is interesting to note parallels in the fact that women in many cultures have traditionally come together to make and talk, quilt making being a particular example. Guss (1989), when working with the Yekuana people, commented that, 'conversation simply did not occur unless someone was making a basket' (p. 2). Craft offers opportunity for reflection not only through the making itself, but also through the social situation constructed to enable the making to take place and the skill to be transferred from one person to another. Crafts people have formed collectives not only for economic reasons, but also because of the interaction of ideas and understandings afforded by them.

GIFT GIVING

Objects have a key role in the process of gift giving. In one sense the object embodies the relationship in which the gift is given. A choice is made in making or selecting the gift that describes the relationship. Gift giving may be about obligations between people, and notions of kinship. When gifts are given it is in response to an emotional, relational link, or, alternatively, an attempt to create one. A sale is a completed transaction, whereas a gift is part of a reciprocal exchange within a relationship and, through the process of the gift exchange, a new value is placed on the object. The object is invested with worth well beyond that of its original price.

Gift giving is probably one of the oldest, most basic and yet potent of human behaviours. 'Before language was written or money minted, humans exchanged gifts' (Hickey, 1997, p. 83). Mauss (1980) refers to archaic societies where gifts were an integral part of social interaction to a point where they ensured internal social cohesion, and intersocietal stability. Through the exchange of gifts social understandings were developed that enabled people to live peaceably and productively. In contemporary society, however, gift giving has become a consumer pastime, part of the shopping experience. Mauss (1980) uses the example of wedding presents to illustrate the point. The shift has taken place from the notion of a 'bottom drawer', where individual items were handcrafted by family members and accumulated over a period of years, to the current 'single store' wedding list, where items are chosen by the couple, bought by relatives (keeping the receipts) and can be returned after the wedding if not deemed suitable, which is indicative of the loss of meaning and personal investment. Relatives do not take the same active part in home creation.

Gifts strengthen relationships and reflect the identity of both the giver and receiver, and for the transaction to be successful, a considerable level of thought needs to be given to it. It does, however, involve risk, and giving an individual craft object is particularly difficult. Craft objects are individual, often unusual, and careful consideration has to be given to making the right choice if it is to reflect the relationship appropriately, but whatever the gift, price, within reason, is not an issue. Pebbles from a beach, for example, may be more valuable than something bought because they have particular properties and embody a sentiment more precisely. It is, quite literally, the thought that counts.

The obligations engendered by gift giving are binding, and involve responsibilities, whereas transactions involving money create distance between people, and involve notions of rights. Beyond the obligation is pleasure. According to Mauss:

> The joy of giving in public, the pleasure of hospitality, social insurance, solicitude in mutuality or co-operation, are better than the mean life afforded by the daily wage handed out by management and better even than the uncertainty of capitalist savings. (1980, p. 67)

Hyperbole, perhaps, but the point is well made. Giving is pleasurable, as indeed is receiving.

CURRICULUM IMPLICATIONS

The school curriculum is language based. Children are inducted into the codes and conventions of language in order that they may derive meaning from it. Langer (1942) suggested that meaning held within language unfolds over time, but that objects are 'presentational', that is, they present all aspects of themselves at one time. While the position on language would appear to be self-evident, I would contest that the same is true for understandings invested in objects; these, too, only become apparent over time.

Children need to be given the knowledge to 'decode' objects, and opportunities to develop interpretative skills, in order to appreciate and value them. The meaning of an object unfolds, as with language, as the object is 'read'. In a developed society the responsibility for developing the necessary skills and knowledge, as with making, lies within the formal education system. The 1988 Education Reform Act recognized this responsibility in requiring a 'broad and balanced' curriculum and spiritual, moral, social and cultural education becoming the right of every child as an integral part of the school curriculum.

Equally questionable is the assumption that because an object can be seen and touched, it can be understood. The adage 'I don't know much about art, but I know what I like' is familiar, but it is probable that in coming to know about art, an individual might like it much more. Art and craft objects need to be understood, to be fully appreciated. To appreciate, according to Hospers (1969), is to 'engage and savour', and to do either would seem to require time and active involvement, together with a knowledge of the codes and conventions of the form. Guss (1989), when faced with the task of coming to understand an unfamiliar culture, suggested that although he could not (yet) understand the myths as told, he could at least see them in cultural objects. Culture is 'objectified' and held in visible and tangible form. He recognized, however, that to understand the complexities of the metaphors within the material culture would require a 'long and active apprenticeship' (p. 2). The objects can be seen but not read and, therefore, not fully understood.

To some extent the strategies suggested by Rod Taylor (1986) to help children deconstruct and understand images are now well established in art teaching, and could be applied directly to objects. Work of a very similar nature has been undertaken with objects in relation to the history curriculum by Durbin, Morris and Wilkinson (1991). Their work suggests ways in which young people might interrogate objects, developing investigative, observational and recording skills, extending their knowledge and developing historical concepts. They suggest that questions are asked of the object, such as: 'How was it made?' 'What material is it made from?' 'Is it coated and decorated?' 'Has it a use?' 'Does it still work?' 'How old do you think it is?' 'Who owns it and how did they come to own it?' The emphasis, however, has been on critical studies, developing specialist vocabulary and cognitive understanding of objects, and their function in time and place. What has been overlooked is the investigation of *meaning*. What is being suggested here is a need to go beyond a conceptual and pragmatic analysis of an object to an understanding of worth to an individual or social group. Appreciation is fed by criticism, but entails personal involvement in a spiritual and emotional sense, reuniting subject with object.

The function and visual appearance of an object is relatively easily tackled in school. What is hidden, implied or invested in an object, however, is more difficult to deal with, partly by virtue of the fact that it is not immediately apparent, but also because it is likely to be more controversial. Description is straightforward, function slightly more ambiguous and meaning is problematic.

At an early age children begin to project values on objects and create powerful associations with them (Hickey, 1997). When children start school they will have already chosen a favourite toy, invested it with all manner of properties and qualities, often to the bafflement of other members of the family, or received comfort from a particular blanket. According to Mauss (1980):

> Things have values which are emotional as well as material; indeed in some cases the values are entirely emotional. Our morality is not solely commercial. (p. 63)

At some level children know this, but they are not necessarily aware that they know it and, all too easily, this knowledge can be cancelled or overtaken by conflicting experiences. Their awareness needs to be fostered and supported. The pleasure in both making and giving objects, and the security afforded by mutuality, are experiences which society should hold dear, and the school curriculum develop. Objects are products of human intention and desire, and help children give form to their conception of themselves, others and abstract ideas. Strategies need to be developed that help children understand what objects mean both to the maker and themselves.

CONCLUSIONS

The school curriculum needs to acknowledge equally all human intelligencies, and their role in the development of the whole child. Through craftmaking and giving, children engage in fundamentally human experiences that develop personal satisfaction, investing themselves and their time for the benefit of particular relationships. Through making, children understand that objects are invested with meaning; through giving and receiving they come to understand their obligations to others.

Children will be socialized through objects and the material culture that surrounds them whether or not the school curriculum takes part. If our contemporary, consumer-oriented, society wishes to perpetuate a notion of worth separate from use and exchange, a space must be made in the formal curriculum of schools in terms of making and appreciating craft. According to Hickey (1997), 'money is at the opposite end of the spectrum from the handmade and the intimate' (p.85). If children do not make, they cannot give something of themselves to those they are close to, and play their part in strengthening relationships. Children need the opportunity to contribute to and enjoy their material world. Engaging with objects enables individuals to reflect on fundamental spiritual issues. The meanings inherent in objects come from both the maker and the giver; as a consequence, meanings are more powerful if the maker and giver are one and the same.

Our current preoccupation with the cognitive, and the narrow range of linguistic, computational and technical competences, neglects those deeper levels of feeling and being which makes us human. Through making, giving and receiving, that sense of worth which we should feel for our fellow humans might be realized. Any comprehensive approach to spiritual, moral, social and cultural education must include opportunities for children to develop this sense through craft.

REFERENCES

Appadurai, A. (ed.) (1986) *The Social Life of Things: Commodities in Cultural Perspective*. Cambridge: Cambridge University Press.

Crafts Council and Roehampton Institute London (1998) *Pupils as Makers: Craft Education in Secondary Schools at Key Stages 3 and 4*. London: Crafts Council.

Dissanayake, E. (1988) *What is Art For?* Seattle: University of Washington Press.

Durbin, G., Morris, S. and Wilkinson, S. (1991) *A Teacher's Guide to Learning from Objects*. London: English Heritage.

Forty, A. (1995) *Objects of Desire*. London: Thames and Hudson.

Gardner, H. (1985) *Frames of Mind: The Theory of Multiple Intelligencies*. New York: Basic Books.

Guss, D. (1989) *To Weave and Sing*. Berkeley: University of California Press.

Hickey, G. (1997) Craft within a consuming society. In Dormer, P., *The Culture of Craft*. Manchester: Manchester University Press.

Hospers, J. (1969) *Introductory Readings in Aesthetics*. London: Macmillan.

Langer, S. (1942) *Philosophy in a New Key*. Cambridge, Mass: Harvard University Press.

Mauss, M. (1980) *The Gift*. London: Routledge and Kegan Paul.

Metcalf, J. (1997) Craft and art, culture and biology. In Dormer, P. (ed.), *The Culture of Craft*. Manchester: Manchester University Press.

Miller, D. (1984) *Artefacts as Categories*. Cambridge: Cambridge University Press.

Miller, D. (1992) *Material Culture and Mass Consumption*. Oxford: Blackwell.

Miller, D. (1994) Artefacts and the meaning of things. In Ingold, T. (ed.) *Humanity Culture and Social Life*. London: Routledge.

Roll, E. (1973) *A History of Economic Thought*. Oxford: Alden and Mowbray Ltd.

Simmel, G. (1968) *The Conflict of Modern Culture and Other Essays*. New York: New York Teachers Press.

Taylor, R. (1986) *Educating for Art*. London: Longman.

Weiner, A. (1976) *Women of Value, Men of Renown*. Austin: University of Texas Press

Weiner, A. (1985) Inalienable wealth. In *American Ethnologist*, **12** (2) 210–27.

CHAPTER 14

Circle Time: a forum for SMSC?

Marilyn Tew

BACKGROUND

Schools have traditionally given consideration to the personal and social education of pupils alongside their academic remit. The 1988 Education Reform Act prescribed a National Curriculum and charged schools with responsibility to, 'promote the spiritual, moral, cultural, mental and physical development of pupils at the school and of society' and to prepare pupils for the 'opportunities, responsibilities and experiences of adult life'. The implementation of a National Curriculum brought about a coherent approach to mental or cognitive learning and development in this country. As a result, many teachers feel that time for affective learning (that which engages the emotions and includes moral, spiritual and cultural dimensions) has been 'squeezed out'. Yet educators and politicians still recognize that to develop children's cognitive faculties is not a sufficient preparation for becoming an adult citizen of our society. Young people, growing up into a rapidly changing pluralistic society, need to develop in the moral, social, spiritual and cultural realms with a socially acceptable set of values and principles. So the last few years have seen renewed affirmation of schools' responsibilities for pupils' personal and social education, with government initiating advisory bodies on personal, social and health education (PSHE), spiritual, moral, social and cultural education (SMSC) and citizenship. The debate on these issues is set to continue into the next millennium with the revision of the National Curriculum in the year 2000.

THE PLACE OF SMSC IN EDUCATION

With the changes and legislation of the past decade, schools and teachers may well feel that they are being asked to compensate for the social and moral ills of society. Whereas it is true schools are uniquely placed to address values concerns in education because of their contact with pupils, families and the local community, it cannot be their role to replace social work. Nor can the development of social, moral, spiritual and cultural education be seen just as a tool to enable teachers to get on with the academic curriculum. Spiritual and moral development with an understanding of socially acceptable values and behaviour must be seen as intrinsic to being human and part of a social context.

The advent of Office for Standards in Education (Ofsted) inspections, brought the terms Spiritual, Moral, Social and Cultural (SMSC) into common parlance, but it was not attached to a timetabled slot in the curriculum. Many schools, particularly those in the secondary sector, cover this area in personal, social education (PSE), sometimes with the explicit inclusion of health education or citizenship. Ofsted inspectors are obliged to evaluate and report on a school's provision for the SMSC development of all pupils 'through the curriculum and life of the school; the example set for pupils by adults in the school; and the quality of collective worship' (Ofsted, 1995, p. 19).

Ofsted produced definitions of spiritual, moral, social and cultural development and their inspections are based on the extent to which the school:

● provides its pupils with knowledge and insight into values and beliefs and enables them to reflect on their experiences in a way which develops their spiritual awareness and self-knowledge;
● teaches the principles which distinguish right from wrong;
● encourages pupils to relate positively to others, take responsibility, participate fully in the community, and develop an understanding of citizenship; and
● teaches pupils to appreciate their own cultural traditions and the diversity and richness of other cultures. (Ofsted, 1995, p. 19)

In July 1996, SCAA (now QCA), produced Discussion Paper No. 6 entitled *Education for Adult Life: The Spiritual and Moral Development of Young People*. This document focused attention on the importance of spiritual and moral development in preparing young people for adult life. It offered definitions and helped to clarify what schools could be doing to contribute to pupils' spiritual and moral growth.

It is unlikely, however, that instruction in moral or spiritual values or information about what is considered right or wrong will bring about change in an individual. There need to be mediating structures and processes, which provide pupils with opportunities to examine their own values, assess them against those of other people and arrive at personal conclusions. Imposing rules on young people as 'right' is unlikely to be effective in producing moral development since knowing the difference between right and wrong does not guarantee choosing to do the right.

An important aim of any course of moral teaching is to develop the *will* of the individual to *do* what is right, not just to inform the mind of what *is* right. Children need to develop skilled moral reasoning, be willing to conduct themselves in a responsible manner and be prepared to take responsibility for their own actions. This will lead to socially acceptable behaviour built on an understanding of why such behaviour is desirable, right or necessary.

The British education system has largely separated the cognitive and affective curricula, especially in secondary education. Yet, recent research demonstrates clear links between emotional and cognitive learning, between metacognition and self-regulated behaviour. The interconnections of brain functioning cannot be ignored (Gardner, 1991; Hannaford, 1995; Goleman, 1996; and Greenhalgh, 1994), so we need to look again at the structures, strategies and opportunities we provide in our education system for developing the spiritual, emotional, cultural, social and moral dimensions of growth and learning.

A COMMITMENT TO THE 'WHOLE' CHILD?

We talk about 'holistic' approaches to health and education. What exactly do we mean? At the end of the nineteenth century, William James (1890) founded the science of psychology and developed enquiry into the 'self'. He saw the constituents of the self as the sum total of all that I can call mine: the material self; the social self; and the spiritual self.

On this early conception of the 'self' is built so much of our current understanding of the interplay between the cognitive and the affective realms in learning. The material, or physical self, consists of the body and the things that are 'mine'. The social self is 'me in society' and is formed and changed by the interaction with other human beings; it contains my moral values and attitudes, my social and interpersonal skills. The spiritual self is the essence of being human, including the capacity to transcend and think beyond ourselves, to love and value others and to have vision, ideals, creativity and imagination. Each part of the 'self' must be developed in a holistic approach to education because they interrelate and affect one another.

Gardner (1993b) has taken this thinking even further. He sees traditional Western schooling as unbalanced in the way it develops knowing and understanding. He refutes the notion of a single intelligence as measured by IQ, and writes of seven or eight different kinds of human intelligence. We can know the world through language, logical-mathematical analysis, spatial representations, musical thinking, the use of the body to solve problems or to make things, an understanding of other individuals, of the natural world and of ourselves. Individuals differ in the strength of these intelligences, and the ways in which they use them to carry out tasks and solve problems.

A holistic approach to education needs to address each area of intelligence and each part of the 'self', enabling every child to use his or her unique profile for learning to best effect.

SMSC OPPORTUNITIES

Clearly a commitment to holistic learning and SMSC development involves all aspects of school life. It begins with the values of the school community, whether implicit or explicitly stated. These values are reflected by the way in which the school community is organized, including the physical and learning environments. They permeate the interpersonal relationships between teaching and non-teaching staff, staff to pupil, pupil to pupil and school to parents and the wider community. The values underpin the underlying and permeating climate or 'ethos' and the ways in which each member of the school community is respected, valued and presented with opportunities to contribute to the life of the whole. Opportunities for SMSC can be curricular and extra-curricular. They can arise in any subject area or any aspect of school life. They are reflected by school policies such as behaviour, equal opportunities or citizenship. The danger is that, because SMSC is not a timetabled subject and it has implications in all aspects of school life, it is not critically examined. It can all too easily become a by-product of school activities so that schools do not offer clearly defined structures and strategies for listening, valuing, respecting and reflecting. Schools need to examine the opportunities available to pupils that mediate the process of acquiring values and examining attitudes and behaviour.

A RATIONALE FOR CIRCLE TIME IN SMSC EDUCATION

One strategy for SMSC education that has received considerable publicity in recent years, is Circle Time.

It is difficult to arrive at a precise definition of Circle Time as there are a variety of different approaches in educational practice. Several models have been proposed (Mosley, 1987, 1993, 1996; White, 1990; Curry and Bromfield, 1994a; Bliss and Tetley 1993). All see it as a system for enhancing children's self-esteem, promoting moral values, building a sense of team and developing social skills. Typically, Circle Time offers children a regular, practical, opportunity to discuss concerns, consider and debate moral values, practise positive behaviours, work out solutions and make action plans in a fun context which is highly motivational. The children sit in a circle so that everyone can see and make eye contact with all the other members of the class. The interactions that take place during a circle meeting create a cohesive and unified group that is able to share common aims and moral values. The teacher acts as a non-authoritarian facilitator and the use of the circle emphasizes equality and collective responsibility while, at the same time, encouraging honesty and trust. The spirit of Circle Time is beautifully captured in the following description, written by a child about the object that was passed round the circle in order to signify a turn to speak.

> *THE MARBLE EGG*
> At circletime we get
> To hold the egg,
> The precious egg,
> The sacred egg.
> The egg that
> Lets you speak,
> To speak freely,
> To let all your problems dissolve
> When others hold the egg.
> We listen,
> We listen, and we show that they
> Are important too.
> That they deserve to be
> Listened to, and treated
> With respect,
> Just like they treat us
> (Aoife Corcoran, age 8)

Rather than write generally about Circle Time in the rest of this discussion,

I have chosen to highlight the model developed by Mosley (1987, 1993, 1996). This model is unique because it sets Circle Time in a whole-school ecosystemic approach as one strategy in a range of recommendations spanning all the school systems that affect a child's day. It seeks to ensure that there is a synthesis between the moral values worked at in the circle and all other practices, encompassing every person in the school and every part of the school day. Research commissioned by Wiltshire Local Education Authority and carried out by the University of Bristol, Graduate School of Education (1998), demonstrated Quality Circle Time to be effective in providing a setting where children:

- are encouraged to behave well
- improve communication
- learn to care
- develop determination and responsibility
- develop decision-making skills
- have damaged self-esteem rebuilt
- increase their ability to empathize

They also:

- learn to appreciate the cultural background of others
- understand a moral code
- take part in a democratic process
- learn that they are valued
- experience positive teacher relationships

MOSLEY'S QUALITY CIRCLE TIME

Mosley calls her specific model Quality Circle Time. It is a group listening system ideally suited to a whole-class context that creates an emotionally 'safe' place for pupils to explore what they think and feel. It is not designed to be a counselling forum nor a place for disclosures. It has been developed as a strategy for encouraging honest communication and the development of positive relationships, self-discipline, self-regulated behaviour, conflict resolution, assertive communication and democratic group process alongside the skills of speaking, listening, observing, thinking and concentrating.

Emotional 'safety' is essential whenever people are being asked to look at any aspect of 'self'. A personality under threat becomes rigid and inflexible. Only when we feel emotionally 'safe' do we feel free to risk perceiving the world differently or trying out new behaviours. Quality Circle Time is 'safe' because it is bound by strict ground rules for teachers and children, based on respect, valuing and reflecting back to participants a positive mirror of their selves. Of paramount importance is the rule that no name may be used negatively, thus keeping parents, pupils, teaching and non-teaching staff safe from exposure or ridicule, while allowing issues to be discussed and problems solved.

GROUND RULES FOR QUALITY CIRCLE TIME

- No one may put anyone down (looks after feelings, affords respect)
- No one may use any name negatively (creating 'safety' for all individuals including teachers and parents)
- When one person speaks, everyone must listen (all views are taken seriously, giving a sense of value and worth to the individual)
- Everyone has a turn and a chance to speak, but anyone can choose to pass
- The teacher/facilitator role models positive, warm, respectful behaviour

Throughout the circle meeting, ground rules strictly apply. Action is taken if someone persists in breaking a ground rule. First a visual warning in the form of a warning card is given, allowing the person to decide whether to continue to break the rule, or to change their behaviour. If he/she persists in breaking the rule, a short period out of the circle follows.

STRUCTURES AND STRATEGIES

Every lesson follows the same general pattern, though the content and activities change each week in order to be appropriate to whatever topic is under discussion. The topics can be infinitely variable. They can follow a set PSE curriculum with progression through the key stages, or arise from the current needs of the group. The content may just as easily relate to topic work in geography, history or religious knowledge; to matters of personal development; or to issues affecting school management. The important thing to remember is that the process matters as much as the content.

Mosley's Circle Time follows a firm structure so that the group moves from *warm-up* exercises and fun into a *round* where every person is given the opportunity to speak individually. The respect afforded to individuals and their choices is very powerful in raising self-esteem. For just a few minutes, they are the centre of attention and a whole group of people is listening intently to everything they say. The round progresses to *'open forum'* where issues and individual problems are aired and brainstormed, an activity which often leads to an individual or group action plan. The next stage is to *celebrate success* and finally to move to *closure*.

Warm-up games

These are designed to provoke laughter and break down the tensions between individuals. Warm-up games unite the class and energize the group. Sometimes, though, if there is an excitable feel to the class, the warm-up game can bring focus, calm and concentration. Each game has its own rules, which reinforce moral values and foster verbal and physical contact between individuals. They break up friendship groups and cause pupils to sit next to and work with new people for each activity. An interesting aspect of most games is that they create the need for positive eye contact (one of the most significant features of relationship building) between group members. They can also be used to release feelings and imagination, which can be explored later on in the circle meeting.

Rounds
A 'speaking object' is passed round as a visual symbol signifying the right to speak and be heard. In order to keep up a good pace and stop the circle 'grinding to a halt' with the vociferous dominating discussion, rounds are usually scripted with a sentence stem such as 'I don't like it when ...'. The majority of people contribute to a round but anyone can say 'I pass' without feeling awkward, and thereby choose not to speak. Every contribution is accepted and valued, creating a climate of trust and genuine interest. In PSE lessons, the rounds are related to the topic under discussion that week and they can be informed by small group work, paired work or individual worksheets. Rounds are used any time opinion is sought or for evaluation and feedback. Expressing personal opinion and hearing other people's views fosters a sense of identity and assertive communication. It also creates a 'window' into someone else's world-view and thereby generates empathic understanding.

Open Forum
At the heart of Circle Time, the Open Forum enables pupils to develop 'inner locus of control'. Rotter (1966) originated the concept of 'locus of control'. Pupils who have an external locus of control feel that they have little or no control over what happens to them. They are the victims of events and circumstances. Those who have an 'inner locus of control' perceive themselves as having control over what happens to them, they are masters of their fate. They believe that they are in charge of their own lives; they can make choices and decisions to get what they want; they feel good about themselves; and are more likely to achieve academically. Open Forum teaches young people to *own* their opinions, values, attitudes and behaviour and thereby increase their perception of being in control of their own lives and actions. They may ask for help with aspects of their life or behaviour and have the power to accept or reject the advice proffered by their classmates. The scripts for Open Forum are 'Would anyone like some help with their behaviour?' Pupils respond with 'I need some help because I ...'. The peer group then offers help 'Would it help if I ...?' or 'Would it help if you ...?' or 'Would it help if we ...?'. The teacher can offer help alongside the peer group.

From the Open Forum comes an action plan that promotes personal responsibility for behaviour and actions plus an understanding of collective responsibility. Various techniques including role-play, scripted drama, discussion and brainstorming can be used for exploring values, attitudes and behaviour as part of Open Forum. I am constantly amazed at the level of sensitive, generous, creative thinking that young people invest in coming up with action plans during this part of Circle Time.

Celebration
Towards the end of Circle Time, pupils are encouraged to thank group members for their contribution to the group dynamics. 'Thank yous' follow Open Forum, as an important vehicle for lightening the group atmosphere and, if necessary, redirecting thinking to more positive things. Any member of the group can nominate another to be thanked, e.g. a quiet member of the group, or a member with a good sense of humour, etc. This activity involves

one-to-one positive and direct communication. It is to do with giving and receiving compliments and is an important component of building self-esteem and positive relationships. An important point for the group facilitator is to check that everyone experiences a 'thank you' at least once in a course of Circle Meetings. Creative nomination categories ensure everyone is included!

Closure
All group experiences need time for closure. Closing activities might encompass some form of reflection or engender laughter. Visualizations can be used to take children beyond the immediate classroom surroundings and to develop imagination, vision and a sense of the ideal. It is important to provide a 'bridge' into the next activity of the day and one useful closure is a quick round of 'One thing I am looking forward to today is ...'.

SCRIPTS FOR QUALITY CIRCLE TIME

Mosley's model of Circle Time uses scripts to ensure helpful communication and emotional 'safety'. The scripts make it very difficult for pupils to sabotage the group process by dominating or using it as a 'get at' forum for another pupil. All rounds are scripted with a sentence stem which children complete, e.g. 'My favourite place is ...' 'I feel angry when ...' 'When I feel angry I ...'. This stops the very vocal or attention-needing child from dominating the discussion and provides a prompt for those who find it difficult to marshal their thoughts.

Similarly, Open Forum uses the scripts already described in the previous section. These model socially helpful forms of offering advice or suggesting ways forward. A 'Would it help if ...?' script addresses the issue and separates it from the person so that giving advice cannot degenerate into a personalized attack. It also allows those seeking help to be in control of the process. They can receive the help or they can say 'Thanks, but that won't help because ...'.

LINKS BETWEEN CIRCLE TIME AND SMSC DEVELOPMENT

A whole-school policy that embraces the use of Circle Time ensures that SMSC education is not left to chance. The structures and strategies used during Circle Time are not age-specific. They apply to primary and secondary education, at any age/stage to engage the individual in personal reflection, create challenges to preconceived ideas and develop pupils' self-concepts.

The development of a self-concept does not happen in social isolation. It arises in a process of social experience and activity, which affects the evaluations applied to the self-concept and adds a cultural perspective (Mead, 1934). It is not fixed, and alters direction and weighting as learning experiences occur (Burns, 1982). The self-concept is constantly monitoring the surrounding environment through self-observation, feedback and interaction with society. Self-esteem is built in the group process and individuals are enabled to 'try out' new behaviour and learning. Maslow (1962) and Rogers (1961) highlighted the need to provide an accepting, non-judgemental milieu in order for individuals to acquire a sense of belonging and to risk making changes to their self-perception and evaluation.

Pupils play games which engender discussion about the need for rules and individual rights and responsibilities in making and breaking rules. Games teach the need for moral imperatives and the consequences of living without personally owned values. They foster co-operation and group identity, producing the sense of belonging that is an essential prerequisite to developing self-esteem. Circle activities involve every group member and the collective 'group'. Individuals see themselves in their social world as similar to and different from other group members; they look at their own behaviour in the light of other individuals and as reflected by the 'generalized other' of the whole group. Many drama strategies can be used to present different ways of viewing situations and alternative ways of responding. This is particularly powerful with older pupils when they examine anger management, conflict resolution and decision-making. Circle activities can also be used to promote stillness, develop imagination and the capacity to 'think beyond' to 'dream dreams' and visualize the ideal. They provide opportunities to rise above ordinariness and collectively move towards helping the more vulnerable members of the community. When children learn to empathize with others' worlds in this way, they move towards a higher self and develop the qualities that lie at the heart of spirituality.

Out of the circle arise two fountains of issues. The first set of issues is personal to the individuals in the group and will result in individualized action plans and target setting. The second set of issues relates to the management of the school. The pupils will highlight school 'hot spots' such as places where bullying frequently occurs, or organizational weaknesses, such as the structure of the school day or the curriculum. They may come up with creative solutions to problems that beset the school community, such as litter control. Unless the management of the school actively hears these issues and takes some action, the power of Circle Time is greatly diminished. Ideally, issues that arise from class Circle Time meetings would be taken to a School Council made up of representatives from every tutor group and facilitated by a senior member of staff.

In an ideal world, Circle Time would be set in the context of a whole-school approach, where it is backed by explicitly expressed values, strong incentives and clear sanctions. These provide a framework to hold Circle Time safely in place. It also needs to be paralleled by a system for listening to pupils one-to-one. The rule of not using a name negatively, while keeping Circle Time 'safe', takes away the pupil's right to say something that might be bothering them on a personal level. In primary schools using Mosley's Quality Circle Time Model (1996), one-to-one listening is set up using a system called 'bubble time'. Each child has a clothes peg in his/her drawer with his/her name written on it. The teacher then makes a circle of thin wood or card which s/he attaches to a piece of wood so that it can stand on a table. The children are told that the circle represents a bubble and if two people get inside the 'bubble' for an undisturbed time together, other children would burst the 'bubble' if they came near. When children want to talk about issues that are not appropriate for Circle Time, they can place their peg on the 'bubble' and so request 'bubble time'. The agreement is that the teacher will arrange for a few minutes with the child either during break time or class time. The other children agree not to disturb this time.

In secondary schools, teachers can set up a surgery system where a member of staff is available in a specific place, during break time, to talk about any work-related or personal issues. If five members of staff could commit themselves to this system, there would be one person available each break time in the week.

Circle Time can also be backed in primary and secondary schools by non-verbal listening. Each pupil can have a 'think book' or 'journal of reflection' in which to write to his/her tutor or teacher. The agreement is that each note will receive a reply.

IS CIRCLE TIME EFFECTIVE? – A PUPIL PERSPECTIVE

Rogers (1983) argued for a difference between 'teaching' and 'learning'. He wrote that significant learning 'combines the logical and the intuitive, the intellect and the feelings, the concept and the experience, the idea and the meaning. When we learn in that way, we are whole.' (p. 20).

Interviews conducted among pupils (Tew, 1998) indicate that they gain considerable insights through taking part in Circle Time. They are happy to take part in the strategies and feel that they benefit from the insights that they gain.

> The circle helped everyone to take part because in my old school when we did PSE we used to sit in rows in desks and in the circle we could see everybody and it was much easier to talk. You didn't feel that you had to turn round all the time, you just looked across the circle; much easier. (Lucy aged 12)

> I like Circle Time because it helps us to get to know each other. (Amelia aged 10)

> Circle Time helped me to stop fighting in a game and to be gentle. Asking for help was a good thing to do. It helped me a lot. (Curtis aged 9)

> I think it did help build friendships because you learn that a lot of people share the same views as you, so you find new friends. (Sasha aged 11)

> I feel Circle Time is a great idea. . . . We have time to just talk and let go of all the things we are holding inside us, without someone breathing down our necks and trying to shut us up. It calms us down and helps us to think better. (Rishabh aged 13)

WHAT DO TEACHERS THINK ABOUT CIRCLE TIME?

> I began using Circle Time in registration with Year 7 groups. I run six 20-minute sessions and include themes of friendship, co-operation, the community, feelings and self-awareness. Even in these short sessions the tutors and myself have noticed an increase in self-confidence of some students. . . . It is intended that tutors will continue to use Circle Time with their tutor groups throughout their school lives, thus providing them with a forum for problem solving and building self-confidence. (Caroline Atherton, Cranford Community School)

> I think the circle increases the number of friendships and relationships in the group. They had opportunities to discover more about one another and more 'in depth' things than in normal discussion. They also sat next to

different people all the time because of the way in which the circle worked. The games mixed them up, constantly changing the pairs for paired work. They did not have a chance to get into friendship groups and stay there as they do in lessons sat at desks. I think that really helped them to find new people and get to know them. (Pricilla Lane, PSE teacher)

I found the egg the best bit. I especially liked the way in which the pupils took part and were willing to say what they thought. It was very powerful and the circle creates its own atmosphere. (Classroom teacher, Year 6)

Ofsted reports also have recognized and commented on the contribution Quality Circle Time is making to spiritual, moral, social and cultural development while encouraging positive behaviour and relationships born out of mutual respect and value. The following comments are typical (emphasis in italics is mine).

The weekly Circle Time for each class enables pupils of all ages, at their own level, to reflect on aspects of their lives, to *discuss moral and social issues* and to express with confidence their *understanding of right and wrong* and their *sense of justice*. Pupils learn to *listen well* to others, to be *tolerant of other viewpoints* and to *respect* fellow pupils. (Ofsted reports, Canberra Primary School, 1995, paragraph 14)

The *excellent* quality of the *relationships* within the school is evidence that pupils feel *respected* and *valued*. Circle Time, an exercise to *raise self-esteem*, is used by form tutors to contribute to pupils *spiritual awareness*. (Ofsted report, Warren Comprehensive, Essex)

Pupils know *right from wrong* ... The pupils are given opportunities to *learn about themselves and others* in order to build up *respect, tolerance, a sense of identity and self-esteem*. (Ofsted report, Phoenix Secondary and Primary School)

CIRCLE TIME ACROSS THE CURRICULUM

This chapter has considered Circle Time as a structured meeting, occupying a discrete slot of time, in which discussion relating to personal, social, moral, behavioural and cultural issues takes place. Circle Time, in this definition, calls on the theory of group dynamics. Group processes have long been recognized as having the power to change the attitudes and perceptions of each group member. Each person, whether adult or child, gains personal insight and the ability to appreciate the world from other people's viewpoints. Such insights make up empathy, one of the core attitudinal conditions identified by Rogers (1983) as fundamental to enabling a personality to change. When each contribution to the circle is valued and listened to with respect, self-esteem is built and children learn to trust and draw on their inner resources, imagination and creativity in order to meet the demands and challenges of life.

The use of a circle need not be confined to this framework however. Circle rituals can be used to begin or end a lesson or the day. These are a quick meeting in a circle to set a personal agenda, a declaration of intent, e.g. 'Today I will finish all my maths worksheets ...' , 'Today I will not interrupt anyone else's learning ...'. Or they can be used to evaluate or reflect on a lesson or the day, e.g. 'One thing I have learnt in this lesson is ...', 'I am really pleased with myself today because ...'.

Many subject areas lend themselves to the use of a circle format when discussion is called for. No discussion can be entirely safe or entirely open if people are sitting behind one another, because the speaker cannot see the reactions to his/her words. The only truly 'safe' format for open discussion is a circle where each group member can see all the others. This promotes honest and direct communication and militates against both verbal and non-verbal put-downs.

Circles and the use of circle ground rules would provide a 'safe' forum for discussion about medical ethics, genetics and health issues in science, or about the relationship between science and religion, evolution and creation. Similarly in English, discussion about characterization, plot development, storytelling and the development of speaking and listening, at all stages of pupil development, are ideally suited to a circle format. In humanities, pupils may explore other people groups, social organization and religious beliefs. All these subjects present challenges to our moral judgements and values. They cause us to re-examine our beliefs in the light of possible alternatives and to appreciate diversity. Here, too, the circle structure can be used to facilitate open debate and to allow the teacher to move into a facilitative rather than a didactic role when moral and cultural issues are considered.

It could be argued that SMSC is the province of every teacher in every subject, yet not all teachers feel comfortable with the facilitative role involved in running a circle meeting. Similarly, not all teachers feel skilled to run a discussion about moral values and, unless they can create the accepting, non-judgemental, empathic 'climate' necessary for risking changes in attitudes and values, it is probably better that they are not required to facilitate such groups.

CONCLUSIONS

Quality Circle Time is a powerful tool for mediating SMSC, PSHE and positive behaviour in schools and as a means of effecting change in the individual. Its contribution is most effective within the framework of a whole-school approach and its implementation has a positive impact on school ethos. It requires teachers who are committed to the underlying philosophies and trained in the structures and strategies. Once in place, however, Quality Circle Time has a powerful impact on the school affecting:

- the quality of relationships throughout the school
- the levels of positive behaviour
- the quality of teaching and learning
- the sense of belonging to, and ownership of the school
- motivation

In contributing to the development of autonomy, initiative and mutual respect, Circle Time may contribute to a much greater outcome than is commonly supposed, for it embodies the means and the values of freedom and equality. Nelson Mandela eloquently summed up so much when he wrote the following extract.

Our deepest fear is not that we are inadequate. Our deepest fear is that we are powerful beyond measure.
It is our light, not our darkness that most frightens us.
We ask ourselves, 'Who am I to be brilliant, gorgeous, talented, fabulous?' Actually, who are you not to be? You are a child of God. Your playing small doesn't serve the world. There's nothing enlightened about shrinking so that other people won't feel insecure around you.
We are all meant to shine as children do. We are born to manifest the glory of God that is within us.
It's not just in some of us, it's in everyone.
And as we let our own light shine, we unconsciously give other people permission to do the same.
As we're liberated from our own fear, our presence automatically liberates others.

Would it be pretentious to claim at least a small role for Circle Time in the process of liberation?

REFERENCES

Bliss, T. and Robinson, G. (1995) *Developing Circle Time: Takes Circle Time Much Further*. Bristol: Lame Duck Publications.

Bliss, T. and Tetley, J. (1993) *Circle Time. For Infant, Junior and Secondary Schools*. Bristol: Lame Duck Publishing

Bliss, T. and Tetley, J. (1995) *Developing Circle Time: An Activity Book for Teachers*. Bristol, Lame Duck Publications.

Burns, R. (1982) *Self-Concept Development and Education*. Eastbourne: Holt, Rinehart & Winston.

Curry, M. and Bromfield, C. (1994a) *Circle Time*. Stafford: Nasen.

Curry, M. and Bromfield, C. (1994b) *Personal and Social Education for Primary Schools Through Circle Time*. Stafford: NASEN Enterprises Ltd.

Gardner, H. (1991) *The Unschooled Mind: How Children Think and How Schools Should Teach*. London: Fontana Press.

Gardner, H. (1993a) *Multiple Intelligences: The Theory in Practice*. London: Basic Books.

Gardner, H. (1993b, 2nd edn.) *Frames of Mind: The Theory of Multiple Intelligences*. London: Fontana Press.

Goleman, D. (1996) *Emotional Intelligence*. London: Bloomsbury Publishing Plc.

Greenhalgh, P. (1994) *Emotional Growth and Learning*. London: Routledge.

Hannaford, C. (1995) *Smart Moves: Why Learning is Not All in Your Head*. Virginia: Great Ocean Publishers, Inc.

James, W. (1890) *Principles of Psychology*. New York: Holt, Rinehart & Winston.

Maslow, A. (1962) *Towards a Psychology of Being*. New York: Van Nostrand Reinhold.

Mead, G.H. (1934) *Mind, Self and Society*. Chicago: University of Chicago.

Mosley, J. (1987) *All Round Success*. Wiltshire: Wiltshire Education Publications.

Mosley, J. (1988) Some implications arising from a small-scale study of a circle based programme initiated for the tutorial period. *Pastoral Care in Education*, **6** (2), 10–17.

Mosley, J. (1993) *Turn Your School Round*. Cambridge: LDA.

Mosley, J. (1996) *Quality Circle Time*. Cambridge: LDA.

Mosley, J. and Tew, M. (1999) *Quality Circle Time in the Secondary School*. London: Fulton.

Ofsted (1995) *Framework for the Inspection of Nursery, Primary, Middle, Secondary and Special Schools*. London: HMSO.

Rogers, C. (1961) *On Becoming a Person*. Boston: Houghton Mifflin.

Rogers, C. (1983) *Freedom to Learn for the 80s*. Merril, USA: Macmillan.

Rotter, J. B. (1966) Generalised expectancies for internal versus external control of reinforcement. *Psychol. Monogr*, **80** (609).

Schools Curriculum and Assessment Authority (SCAA) (1996) *Education for Adult Life: The Spiritual and Moral Development of Young People*. SCAA Discussion Papers 6.

Taylor, M. (1998) *Values Education and Values in Education*. (A guide to the issues commissioned by the Association of Teachers and Lecturers.) London: NFER.

Tew, M. (1998) Using Circle Time in personal and social education. Unpublished MEd dissertation, University of Bristol.

White, M. (1990) Circletime. *Cambridge Journal of Education*, **20**, (1), 53–6.

CHAPTER 15

A collaborative approach to researching teacher work in developing spiritual and moral education

Jane Erricker

INTRODUCTION

This chapter will deal with the issue of spiritual and moral education, and in particular the problems teachers have in addressing it as part of the normal school curriculum. The insights that I offer arose out of the work of the Children and Worldviews Project which has been developing a particular approach to the issue.

Spiritual and moral education, as an area of the school curriculum, was highlighted by the 1988 Education Reform Act and again in Circular 1/94. The first paragraph of the circular provides the context for the curriculum in relation to the overarching aim of education:

> The Education Reform Act 1988 sets out as the central aim for the school curriculum that it should promote the spiritual, moral, cultural, mental and physical development of pupils and society, and prepare pupils for the opportunities, responsibilities and experiences of adult life. (DfE, 1994, p. 9)

As most of us in education would acknowledge, there are a great many questions that can be posed now, more than ten years after the Act, about the degree to which this overarching aim has been addressed. Spiritual and moral education, as a defined aim and as an area of the curriculum, has been debated in conference (e.g. the annual Roehampton conference on Education, Spirituality and the Whole Child, conferences of the Association for Moral Education and the biennial International Seminar on Religious Education and Values), pronounced upon by government (e.g. SCAA, 1995, 1996) and researched in the intervening years. But teachers are still unsure about what the terms imply and what they themselves could or should be doing in the classroom. It was in this climate that the Children and Worldviews Project began investigating children's spirituality, or, as the team prefer, children's *world-views*.

The previous research (Erricker *et al.*, 1997) done by the project team involved establishing conversations with primary aged children ('interviews') around issues that are of importance to them. The nature of these issues was decided by the children themselves, in response to a variety of stimuli. The conversations took place in schools and normally in small groups, though some whole-year assemblies were involved. Over the course of the last three years, the project team has 'interviewed' approximately 200 children ranging in age between 6 and 11 years.

Analysis of the transcripts has resulted in the identification of particular themes that the children find important, such as relationships, secret places, ethnic identity, religious affiliation, death, separation and the environment. The analysis has also revealed the process that the children go through as they attempt to verbalize what they think and feel. The process not only involves finding the right words or metaphors to express complex and deeply felt issues, but shows also that the verbalization is a part of the process of the child's self-understanding. As they express themselves their feelings are made clearer to themselves and this self-discovery is evident in what they say. Sharing these feelings and the process of discovering them allows the children to find that other people have these feelings too, revealing and facilitating the development of empathy and understanding as the children discuss and help each other (Erricker *et al.*, 1997).

This process forms the basis of what we understand spiritual and moral education to be. In order to enlarge on our understanding, I would like to use a term that is beginning to be recognized as useful, that is *emotional literacy*. The exact meaning of this term differs according to the source; within psychological literature its origin appears to be Daniel Goleman (1996, 1998), whose work on emotional intelligence draws on Howard Gardner's (1984) theory of multiple intelligences. The pressure group Antidote, which campaigns for the recognition of emotional education as a valid part of the curriculum, also uses the term (Parks, 1999) but does not clearly define its meaning.

I would like to suggest that emotional literacy involves the development[1] of the following skills:

1. reflection on one's own emotions
2. self-knowledge (understanding *why* one does something)
3. understanding of consequences
4. self-criticism (according to one's own recognized principles)
5. self-control
6. reflection on the emotions of others
7. empathy
8. criticism of others (according to one's own recognized principles)
9. understanding why others do things
10. recognition of relationship
11. recognition of difference
12. recognition of the complexity of social discourse

The skills can be divided into three groups: numbers 1–5 are centred around the self, 6–9 are concerned with others and 10–12 with society. It is these skills that the children will be developing as a result of conversation with a facilitating adult and/or with other children.

I do not suggest that the terms spiritual and moral education and emotional literacy are necessarily synonymous. Spiritual and moral education could be taken to mean very much more than this. However, I would suggest that spiritual and moral education *must* include emotional literacy.

This idea of emotional literacy and the skills that make it up is very different from the notion of an imposed moral framework. The 'rules and regulations' are self-determined and self-imposed and there is no conforming to specified values. It is not about knowing, or being told, about how one should be or how one should behave. Instead, the recognition and practice of the skills should result in a recognition of the complexity of social discourse, a recognition of one's own agency within it and one's responsibility for its successful functioning (in Aristotle's sense of the maximum happiness). This is not to deny the possibility of conforming to a set of values or a spirituality derived from a religion, if that is what the individual wants and needs, only that that course of action should be pursued mindfully, in the knowledge that this is a choice and a positive decision that one is free to make. This represents a different position and process from that often found in school PSE or RE lessons where the values are suggested and then discussion is invited. The discussion takes place within a context that recognizes implicitly that no significant change in position is allowed. The value has already been stated. Interestingly, this process was mirrored in the procedures of the 1996 SCAA Forum on Values in Education and the Community. Here discussion was invited, with the suggestion that a consensus was sought, but the agenda had already been decided (see Erricker, 1997). The issue is one of power; we, the authorities, have decided how you should behave, we will allow you to discuss it but we will allow you no power to change it.

Within the framework of understanding detailed above, the project team decided to involve teachers in schools, encouraging them to take on the role of 'interviewer' which we now felt we could redefine as the facilitator of the children's development in this area. This represented the first step in establishing a provision within the curriculum for spiritual and moral education/emotional literacy.

WORKING WITH THE TEACHERS IN PRIMARY SCHOOLS

The teachers with whom we decided to work in the phase of the research reported here were either self-selected, or were teachers in schools with which we already had close relationships and which we had used for interviewing previously. Four schools were used, with one teacher in each school. Each teacher is identified by the initial letter of her name. Teacher C worked with reception children in an urban school, teacher P with Years 1 and 2 in an inner-city school, teacher G with reception in an inner-city school in a different city and teacher N with Years 4 and 5 children, from a mixed-year class in a small rural school.

All the teachers expressed a commitment to child-centred education. They all felt an unease with the weight of curriculum requirements (and this was before the advent of literacy and numeracy hours) and expressed a desire to spend more time in general conversation with the children. In a sense the teachers were self-selected because of this unease and desire. In two of the schools, the school with teacher N and the school with teacher G, the catchment included areas of recognized social deprivation and the teachers felt a need to try to compensate for the problems in the children's home lives.

We began the process by visiting the schools for a meeting as a project team.[2] In all schools the first meeting was with the head, then the class teacher concerned and subsequently the whole staff. In these meetings the work was described, and the involvement of the school negotiated. Some schools preferred the involvement to be with just the one teacher, others would have wanted as many staff as possible working with us, or at least knowing what we were doing and supporting it. In practice, it has been difficult to involve more than one teacher in each school to date and that is what we have done. The teachers were expected to talk to the children and tape-record the conversations, transcribe the tapes, keep a research log and attend meetings together to discuss progress. The meetings took place approximately every two months and were recorded and transcribed. Between meetings a member of the project team went into each school to work with the children or talk with the teacher. We provided written guidelines to help the teachers with the process, and further guidelines were issued as we recognized some of the difficulties teachers were experiencing.

The teachers were encouraged to find a format for talking with the children which suited their own situation. Where they spoke, when and with how many children, depended on the teacher, as did the nature of the stimulus used to promote the discussion. The teachers needed to find a method that worked for them.

In a previous stage of our research we had produced children's 'stories' by removing the interviewer's questions from each transcript so that a continuous piece of prose was produced. We had used these stories as stimuli to promote discussion by other children and encouraged the teachers in this phases to follow suit. Some also used picture drawing and annotation.

Teachers C, G and P used a story, asked for a picture and then annotated the picture during discussion with the child. Teacher P also used a story on its own for discussion with a small group of children and used the existing format of Circle Time to have a conversation with the whole class. Teacher G also made use of unsought opportunities when the children were doing ordinary curriculum tasks and brought up particular issues. The teachers kept a research log where they recorded any extra information about the conversations and any thoughts that they had about the work. These logs formed the basis of the discussions at the meetings with the project team. Members of the project team also visited each school and interviewed some children themselves, in order to help the teachers with the interviewing process.

There were, therefore, five distinct data sets that were available to me.

1. Transcripts of interviews done by the project team
2. Transcripts of interviews done by the teachers
3. Annotated pictures drawn by the children
4. Teachers' logs
5. Transcripts of teachers' meetings with the project team

And there were several different levels at which the analysis could be done:

I.   We could look at the content of what the children say: what things they talk about, what issues are important to them, frame their understanding and give meaning to their lives.
II. We could look at how they say it: how the content and way of expressing themselves changes over the course of the conversation, how they develop the skills of emotional (spiritual and moral) literacy.
III. We could look at how the teachers question and facilitate the conversations and how this has changed over time.
IV. We could look at what the teachers think about what they are doing.

In this chapter I concentrate on the teachers and the way in which they carried out the process (II, III and IV above).

ISSUES IN THE TEACHERS' DEVELOPMENT

The teachers with whom we worked became involved with us because they had an idea of their role that resonated with the philosophy underlying our research. They were all concerned that the demands of current educational policy made it difficult to fulfil the role to their own personal satisfaction and they were eager to work with people who appeared to affirm their vision. However, they found that they had become accustomed to a style of teaching that had distanced them from their ideals, and to return to those ideals in practice (if they had ever practised them at all) was more difficult than they expected.

In the following sections I discuss the difficult issues that I identified.

Epistemological issues

Teachers understand themselves to be the purveyors of knowledge. They have knowledge and their job is to pass this on to the children. However, this statement presupposes that teachers understand what knowledge is or at least what type of knowledge their teaching is concerned with. The French postmodern philosopher Jean-François Lyotard (1984) identifies two types of knowledge: scientific and narrative. Scientific knowledge is that which is considered to be 'verifiable' or 'falsifiable', legitimized by the 'expert' and passed on didactically from 'sender' to 'addressee' (p. 24). Lyotard objects to this 'unquestioning acceptance of an instrumental conception of knowledge' (p. 18) and suggests, by contrast, the value of narrative knowledge.

> Knowledge in general cannot be reduced to science, nor even to learning. Learning is the set of statements which, to the exclusion of all other statements, denote or describe objects and may be declared true or false. Science is a subset of learning ... But [knowledge] ... also includes notions of 'know-how' (savoir-faire), 'knowing how to live', (savoir-vivre), 'how to listen' (savoir-entendre), etc. (Lyotard, 1984, p. 18)

Lyotard's ideas allow us to include under the umbrella of knowledge the stories that are told in order to cement the social bond between people, and which bind them together by their 'three-fold competence' in 'the speech acts' of 'know-how, knowing how to speak and knowing how to listen – through which the community's relationship to itself and its environment is played out' (Lyotard, 1984, p. 21).

We use Lyotard's ideas as a legitimation of the valuing of the children's narratives and we ask the teachers to do the same. Thus we are asking them to act in opposition to the demands increasingly made by the National Curriculum to concentrate on objective knowledge and instead to value subjective knowledge in the form of the narratives, or stories that the children tell. The teachers are not used to this (except perhaps in the teaching of skills, though I am not sure if they would identify this as subjective knowledge)[3] and to differing degrees they found it difficult to adjust their working practices, and to identify clear learning objectives beyond those which normally derive from the 'objective' knowledge paradigm.

This quotation from one of our teachers shows the conflict for them. While working on a Maths topic one child 'poured her heart out':

> I then asked myself ... why feel guilty about going with the mood and needs of the group and abandoning a core subject! (Teacher G, log, May 1998)

As well as demanding a valuing of, and commitment to, objective knowledge, the National Curriculum also demands the valuing of the purveyor of that knowledge, the 'one who knows', the teacher. Thus by asking teachers to shift their commitment to a particular knowledge paradigm we are also asking them to yield their position of power and authority within the classroom. We are suggesting that children can be allowed to know as much or even more than the teacher, can publicly claim the position of the repository of that knowledge and have it acknowledged by the former holder of that exalted rank – the teacher.

I shall return to the issue of power in the next section.

Methodological issues

If 'objective knowledge' is an inappropriate category to use when developing emotional literacy then the transmission model of teaching is no longer appropriate either. This meant that the teachers working with us had to learn a different way of relating to the children in what could be called a 'teaching' situation and this was difficult for them. We asked the teachers to talk to the children in a comfortable and non-threatening environment. This they achieved in different ways but it is best illustrated by a quotation from one of their logs. This quotation is from Teacher G.

> She [the child] just poured her heart out while working on a Maths topic. It was too important not to pick up on and certainly something which could be talked about together. Out came the cushions, and there was a good feeling of togetherness as we sat in the circle and started talking. (Teacher G, log, May 1998)

Some found it more difficult than others because of their personalities, their experience and their confidence. Some found it difficult to relinquish the control and their position as the powerful one in the classroom. The following is not intended as a criticism of the teacher involved but an interesting example of the complexity of the process. Teacher C retained the power and control by editing one of the stories that acted as a stimulus for discussion by the children. One of the stories contained a paragraph about the devil and the teacher did not want to use this paragraph because she claimed that the children would be disturbed by the reference. However, in discussion at the subsequent teachers' meeting it became apparent that it was she herself who was disturbed by the reference.

> *Teacher C* I left out the bit about I believe in the devil ... I was just scared really (scared of the devil!). Scared of doing the devil with four-year-olds unless they brought it up. (Teachers' meeting, 26 March 1998)

It took about nine months for all of them to be comfortable with the way of working that we were suggesting.

One recurring issue was the use of the tape recorder. It took the children a while to get used to being recorded and the teachers a while to find the right position for the machine. This was solved in a variety of ways by the individuals concerned.

A more pressing issue was the time needed to do the interviews with the children, to transcribe them and to come to the teachers' meetings. It was difficult to find the space in the curriculum for the conversations. One teacher used Circle Time, another RE time and the others just fitted it in somewhere. One teacher, P, found that some children liked the idea of talking so much that they suggested an after-school talking club. One child has attended regularly and two more (all girls) occasionally.

The teachers' meetings (of which four have been held to date) are particularly important. They are a forum for discussing the 'results' of their own work – the children's narratives, pictures, etc, for the joint interpretation of the transcripts and pictures, and for discussion of problems and issues. They also provide opportunities for reflection on their own narratives, the stories of their experience of doing the research, which might not have otherwise occurred (like the reflection on the devil).

Interpretative issues
After the work of collecting the children's narratives has been done, the next task is to analyse and interpret them. There are several different ways in which this can be done.

- We could look at them from a psychological perspective by applying, for example, theories of cognitive development.
- We could code and categorize them according to the issues raised, according to the metaphors used, according to the other ways in which children express themselves.
- We could look at them from a 'developmental'[4] perspective, though this is unlikely because as yet we have no longitudinal data.
- We could look within the transcript of a single conversation for evidence of the children wrestling with particular issues.

This last option was the one that we chose in this particular phase of our work. We looked in the transcript for how the children expressed the issues in metaphor, communicated and explained them to the other children (a very important reason for interviewing in small groups) and came to a position on the issue in question (remembering that the 'issue' is one that has been raised by the children themselves in response to a stimulus, not an issue that has been raised by the teacher). It does not matter if the position reached is only temporary, or even particular to the time and place in which it is expressed and therefore ephemeral, because that is the nature of learning: as we experience so our position changes. The important thing is not the position, but the *process* of coming to that position. What we are trying to do with the children is to allow them to practise 'reasoning' themselves into a position. However, the position and the process we are talking about is one which involves the emotions as much as (or even more than?) the powers of rational thought.

The interpretation of the children's conversations also depends upon the experiential, ideological and epistemological position of the one who is the interpreter. This interpreter is the teacher while the conversation is going on, because the interpretation of the conversation guides the conversation, as the teacher decides what to say next and how to respond. The teacher will also look at the tapes afterwards and decide the next step in the process of facilitating the children's 'development'. It is therefore vital that the teacher reflects on her own position and that these reflections are shared with other members of the team. This is achieved by the research log which is in effect the teacher's narrative. In addition, as the writer of this chapter my own narrative is a consideration.

The relationships between these narratives is layered and hermeneutical. In the transcripts and the research logs of the teachers we have the representation of two narratives (discourses). The first is the one that the research is intended to uncover – the narrative of the child. This narrative is exposed by the mechanism of the interview, and captured and ossified by the mechanics of recording. But this exposure and capture is only revealed by the intervention of a third narrative, that of the interpreter of the transcript. Without the third narrative the other two are not represented, in that their existence is ephemeral and their meanings, as they collide, are not revealed. The second narrative is that of the teacher, the interviewer, the facilitator of the exposure of the narrative of the child, but also the subject of exposure herself, both in the interview and in the research logs. Likewise the narrative of the interpreter of the narratives of the teacher and the child is revealed in the act of interpretation.

Although in the role of 'interpreter' as characterized above, embedded in the process, I must nevertheless try to pull apart the 'pile-up' resulting from multiple narrative collision, to open up the spaces between them and reveal the nature of the relationships and influences. Without revelation of the nature of those influences, the process cannot be understood and judgements cannot be made about the value of the exercise.

Ethical issues
Prior to taking this research to the teachers we had, as a team, identified and been confronted with various ethical issues surrounding the work. We discussed these with the teachers and they identified more specific ones as the conversations with children progressed.

The whole process was seen as 'risky'. The teachers felt that they were potentially 'opening a can of worms' by asking the children to narrate and reflect on their experiences. Yet they felt that this was valuable and necessary as these issues were part of the children's lives, and affecting their performance in the classroom and their growth as personalities. They were also committed to the process as a part of spiritual and moral education. This type of conversation occasionally took place in the classroom anyway, but the Project work was different because it 'invited it', as the following quotation from teacher N illustrates:

Teacher N We have an NTA (non-teaching assistant) who was at the meeting. She is also a parent and she was very much [concerned] about what would be said and whether she would be happy as a parent for her children to say it. The children are saying those things anyway and the staff, whether or not it's research, are dealing with it on a day-to-day basis. Why should the research make any difference? (Teachers' meeting, 14 Jan. 1998)

That it was worthwhile was made clear on another occasion when teacher G reflected on a particular conversation with the children.

Teacher G I was afraid of taking a risk. I find this is still one of my big problems. Am I prepared to take a risk?
Researcher It was interesting what came out of that.
Teacher G Yes, it was, and it proved that you can [take a risk]. (Teachers' meeting, 26 March 1998)

A very substantial ethical issue is whether or not we, as the facilitators of the conversations, should *do* anything with the information we are given. For example, should we try and solve the children's problems? Should we tell parents if the children say something about them? Should we report suspected abuse? Should we report confessions of illegal activities?

In our view it is not our place to solve problems. Although it has been suggested that our methods are those of counselling, the children have shown that they do not see us in that way. They are aware that we cannot solve problems, and do not want us to. One child in particular showed his antipathy to such attempts (see Erricker *et al.*, 1997). We always discuss the conversations with the head teachers of the schools involved and take their advice, but as a general principle we do not tell parents what the children have said. In this way we respect the confidentiality of the children, but if abuse or illegal activities were suspected we would take the head's advice as to the action. Teacher N, herself the head teacher of the school, had to make a difficult decision when some children she was interviewing confessed to some criminal damage. She decided to tell the parents of the children and the owners of the property that she had the evidence, the children confessed and she destroyed the incriminating tapes so that they could not be used as data. It is particularly interesting that the children disclosed this information to her, knowing that she was the head and knowing that she had been investigating the damage, but seeing their relationship to her as interviewer as different and separate. Her opinion was that the children regarded the interviews as storytelling and therefore not directly related to real life. This opens up another issue regarding the nature of 'truth' for the children which has been discussed in previous publications (Erricker *et al.*, 1997).

CONCLUSIONS

The teachers have now been trying out this methodology for approximately nine months. They report that they feel comfortable with it and they think that the children are benefiting. The exact nature of that benefit will be the subject of future longitudinal study. The teachers also feel that they themselves have benefited, as the following quotation shows:

> *Teacher C* It's been really enjoyable to do with the children and I feel that I've developed skills in the kind of interviewing, trying not to direct it too much. You know, stepping back as we've discussed before, not being, you know, knowing exactly the way something's going to go, you plan all the outcomes, with this it's letting go of that, and it's quite liberating to do that for a session ... let the children take it where it's going. (Teachers' meeting, 20 May 1998)

We have observed that teachers find it difficult (but ultimately rewarding) to be researchers. These difficulties are both practical and philosophical. Practically, with the demands of the National Curriculum and the accompanying administration, there is not enough time in a teacher's working day to do both jobs well. Research requires not just the time to collect the data but also to read the necessary literature. Collaboration is essential. Teachers will not be successful as researchers if they do not have the time to seek out and receive support from other teacher researchers and experienced researchers from higher education establishments and this needs commitment from the heads in the form of funds for supply cover. Those who, like David Hargreaves at a 1996 TTA conference, advocate teaching as a research-based profession, just like medicine, overlook the time-consuming and resource-consuming nature of constant curriculum change. Where funding for classroom-based research is available, the constraints on teachers' time and energy make it very difficult to produce work of quality, as the first research reports of TTA funded projects show (TTA, 1996). The first step must surely be some lightening of the teachers' workloads by curriculum stability and smaller class sizes. Poor research done by overworked teachers in the classroom does the profession no favours.

In carrying out the process I have described, the teachers were both researching and attempting some new classroom practice. When engaged in the process with the children they found it difficult to relinquish the power and control of the classroom situation. When we discussed the method with them, they were committed to the idea of child-centred, child-led education, but in practice they found it hard to do. Their role as teachers was to be in control, to guide the lesson and to achieve the learning objectives. However, they believed that the children learned best when education was in their (the children's) control. There appeared to be a tension between the method that was best for *teaching* and that best for *learning*. In other words, they believed that teaching is best done by control but learning is best done by facilitation. Put another way, learning is something children do for themselves, with help. This contrasts with the paradigm underpinning the National Curriculum, that of learning being knowing what you have been taught.

Thus our teachers had to work through the stresses working in a different paradigm from that required of them in their normal teaching, but one which they felt was right for their children. The comments of teachers at the last teachers' meeting show that they can do so:

Teacher C You don't need them [the stories] in a way. You can start at any point ... It takes shape all on its own. We need to learn that you can't always ensure the outcome ... We need to be open to any outcome ...

Teacher G I wouldn't be surprised that they [the children] might be more developed [spiritually] than when we're older. ...

Teacher N You don't stop playing because you grow old, you grow old because you stop playing. And this is playing with talk. You have to have a certain confidence and reflection to be able to do it and that's maybe why our colleagues don't want to do it. We're the enlightened ones.

NOTES

1 I am unhappy with the use of the word 'development' mainly because of the linear and hierarchical connotations that it has. It also suggests that I have an end point in mind – the completely 'developed'? 'mature'? emotionally literate? person. I do not think I have defined that person at all. Carol Gilligan (Hekman, 1995) defines development as the realization of potential, and although I am still not completely happy with this because there is still an end point implied, it is the best so far. I will continue to use the word with these reservations in mind.

2 The Children and Worldviews Project team consists of Jane Erricker (Director), Clive Erricker (Director) and Cathy Ota (Research Assistant). The Project is funded by the Calouste Gulbenkian Foundation, King Alfred's College, Winchester, and Chichester Institute of Higher Education.

3 I would see the difference being that we are asking the teachers to encourage children's narratives and to value their experiences as being a genuine and valuable aspect of knowledge.

4 By 'developmental' here I mean looking for increasing complexity and depth in the children's conversations.

REFERENCES

DfE (1994) Circular 1/94. London: HMSO.

Erricker, C. (1998) Spiritual confusion. *International Journal of Children's Spirituality*, **3** (1).

Erricker, C., Erricker, J., Ota, C., Sullivan, D. and Fletcher, M. (1997) *The Education of the Whole Child*. London: Cassell.

Gardner, Howard (1984) *Frames of Mind: The Theory of Multiple Intelligences*. London: Heinemann.

Goleman, Daniel (1996) *Emotional Intelligence: Why It Can Matter More than IQ*. London: Bloomsbury.

Goleman, Daniel (1998) *Working With Emotional Intelligence*. London: Bloomsbury.

Hekman, S. (1995) *Moral Voices, Moral Selves*. Cambridge: Polity Press.

Lyotard, J. F. (1984) *The Postmodern Condition*, Manchester: Manchester University Press.

Parks, J. (1999) Emotional literacy: education for meaning. *The International Journal of Children's Spirituality*, **4** (1).

School Curriculum and Assessment Authority (SCAA) (1995) Discussion Paper 3: *Spiritual and Moral Development*. London: SCAA.

School Curriculum and Assessment Authority (SCAA) (1996) Discussion Paper 6: *Preparation for Adult Life*. London: SCAA.

Teacher Training Agency (1996) *Summaries of Findings of Teacher Research Grant Projects*. London: TTA.

CHAPTER 16

Reflections on inspections

Margaret A. Warner

INTRODUCTION

The present inspection process has both supporters and critics (see Hackett in TES, 1999). The following chapter is written in the hope that it will add further to an understanding of what those working in this field are trying to do. Many Ofsted inspectors have spent a lifetime in education, as class teachers, head teachers and then as inspectors doing, conscientiously, their own part in helping children on their journey to adulthood. Inspectors bring a considerable range of experiences to help others run and work in their respective schools. Those who have chosen to be independent inspectors prefer not to be part of a group who know each other too well, believing that more independent judgements can be made in this way and a wider view of education is brought to schools from inspecting schools across the country.

This chapter focuses on the aspect of inspections relating to the provision schools make for pupils' spiritual, moral, social and cultural (SMSC) development. It is informed by my own experience as an inspector on over one hundred primary, secondary and special school inspections, often taking the lead and collating the evidence for the SMSC paragraphs in the report. The inspections have been in state and voluntary schools; Church of England and Roman Catholic. It is, inevitably, also informed by my own religious convictions.

THE OFSTED FRAMEWORK FOR INSPECTION

The 'Framework for Inspection' clearly points out the links there are between pupils' attitudes and responses, the curriculum, teaching and the provision made for pupils' spiritual, moral, social and cultural development, with each influencing the other. The Framework also provides ample opportunities for inspectors to look for good provision: through attending assemblies; looking at displays and other evidence of pupils' work; through discussions with teachers and pupils; and through observation of lessons and the everyday life of the school.

Possibilities for pupils' spiritual development will also be through the daily act of collective worship, when that moment of silence speaks louder than words, when hymns are learned and sung with joy or sorrow and when mysteries are explored. How often in future life will the words of an appropriate hymn or prayer, learned as a child, bubble to the surface or come to mind at different adult times of joy or trial? What a vacuum there will be if we do not have these to recall.

Pupils' spiritual development will be promoted through: the poetry they read and write; the art they create or learn to appreciate; through experiences in physical education and geography, which take them into the natural environment and wider world when cross-country running and on field trips; through the aesthetic, associated with music, art, dance and drama; and through the study of religious belief in history, geography or religious education. Pupils should begin to realize that the power of the Spirit is evident in all cultures and countries and they need to find their own way of following and walking with it. To ignore it is to ignore what is of great value to, and has influenced, vast numbers of people across the world and down the ages. What are the pupils' responses going to be? God either exists or does not. By far the majority of people in the world believe, and very many experience, that He does. All major world faiths believe there is one God or Supreme Being, although their understanding of Him may differ. If all believe there is one, then He must be the same one. You cannot run away from the Spirit by pretending He does not exist, any more than you can avoid the break of day or the fall of night. Life moves on and we all have to move with it, passing the baton on to the next generation, for their turn through the journey of life and their own relationship with the Divine.

Although one inspector, other than the registered inspector, has ultimate responsibility for writing the allocated SMSC paragraphs in a report, if the report is to be truly representative of the whole school, he or she is dependent on colleagues for information. Because of this, it is often a learning experience for this lead inspector who, while giving a lead, allows colleagues to bring their own interpretations to this aspect of pupils' development and seeks to reflect these interpretations in the report. This is particularly so in secondary schools where inspectors usually inspect one subject only. In my experience of working with the same secondary team over three years, the increase in understanding there has been, by all of us on the team and by the departments we have worked with in the schools, is because all of us have had to think through what we mean, in order to collect the appropriate evidence. It is not only the subject inspectors who contribute to this section of the report; those looking at other aspects contribute as well. For example, an inspector reporting on accommodation considered that in one school the environment did not promote the spiritual development of pupils as well as it could. Pupils' work was not much in evidence around the corridors of the school, and thus probably little valued, paintwork was chipped and minor repairs needed to be carried out on the building. Others found in the same school that pupils' conclusions to discussions on values needed at times to be challenged, as they were often self-centred. One wonders how far the former had influenced the latter.

Inspection is indeed a learning process, and rightly so, for although some are further along the road of understanding than others, none of us has full knowledge. Having to inspect provision for the spiritual development of pupils is rightly done by all inspectors. There are no specialists in spirituality, save God. Unlike a subject, including religious education, where the acquisition of knowledge determines whether one is a specialist or not, inspectors, head teachers, teachers, and pupils all learn through the inspection process and, one hopes, become the better for it.

Both the original 'Framework for Inspection' and the revised Framework placed provision for the spiritual, moral, social and cultural development of pupils high on the school's and inspection's agenda. The original Framework divided the inspection report, as well as individual subject findings, into: 'standards; quality of learning; efficiency; and spiritual, moral, social and cultural development'. The revised headings were: 'educational standards achieved; quality of education provided; and the management and efficiency of the school'. The most recent Framework includes 'pupils' spiritual, moral, social and cultural development', not as a discrete section to be inspected under the wider umbrella of 'quality of education', but as part of the total curriculum offered by the school. If this provision were not included, much would be missing from many pupils' lives and from the school community of which they are a part.

When inspecting, evidence for provision in each of the four, be it spiritual, moral, social or cultural development, has to be collected separately, as provision for each has a purpose in its own right. Yet all overlap. One might add 'collective worship' as a fifth section, as assemblies often contain elements of the other four, but stand alone in terms of worship. The intertwining of these five elements contribute to the character of the school and often create its ethos. To leave any of them out would leave a 'black hole' in the overall education of the child.

DIFFERENT SCHOOLS – DIFFERENT WAYS FORWARD

As with all other aspects of a school, much will depend on the priorities of the head teacher and staff of the school and, increasingly, those of the governors and parents. Schools are at very different stages of development in this aspect of the curriculum and ways forward have to match the stage the school has reached. We need always to be aiming for the best, but realize that small steps may have to be taken where little provision has previously been made. Only the school in its own community can plan those steps appropriately, but plan they should, if they are not to fall short of providing their pupils with the quality of education others enjoy.

In one secondary school, pupils experienced a sense of the spiritual through pilgrimage in religious education lessons. They learned about pilgrimage through experiential activities, such as a walk through the school grounds collecting feathers. They then considered the different experiences each brought back with them. In the same school, pupils were also encouraged to view mathematics as an aspect of life in more than a material way, and in design and technology, students were encouraged to be curious and perceptive about the natural and man-made world and appreciate man's skill and inventiveness.

In another school, where the overall provision for pupils' spiritual, moral, social and cultural development was said to be good, provision for their spiritual development was considered sound and reported thus:

> Clear, positive values, with a spiritual dimension, are promoted in the school. These are based on the school's aims and a planned programme of

assemblies, and are reinforced through the school's rules. These values are clearly evident in pupils' attitudes, behaviour and good relationships.

Pupils' spiritual development is often promoted in lessons. In RE, for example, pupils consider the religious and spiritual dimensions of life and their own views of them. In art pupils are encouraged to make a personal response to different themes. In music their aesthetic and spiritual development is promoted, especially through sensitive and expressive string-playing in both lessons and the orchestra. In English and modern foreign languages there are uplifting experiences through, for example, poetry. (Ofsted, March 1998, p. 24)

Even where the school does not meet legal requirements to provide pupils with a daily act of collective worship, pupils do have the opportunity to reflect deeply on significant influences in life, and on such matters as the value of the human spirit in regard to the material aspects of life.

In schools where provision for pupils' spiritual development is said to be poor, departments are often unaware of the opportunities available to them to provide for this area of pupils' development. Much depends on individual teachers carrying out legal requirements and providing pupils with the depth of education expected of them. For example:

The school plans specifically for whole school assemblies. It provides an act of collective worship each Monday and Friday, and these are clearly based on Christian moral values. Whilst the sixth form assembly does not have an act of collective worship, it gives a clear moral lead to pupils, sometimes showing how the Bible is relevant in today's world. Other assemblies frequently do not meet statutory requirements. The 'Thought for the Week', available for tutors to use with their classes, is often ignored and the school's published policies on assemblies and tutor times are often not followed. (Ofsted, February 1998, p. 23)

Head teachers at the National Association of Head Teachers' annual conference asked for the requirements for collective worship to be lifted. Head teachers are not people who would wish to flout the law, but when they depend so much on the knowledge and understanding of their many form or year tutors to implement it, difficulties arise. In the majority of schools I have inspected, the tutor time at the start of the day is poorly used for any purpose, let alone collective worship. It is not possible for many large comprehensive schools to meet as a school very often, but most could use the time when pupils first arrive at school in the morning in a more productive, positive and even reflective way. Not meeting the requirements for collective worship often goes hand in hand with a poor use of tutor time first thing in the morning. To start each day either offering the day to God or reflecting on how one is going to use it, is hardly something which should be controversial, but embraced as a move towards leading a worthwhile and positive life. Such daily experiences should not only serve pupils well at school, but also equip pupils for their lives outside school when they leave.

In some schools the difference between departments is strongly evident. For example:

Only in English, music and RE is there evidence of the spiritual element being experienced or studied explicitly. In English, themes such as life and death, and love and loyalty, are discussed through a wide range of poetry. Pupils often listen well and reflect quietly on the music they hear. In RE, pupils in Years 10 and 11 consider the spiritual experiences of people of different religions and examine their own beliefs. Opportunities to promote pupils' spiritual development are often missed in other subjects, although incidental opportunities do occur through the teaching of the National Curriculum – for example, the study of the Romans and Middle Ages in history, and in fieldwork in geography. Subjects have not, in the main, analysed or planned specifically for pupils' spiritual development. The school's stated values, however, are displayed in all classrooms and are a good basis for enhancing the spiritual aspect. (Ofsted, March 1997, p. 16)

In other schools only a little progress has been made since their previous inspection, and provision for pupils' spiritual development is still unsatisfactory. Even so, within some departments in such schools, teachers are beginning to plan for, and respond to, incidental opportunities for developing spiritual awareness. In some schools, local education authority guidelines are beginning to be used well. Progress can be made when schools are given clear guidelines as to what it is they should be doing and teaching, and it is not left to the personal knowledge and experience of teachers. Schools should not be run according to what teachers do not know and understand, but should strive, through planned INSET and other systematic staff development, to educate those who educate the pupils. Too often in the past we have fallen short of providing pupils with the education they deserve through inadequate teacher knowledge and understanding. It would seem that many of the present generation of teachers have had restricted education themselves.

Where this aspect of school development has been taken seriously, progress is being made. In one school, a deputy head has been appointed to take responsibility for co-ordinating the provision for pupils' spiritual, moral, social and cultural development. An audit has been made across the school to establish the extent of coverage of these areas. This comprehensive overview forms the basis for the next stage of planning future developments.

In the same school, the inspection report asserts:

Relationships in the school are very good and the school promotes well the worth and dignity of all pupils. There are opportunities for spiritual development particularly in English, PSHE, history, geography, music and RE. Pupils are encouraged to consider their own values and beliefs. In RE, they reflect on their own and other peoples' beliefs, valuing a non material dimension to life, and they develop an understanding of themselves in PHSE. There are, however, many opportunities that are missed. Collective worship is strongly led by the headteacher, who provides a valuable model. There is a good record of the content of school assemblies, which are held for parts of the school in four days each week. Careful thought has gone into the use of tutor times, to include an act of worship on days when pupils do not attend assemblies in the hall, but these opportunities are seldom taken up. The school does not meet the legal requirement to hold a daily act of collective worship for all pupils. (Ofsted, January 1998, p. 13)

In spite of all the head teacher is doing, he is still dependent on his staff carrying out the letter of the law. Surely the law should not bend to those who wish to ignore it, but should support the head who is doing all in his power to fulfil it.

THE TYPE OF SCHOOL AND ITS ENVIRONMENT

My work has taken me to a wide variety of communities, ranging from the Scottish borders, where pupils are bussed in from remote farms each morning, and the school car park at a quarter to nine each morning looks more like a coach or bus station, to close-knit, ex-mining villages, where employment expectations have changed, and the school has to respond to this, as to other changes. It has taken me to inner-city primary schools that serve a neighbourhood community and to schools which, because of voluntary aided status, take pupils from a distance, who do not belong to the local community but are members of the faith community. Each school has to take its own context into consideration when planning for pupils' spiritual, moral, social and cultural development. Schools get 'caught up' in the trials and tribulations of their own communities, be they the closing of a mine or the murder of a black teenager. When inspecting, it is vital that one is aware of the context of the school and why particular emphasis needs to be placed on one aspect of the curriculum rather than another. Greater provision for social development may be the priority for one school where pupils go home to remote farms, while multicultural developments may be top of the agenda, both in the choosing of an inspection team and in the focus of the school, where racial incidents are topical or prevalent. While all schools need to cover all aspects, wherever they are situated, emphasis will always differ, according to the context of the school and its intake. Spirituality in a rural, farming community may well be understood more through the natural world, while that of the city school may be better understood through human relationships. Each has its place in God's world and will understand the spiritual in its own way.

While primary, secondary and special schools will make different provision to meet the age and developmental needs of the pupils in their schools, all should provide well-planned opportunities.

The previous inspection Framework stated, 'For primary pupils acts of collective worship play a particular part' (Ofsted, 1995). This, I believe, reflects a lack of understanding, that spirituality is not something that children grow out of, but a relationship which continues and possibly deepens with knowledge, understanding and practice. Secondary schools should be providing an equal or deeper experience, building on what pupils have already experienced. No doubt the writers of the inspection Framework meant well, with a positive message about primary schools, but its interpretation is such that it does not show a full understanding of what spirituality really means: that God is in all His creation and we see and begin to understand Him through the subjects we learn, the experiences we have and the worship we offer, be it collective or personal worship. (Framework 2000 corrects this as well.)

MEASURING PROVISION AND COLLECTING EVIDENCE

Collecting evidence for this aspect of an inspection report is in some ways more difficult than in others and is often more extensive. Head teachers and sometimes members of the senior management team need to be interviewed by the lead inspector to gain an overall picture of the context in which they are inspecting. All inspection team members need to interview the heads of departments to ascertain how much thought the department has put into their provision. Pastoral tutors will need to be seen by one of the inspectors to gain a picture of the provision for moral and social development and those in the English, art, dance and music departments may well provide more fully for cultural development. For example, in what depth and breadth do pupils learn about the cultural heritage of the British Isles and other countries through music and dance?

It is evident that European artists have enjoyed an increased degree of popularity since the National Curriculum was introduced. But inspectors will need to look also at provision for cultural development in terms of understanding the multicultural nature of Britain today. The culture of the school's own community will include distinctive events, be it horse racing in Doncaster or a music festival in Surrey. Does the school provide opportunities for pupils to learn about the business culture of enterprise, particularly in places where there is unemployment, and how does religious belief influence culture in multi-faith environments? The spiritual, moral, social and cultural development of pupils is extensive, and clear guidance needs to be given both to schools and inspectors if inspections are to help schools develop this provision.

Evidence will be collected from the different departments in secondary schools, and usually from the head teacher in primary schools, and the results given to the lead inspector for that aspect. Departments respond in very different ways and often welcome the opportunity to think further about provision, which they make implicitly, but have not thought to make explicit. The inspection experience is necessarily fragmented, but if all the team have done their part faithfully, the paragraphs in a report can truly represent the school's provision. Further training of inspectors may be needed if all are responsible for collecting this evidence, rather than one person. The richness of different inspectors' experiences and understanding, or lack of them, will also contribute to building up a picture of what spirituality is, and how it is understood. Naturally, the observed experience of the children themselves is highly significant. The way pupils conduct themselves about the school and their responses to lessons provide some evidence for inspectors, but the inspection is as much about provision as about response in this particular aspect of the school report. Personally, I almost always have a school dinner, so that I can chat to the children in the school and learn about them, their likes and dislikes, and in this context the question to pupils, 'what would you most like to change in the school?' often brings enlightening responses!

THE PARTICULAR CONTRIBUTIONS OF RELIGIOUS EDUCATION AND PERSONAL, SOCIAL EDUCATION

Although all departments will contribute to the spiritual, moral, social and cultural development of pupils, the religious education department and the

PSE programme will probably make a major input. For example, I was present recently at a most spiritual experience when a primary school teacher re-enacted part of a Shabbot meal with her class. There was a real sense of expectancy as she lit the candle and passed round the herbs for them to smell. A little, perhaps, was now understood of the Jewish meal and the spirituality and tradition lying behind it. Equally enlightening was another lesson when the teacher talked about St Paul's conversion and the significance of light, and children led each other round the classroom taking turns 'to be blind', and then watched a candle flame shed light around it, when the classroom lights were turned off.

It is in RE and PSE that questions will particularly be asked and answers sought. Why is it that people believe in different things, live in different ways and react differently to the similar situations? What is morally right and wrong? What is it that helps the school to become a cohesive community, a class to be a supportive group or a pupil to grow to be a responsible adult? What is our local culture, how can we widen our understanding of culture and what do others consider to be their culture? RE and PSE both attempt to answer these questions, and other subjects will contribute in their own way.

In almost all schools now, I am constantly reading that different 'Issues' are to be considered. Everything nowadays seems to have become an 'issue' and probably not far short of becoming a 'problem'. While this is probably an appropriate term when discussions take place in PSHE, I should prefer not to see it emphasized in religious education lessons. I would rather teachers refer to 'questions that are asked and answers that are given', within the belief of any particular religion. To call them 'Issues' within the religious education context is to undermine the authority that religion should hold. One very good RE lesson on making moral decisions comes to mind. Twelve sixth form pupils, in pairs of a boy with a girl, were given a real-life situation to discuss with each other, and were expected to come to a conclusion as to how a decision would be made by people of different faiths. Each pair was allocated the name of a specific faith or the law of the land to guide them. The discussions were both serious and knowledgeable and decisions changed as they discussed with each other. The one boy still giving an irresponsible answer at the end was brought up short by the teacher, realizing how his answer showed cowardice rather than the macho view he had intended. These pupils were learning to make decisions based on sound information in a guided situation. They should be well equipped and able to apply their knowledge and these skills on leaving school.

It is, I believe, because of a lack of religious knowledge and this loss of respect for religious authority, that the world flounders, without any moral absolutes. Christ's command, to love God and secondly love others as oneself (Matthew 22.37–40) has lost the Jewish foundations it was built upon. Jesus said, 'Think not that I have come to abolish the law and the prophets; I have come not to abolish them but to fulfil them' (Matthew 5.17, RSV). Nor is this, as with so much else, an exclusively Christian concept: 'Whenever the Law declines and the purpose of life is forgotten, I manifest myself on earth. I am born in every age to protect the good, to destroy evil, and to re-establish the Law' (Bhagavad Gita, 4.7–8). When I said somewhat hurriedly that something had to be done 'because it was the rule', a ten-year-old boy recently replied,

'But rules are there to be broken.' One first has to know what the rules are, before one can consider breaking them. Jesus knew them well. A change seen in the RE lessons I have observed over the last two years has been the teaching of the Ten Commandments. I observed no lessons on them before then. The quality of the teaching is variable, but at least children are beginning to know what the basic rules of an ordered society are. The Christian interpretation (for that is what all Agreed Syllabi lay down should be emphasized) can follow after.

THE LAW AND COLLECTIVE WORSHIP

A daily act of collective worship is the law, and many find it difficult to keep when adequate accommodation is not available. Where there is a will, however, there is always a way, and many schools *do* find ways to provide a time when pupils can meet together, usually at the start of the day, to reflect quietly and sometimes worship. Some secondary schools allow pupils to go straight to the hall and sit in their own places as they arrive before school in the morning, so that when the bell goes all are already present and no time is wasted moving from tutorial classes to the hall. Others meet in year groups and a smaller sense of collectiveness is experienced. In other schools, the tannoy is used to bring the school together first thing in the morning. Different schools will find different ways – if they want to. It is a matter of will rather than lack of hall provision, it would seem. That collective worship should always be a full-blown performance of some kind is, in my thinking, mistaken. In some schools, acts of collective worship have become no more than this and difficulties of timetabling and space become the excuses for not having one daily. If this is what schools expect, then a daily act would appear to be too much to ask. To me it is a simple offering of the day to God. This may be in the form of a well-prepared assembly with various parts to it, or it may be in the form of a quiet time of reflection or prayer before going to lessons. To meet requirements, however, God must be addressed, so pupils (and staff if present) may choose whether to respond to a Greater Power or take all the responsibility on their own shoulders. The option must be given, not avoided.

SMSC AND THE ETHOS OF THE SCHOOL

The ethos of the school is very closely related to the provision the school makes for SMSC and, in particular, for three aspects of school life: spiritual, social and cultural development. Provision for pupils' moral development is often linked to one of the others, and has different links dependent on whether it is a county or voluntary school. When writing up paragraphs for reports of county schools, and in particular, county secondary schools, I often find that provision for pupils' moral development can be written within the paragraph on social development as it is often taught in PSHE lessons. In voluntary schools, it can often be written within the paragraph on spiritual development, relating directly to religious education. Where it is taught across the curriculum it is given a discrete paragraph.

As the emphasis on academic excellence will be greater in some schools than others, so also will the emphasis the school lays on provision for pupils' spiritual, moral, social and cultural development vary. Not only will it reflect the aims of the school, but also the practice itself and thereby its ethos. Social development will, it has to be admitted, be influenced perhaps more than any other aspect of school life by what pupils bring to school from their homes and the environment they live in. The school, however, has a role to play in providing a social setting for pupils to meet, eat, work together and generally learn what it is to be a social being.

Provision for pupils' social development is observed in lessons where they learn to take turns in answering questions, work together with a partner or in groups, or debate matters formally. Specifically planned teaching will take place in lessons such as PHSE and in 'Circle Time' when each pupil is given time to speak to the rest of the class about a given matter of concern. Time is wrongly used, as I have observed, when the school has made 'Circle Time' into a subject in its own right to replace religious education.

MEASURING THE UNMEASURABLE

So how does one grade provision for pupils' spiritual development? It is not unknown for teachers to read their inspection report and say, 'It says that we provide well for SMSC, but I don't know what it is we are doing well.' If this is the case, then the report and 'feedbacks' to staff have not shown clearly enough how judgements have been made. This is sad, because it is by stating clearly what it *is* that is good, and what it is that is missing, that teachers and head teachers are helped in their search for excellence in their own schools.

As has already been stated, the provision for pupils' spiritual development should be made through the whole life of the school. Assemblies and collective worship are only one aspect of it. Excellent teachers are often as unaware of their good teaching as others are unaware that their positive relationships, shared sense of wonder and excitement in learning and of the world about them, and their willingness to value pupils' ideas, all contribute to providing for pupils' spiritual development. The curriculum they provide, the poetry they read, the art to which they introduce children and the music they play to them and help their pupils to sing and play themselves, all contribute to the rich provision for spiritual development. The wonders of mathematics, science or design, or the pleasure of dance or physical activity all provide for the development of the human spirit as well as for the mind and body. A rich curriculum will not only enliven the spirit of the child, but will point them towards the true, the beautiful and possibly towards ultimate goodness.

Pupils' responses, whether to the curriculum and whole life of the school or specifically to collective worship, will also have some bearing on inspection judgements. In religious education, inspectors note whether pupils show respect for other people's beliefs, and in assemblies, if appropriate respect or reverence is shown during collective worship. It always surprises me that those who want to do away with collective worship are often the same people as those who think they are particularly tolerant towards other people. In some schools I have visited, where collective worship does not necessarily come naturally to the adults, assemblies have still been provided with time for an act of collective worship. Pupils have been asked to 'think about or pray for ...', enabling all to take part and opening the door a crack to those who would otherwise never experience what it is to pray. They may one day open it further, or may choose to stay on the other side, but the opportunity has been offered. It is difficult to respond to someone you do not know. May we, working in schools, at least introduce pupils to what means most to us, and give them the opportunity to respond or not. In one school where a head teacher was not at all happy about an act of collective worship, she did not suggest that pupils say anything at the end of the 'thought', but the pupils most firmly said 'Amen'. They were in no doubt. In some schools they seem to 'say prayers' in assembly, in others they pray. In this particular school, in spite of the head's reluctance – they prayed.

In another:

Prayer is understood by pupils from an early age and is a powerful spiritual experience. Music is used very well as an integral part of worship, creating not only tranquillity, an inner peace and reverence, but also joyful participation by children and adults alike.

The spirituality of other cultures, such as those found in the Far East and among the Australian aborigines, are reflected upon through poetry and in art. The school celebrates major world faith festivals such as Diwali with displays of pupils' work. (Ofsted. May 1998, p. 14)

One cannot measure a person's response to the Creator, the Spirit who embodies 'goodness, truth and beauty', as the hymn which used to be sung in many primary schools describes him. But when that response is as a result of belief, the power of it cannot be denied. I have experienced such only twice on inspections, once in a county and once in a voluntary school. Where the inspection team came from a variety of faith backgrounds the response was understood most fully and a unanimous Grade 1 was given. Contact had been made! It was obvious to all. It is that moment of total silence, when you can hear a pin drop, of total concentration and handing over to God in prayer, that the 'still, small voice' of the Old Testament can be heard in the hurly-burly of modern-day life. Few are Grade 1s in any aspect of school inspections, but that does not prevent any of us from striving to provide for and reach the Highest.

REFERENCES

Hackett, G. (1999) Cautious welcome for inspections. *The Times Educational Supplement*, 8 January 1999.

Ofsted (1995) *The Handbook: Guidance on the Inspection of Nursery and Primary Schools*. London: HMSO.

Ofsted (January 1997) Hungerhill School. Inspection Report. London: Ofsted, p. 13.

Ofsted (March 1997) Howden School. Inspection Report. London: Ofsted, p. 16.

Ofsted (February 1998) Campsmount School. Inspection Report. London: Ofsted, p. 23.

Ofsted (March 1998) Gosforth High School. Inspection Report. London: Ofsted, p. 24.

Ofsted (May 1998) Rosary RC Primary School. Inspection Report. London: Ofsted, p. 14.

Ofsted (1999) *Handbook for Inspecting Primary and Nursery Schools*. London: HMSO.

Conclusion
Ron Best

In these brief closing comments, I want to revisit some of the key themes and issues which have run through this book and to indicate where further thought and action is needed. The first issue is that of *the crumbling 'bedrock' upon which our thinking about, and planning for, spiritual, moral, social and cultural development is based.*

I recall my first brush with postmodernism at a conference of the British Educational Research Association at Nottingham in the early 1990s. I sat in a packed room and listened to academic after academic worrying away at the problems of relativism and uncertainty. That they did this in a shared language, presuming a common belief that we exist, and deduced and conjectured in Cartesian fashion seemed self-contradictory. I was torn between a feeling that postmodernism was a lot of fuss about nothing, since we could reason about it and critique it by the traditional methods of modernity, and the feeling that I stood on the brink of the abyss in which the very procedures of science and philosophy were self-destructing before my eyes. The contradictions in applying logic and a common language to speculation about a reality whose character, if not existence, was in some way no more than a matter of opinion (or, at best, a matter of definition according to the untestable assumptions of some paradigm), was more than I could cope with.

I cannot help wondering to what extent the preoccupation with the idea of a postmodern society with all its uncertainty and insecurity was attributable to a *fin-de-siècle* mentality of reassessment and revisionism as the turn of the millennium approached. However that might be, one certain feature of life in what some commentators prefer to call 'late modernity', is the tension between absolutism and relativism, and one place where this tension is very much in evidence is education.

Now, because we have an inherited corpus of knowledge – the facts, concepts and skills that make up the disciplines and fields of study comprising the school curriculum and which are conceived of as standing outside the teacher and learner – the problem of relativism within these subjects may appear to be no more than a dispute as to which facts to transmit and which competences to develop. The recent (and ongoing) debates about the selection of literary texts for inclusion in National Curriculum English, and whether or not the Romans, Saxons and Normans are essential to any history programme worthy of the name, are cases in point. The 'traditionalists' are resolute in their belief that both literary quality and historical significance are more than matters of taste or cultural preference, while the 'progressives' are keen to advance a view of cultural relativity which can accommodate emerging and revisionist forms alongside established canon. Whether either an objective aesthetic or a properly scientific determination of historical significance is possible remain unanswered questions.

In any case, such debates go on in an arena whose boundaries have been predetermined by a view of education which separates knowledge from the knower, learning from the learner. As Jack Priestley argues in Chapter 7 of this volume, we need to restore the balance between the subjective creativity of the spirit and the objective realities of knowledge (however defined) in the sciences, arts and humanities if we are to achieve real progress in educational provision.

Once we leave the realm of the traditional subject disciplines, the problem becomes much greater because the subject matter of the curriculum is no longer 'outside of' or remote from the learner. As I tried to indicate in my Introduction to this book, if we are to take the opportunities, responsibilities and experiences of adult life as a significant orientation for education, then matters of values, morality and the emotions are immediately on the agenda. If education for life is to be more than the transmission of facts and the practice of skills, then the procedures of moral thinking, political debate and community involvement take centre stage. Perhaps the problem of relativism can be overcome through the rediscovery of *process* in an educational world which has become dominated by outcomes and accountability. In this context, absolutist calls for the teaching of 'right and wrong' or for the promotion of moral codes derived from religious dogma would seem to have little to offer. If there is a 'bedrock' to planning for SMSC, it seems more likely to reside in some analysis of the nature of human experience than in the nature of human knowledge. The chapters by Law, Bigger, Tew, Rowe and Ford each in their own way demonstrate the folly of trying to *instruct* children in values, as opposed to trying to provide the experiences through which such values develop within the individual's personhood.

The second major issue which this volume raises is *whether or not the idea of education as preparation for adult life is an acceptable focus for what schools should be trying to do.* As I tried to show in my Introduction, that part of the curriculum to do with the personal-social development of the child seems to have been particularly susceptible to the ebb and flow of postmodernist uncertainty, to the extent that there is now even less agreement about what it should be called than was the case in the past. No sooner were moral education, health education and personal and social development (PSD) integrated under headings of PSME and PSHE, than Ofsted and the SCAA/QCA initiatives replaced it with 'SMSC'. But within the last two years 'SMSC' seems to have been eclipsed by 'PSHE and Citizenship' as a combination with backing from the Secretary of State, while the report of the National Advisory Group on Personal, Social and Health Education chose 'Preparing Young People for Adult Life' as its title. This inability to agree a name is not just because any disaggregation and recombination of aspects of the person fails to do justice to the complexity and unity of personhood; it seems also to be the case that we cannot decide whether it is personhood here and now or the adult of the future which should orient our curriculum. The political pressure seems to be for the latter, but there is a very strong argument that a preoccupation with the challenges of adulthood is less helpful for this purpose than asking: what does a *child* need? What does a *teenager* need? What does this *person*, here, in front of me at this moment, need? As the contributors to a recent volume in this series (Decker *et al.*, 1999) argue, we are unlikely to achieve very much by way of teaching the academic curriculum if we do not take children (and childhood) seriously, especially where children come to school with emotional and behavioural difficulties which require sensitive handling. It seems to me that many of the chapters in this volume, and particularly those of Tew, Gill and Smith, are implicitly or explicitly concerned with how we meet the needs of children *qua* children, while Erricker's chapter shows how researchers can support teachers as they try to find more effective ways of doing so.

A third issue has to do with *procedures for designing the curriculum*. The chapters by Smith, Roberts, Talbot, Yates and Cooper can be read as explorations in the problematics of curriculum design. Their deliberations are particularly welcome because this is one place in education where the opportunities for disagreement are legion, and where the dangers of politics and bureaucracy are apparent.

Clearly, if our starting point is some presumed body of concepts, facts and skills which we want to transmit then a rational-objectivist model of curriculum planning is logical. If we begin with the needs of the learner, here, now, then we are likely to come up with a very different approach and one which emphasizes process rather than outcome, pedagogy rather than content. Yet the temptation to polarize the debate by such simple oppositions as those of 'traditionalist' and 'progressive', 'process' or 'product' is not necessarily helpful. Surely we need to accept that without concepts, facts and skills, experience will be without form and meaningless? But equally surely, we need to recognize that concepts, facts and skills are inert and unachievable without the processes of experience by which the learner engages the world. One challenge for the curriculum designers is how to accommodate this blindingly obvious dialectic rather than play polemics.

That said, *it is the category of 'experience' that I think offers the most hope for progress*. Spiritual experience remains a particularly significant focus for many of the contributors to this book (notably Gill, Warner and Ogden). But it is clear that other forms of experience are also significant and McCarthy's chapter on the emotions and the need to develop 'emotional literacy' is particularly helpful in this regard. Here, too, there is a challenge for the curriculum designers: what sorts of experience should we be providing in SMSC if we are to develop children's capacity to explore, acknowledge and manage their emotions?

A much neglected concept in all of this is that of *empathy*. By this I do not mean simply 'putting oneself in the shoes of another' – although this in itself is a prerequisite for both moral reasoning and successful social interaction – but a deep and meaningful relationship through which might come personal growth, mutual support and shared enrichment, much as described, in the context of counselling, by Carl Rogers:

Empathy involves being sensitive, moment to moment, to the changing felt meanings which flow over this other person, to the fear or rage or tenderness or confusion or whatever that s/he is experiencing. It means temporarily living in his/her life, moving about in it delicately without making judgements, sensing meaning of which s/he is scarcely aware, but not trying to uncover feelings of which the person is totally unaware, since this would be too threatening. It includes communicating your sensings of his/her world as you look with fresh and unfrightened eyes at elements of which the individual is fearful. It means frequently checking with him/her as to the accuracy of your sensings and being guided by the responses you receive. You are a confident companion to the person in his/her inner world. (quoted in McLaughlin, 1995, p. 60)

Again, a greater attention to the nature of human experience seems essential for real progress to be made. It is within experience that the spiritual, moral, social and cultural come together in ways which their analytic separation would seem to deny. In particular, if we are to take the spiritual as having to do with the quality of lived life, of the essential becoming-ness of personal growth and as the transcendence of the mundane world of routine existence, then schools must be much richer sources of experience than they currently are. In the face of pressures to school children in 'the basics' of numeracy and literacy, to develop competences in information and communications technology and to improve performance across the 'academic' curriculum, we need to protect and extend opportunities for children to engage the world emotionally, aesthetically and morally, in the hope that they come to understand much better themselves, their fellow human beings and that greater whole of which we are all part.

I hope this volume will, in some small way, help to focus the debate on such issues. If it does not, it will not be the fault of the contributors, whose work, without exception, has caused me to question and extend very considerably my understanding of what education might be.

REFERENCES

Decker, S., Kirby, S., Greenwood, A. and Moore, D. (eds) (1999) *Taking Children Seriously. Applications of Counselling and Therapy in Education.* London: Cassell.

McLaughlin, C. (1995) Counselling in schools: its place and purpose. In Best, R., Lang, P., Lodge, C. and Watkins, C. (eds), *Pastoral Care and Personal-Social Education. Entitlement and Provision.* London: Cassell.

Index